Exchange and transport

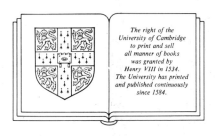

The right of the
University of Cambridge
to print and sell
all manner of books
was granted by
Henry VIII in 1534.
The University has printed
and published continuously
since 1584.

CAMBRIDGE UNIVERSITY PRESS

Cambridge
London   New York   New Rochelle
Melbourne   Sydney

Contents

Published by the Press Syndicate of the University of Cambridge
The Pitt Building, Trumpington Street, Cambridge CB2 1RP
32 East 57th Street, New York, NY 10022, USA
296 Beaconsfield Parade, Middle Park, Melbourne 3206, Australia

© Cambridge University Press 1984

First published 1984
Printed in Great Britain at the University Press, Cambridge

Library of Congress catalogue card number: 84-1837

British Library cataloguing in publication data

Exchange and transport.—(Advanced biology
alternative learning project; unit 5)
1. Biology
I. Advanced Biology Alternative Learning
Project   II. Series
574   QH308.7

ISBN 0 521 28822 3

Preface

The Inner London Education Authority's Advanced Biology Alternative Learning (ABAL) project has been developed as a response to changes which have taken place in the organisation of secondary education and the curriculum. The project is the work of a group of biology teachers seconded from ILEA secondary schools. ABAL began in 1978 and since then has undergone extensive trials in schools and colleges of further education. The materials have been produced to help teachers meet the needs of new teaching situations and provide an effective method of learning for students.

Teachers new to A-level teaching or experienced teachers involved in reorganisation of schools due to the changes in population face many problems. These include the sharing of staff and pupils between existing schools and the variety of back-grounds and abilities of pupils starting A-level courses whether at schools, sixth form centres or colleges. Many of the students will be studying a wide range of courses, which in some cases will be a mixture of science, arts and humanities.

The ABAL individualised learning materials offer a guided approach to A-level biology and can be used to form a coherent base in many teaching situations. The materials are organised so that teachers can prepare study programmes suited to their own students. The separation of core and extension work enables the academic needs of all students to be satisfied. Teachers are essential to the success of this course, not only in using their traditional skills, but for organising resources and solving individual problems. They act as a personal tutor, and monitor the progress of each student as he or she proceeds through the course.

The materials aim to help the students develop and improve their personal study skills, enabling them to work more effectively and become more actively involved and responsible for their own learning and assessment. This approach allows the students to develop a sound understanding of fundamental biological concepts.

Acknowledgements

Figures: 2, 6, 9, 13, 17, 21, 23, 58, 59, 71, 166, 167, 172, 190, 235, Biophoto Associates; 12, J.Z. Young (1975) *Life of Mammals*, Oxford University Press; 25, based on Nuffield Foundation (1970) Nuffield Advanced *Study Guide*, Longman; 30, 31, 32, 33, 34, 35, 36, 37, 38, 39, 40, 44, based on Nuffield Foundation (1970) Nuffield Advanced Science *Maintenance of the Organism*, a laboratory guide, Longman; 66, 67, 68, A.C. Shaw, S.K. Lazell & G.N. Foster (1965) *Photomicrographs of the Flowering Plant*, Longman; 86, 94, 119, 120, 123, 124, 128, 138, 140, based on Nuffield Foundation (1970) Nuffield Advanced Science Topic Review *Circulation*, Longman; 87, J.A. Ramsay (1955) *A Physiological Approach to Lower Animals*, Cambridge University Press; 97, reprinted with permission from *Comp. Biochem. Physiol.* 5, K. Johnson & A.W. Martin, *Circulation in the cephalopod Octopus dofleini*, copyright 1962, Pergamon Press Ltd.; 121, F. Winton & O. Lippold (1979) *Human Physiology*, Churchill Livingstone, Edinburgh; 129, J.J. Head (1976) *Science Through Biology*, Edward Arnold (Publishers) Ltd.; 131, 173, courtesy of D.G Mackean; 135, Nuffield Foundation (1975) Revised Nuffield Biology Text 2 *Living Things in Action*, Longman; 143, J.A.C. Nichol (1960) *The Biology of Marine Animals*, by permission of Pitman Publishing Ltd., London; 161, J.W. Kimball *Biology* © 1965, Addison-Wesley Pub. Co. Inc., Reading Ma., page 234, figure 14.9, reprinted with permission; 174, 175, C.J. Clegg & Gene Cox (1978) *Anatomy and Activities of Plants*, John Murray; 193, 194, courtesy of Dr J.W. Hannay, Imperial College of Science and Technology; 207, 208, Redrawn with permission from the Blackie Publishing Group Ltd.; 212, W.J. Garnett; 213, from *Biology, a Modern Introduction*, 2nd ed., by B.S. Beckett, published by Oxford University Press © B.S. Beckett 1982; 231, 267, M.B.V. Roberts (1971) *Biology, a Functional Approach*, 2nd ed., Thomas Nelson.

Examination questions: By permission of the University of London University Entrance and School Examinations Council, the Associated Examining Board and the Nuffield Foundation.

How to use this unit

This is not a textbook. It is a guide that will help you learn as effectively as possible. As you work through it, you will be directed to practical work, audio-visual resources and other materials. There are sections of text in this guide which are to be read as any other book, but much of the guide is concerned with helping you through activities designed to produce effective learning. The following list gives details of the ways in which the unit is organised.

(1) Objectives

Objectives are stated at the beginning of each section. They are important because they tell you what you should be able to do when you have finished working through the section. They should give you extra help in organising your learning. In particular, you should check after working through each section that you can achieve all the stated objectives and that you have notes which cover them all.

(2) Self-assessment questions (*SAQ*)

These are designed to help you think about what you are reading. You should always write down answers to self-assessment questions and then check them immediately with those answers given at the back of this unit. If you do not understand a question and answer, make a note of it and discuss it with your tutor at the earliest opportunity.

(3) Summary assignments

These are designed to help you make notes on the content of a particular section. They will provide a useful collection of revision material. They should therefore be carried out carefully and should be checked by your tutor for accuracy. If you prefer to make notes in your own way, discuss with your tutor whether you should carry out the summary assignments.

(4) Self tests

There are one or more self tests for each section. They should be attempted a few days after you have completed the relevant work and not immediately after. They will help you identify what you have not understood or remembered from a particular section. You can then remedy any weaknesses identified. If you cannot answer any questions and do not understand the answers given, then check with your tutor.

(5) Tutor assesssed work

At intervals through the unit you will meet an instruction to show work to your tutor. This will enable your tutor to monitor your progress through the unit and to see how well you are coping with the material. Your tutor will then know how best to meet your individual needs.

(6) Past examination questions

At various points in the unit you will come across past examination questions. These are only included where they are relevant to the topic under study and have been selected both to improve your knowledge of that topic and also to give you practice in answering examination questions.

(7) Audio-visual material

A number of activities in this unit refer to video cassettes which may be available from your tutor. They deal with topics which cannot be covered easily in text or practical work as well as providing a change from the normal type of learning activities. This should help in motivating you.

(8) Extension work

This work is provided for several reasons: to provide additional material of general interest; to provide more detailed treatment of some topics; to provide more searching questions that will make demands on your powers of thinking and reasoning.

(9) Practicals

These are an integral part of the course and have been designed to lead you to a deeper understanding of the factual material. You will need to organise your time with care so that you can carry out the work suggested in a logical sequence. If your A-level examination requires your practical notebook to be assessed, you must be careful to keep a record of this work in a separate book. A hazard symbol, ☠ is used in the Materials and Procedures sections to mark those substances and procedures which must be treated with particular care.

(10) Discussions

Talking to one another about biological ideas is a helpful activity. To express yourself in your own words, so that others can understand you, forces you to clarify your thoughts. When a sufficient number of your class (at least three, but not more than five) have covered the material indicated by a discussion instruction, you should have a group discussion. Question individuals if what they say is not clear. This is the way that you will both learn and understand.

(11) Post-test

A post-test is available from you tutor when you finish this unit. This will be based on past examination questions and will give you an idea of how well you have coped with the material in this unit. It will also indicate which areas you should consolidate before going on to the next unit.

Study and practical skills

The ABAL introductory unit *Inquiry and investigation in biology* introduced certain study and practical skills which will be practiced and improved in this unit. These included
(a) the QS3R method of note-taking;
(b) the construction of graphs, histograms and tables;
(c) the analysis of data;
(d) drawing of biological specimens;
(e) use of the light microscope;
(f) the design of practical investigations;
(g) comprehension of written reports;
(h) discussion groups.

Pre-knowledge for this unit

You should have a basic understanding of the following:

Photosynthesis and respiration.
The structure of a typical plant cell.
The relationship between changes in gas pressure and volume in an airtight chamber.
Anaerobic respiration in mammalian muscle and oxygen debt.
An elementary understanding of receptors.

Introduction to the unit

All living things are surrounded by barriers of one form or another. These barriers such as cell membranes in protozoa, cell walls and membranes in plants, the chitinous cuticle of arthropods and the skin of vertebrates help protect the organism from the external environment. This protective function of the surface layers however poses problems for the organism. Living things cannot exist in isolation from their environment. A constant supply of raw materials is required for the processes of metabolism and a constant supply of waste materials must be removed. This unit looks at some of the mechanisms and problems associated with the exchange of substances between organism and environment.

In unicellular organisms, the rate of production and consumption of substances by the cytoplasm is sufficiently slow for the process of diffusion to remove or supply materials. There has been, however, an evolutionary trend towards larger and more active multicellular organisms in which diffusion is no longer adequate for movement of materials around the body. These larger animals and plants have come to rely on the mass flow of air and water for the transport of materials. This unit looks at the structures associated with diffusion and mass flow in animals and plants.

Section 1 Overview and principles

1.1 Introduction and objectives

A living organism is active, changing and dynamic. Part of this activity involves the exchanging of substances between the organism and its environment.

In animals, oxygen is usually taken up for the process of energy release in respiration and carbon dioxide, an end product of the process, is passed out. Food and water are also taken up from the environment. Part of this is returned to the environment unused (egestion). The rest is digested and absorbed into the body and used for growth, repair and energy release. Waste products, including nitrogenous waste and excess salts are formed in the body as a result of metabolic processes. If allowed to accumulate, they would become toxic. Therefore, they are eliminated from the body and pass back into the environment. This is called *excretion*.

In plants and animals respiration occurs continuously. In plants, however, photosynthesis also takes place during the day. Hence, in the day, carbon dioxide is absorbed and oxygen is evolved while at night, the uptake and evolution of gases is reversed.

The material requirements for plant nutrition include water and minerals in addition to carbon dioxide. These are taken up from the environment. Unlike animals, which take in complex foods, part of which are unusable and are eliminated, plants manufacture their own sugars, proteins, etc. according to their requirements. This means plants have less waste to be eliminated than animals. Plants do, however, lose considerable amounts of water from their aerial parts.

These exchanges are summarised in figure 1. In simple organisms the materials taken into the body can pass to all regions by diffusion. In the larger organisms, special transport systems have been evolved to circulate materials within the body.

1 Exchanges between living organisms and the environment

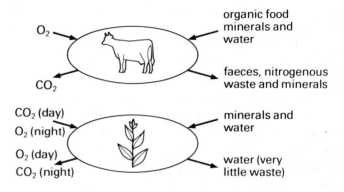

At the end of this section you should be able to do the following.

(*a*) Name the processes which entail exchange of substances between the organism and its environment and state the substances concerned.

(*b*) State the surface for gas exchange in *Amoeba, Spirogyra, Planaria,* a moss and earthworm.

(*c*) Explain how increase in size of an organism affects the use of the body surface as a respiratory surface.

(*d*) Explain how body shape affects the surface area/volume relationship.

(*e*) Name and describe the mechanism of gas exchange at the respiratory surface.

(*f*) List the three characteristics of a respiratory surface.

(*g*) Explain why some organisms need an internal transport system.

(*h*) Explain how molecules move by mass flow.

(*i*) List the advantages of internal respiratory surfaces for terrestrial organisms.

(*j*) State the regions for food and water absorption in *Amoeba*, *Planaria*, earthworm, human, *Spirogyra*, a moss and a grass.

(*k*) State the regions for waste elimination in *Amoeba*, *Planaria*, human and a grass.

(*l*) Explain the necessity for ventilation mechanisms.

1.2 Gas exchange in living organisms

The process by which some gases are absorbed from the environment by organisms and others are excreted is known as **gas** (or **gaseous**) **exchange.** The word 'exchange' could be misleading here — it does not mean that one gas is actually exchanged for another — merely that there is a two-way transport of gases in and out of the organism.

SAQ 1 What processes involve gas exchange (*a*) in plants, (*b*) in animals?

SAQ 2 Which gases are taken up and which are evolved (*a*) in plants, (*b*) in animals?

Figure 2 shows *Amoeba* and *Spirogyra*. Both are aquatic organisms living in ponds. They both carry out respiration, obtaining oxygen from that dissolved in the water, and passing carbon dioxide in solution back into the water. In *Spirogyra* during the day, photosynthesis causes a movement of gases in the opposite direction, carbon dioxide being absorbed and oxygen being given off.

SAQ 3 What is the surface for gas exchange (*a*) in *Amoeba*, (*b*) in *Spirogyra*.

2   (a) *Amoeba*

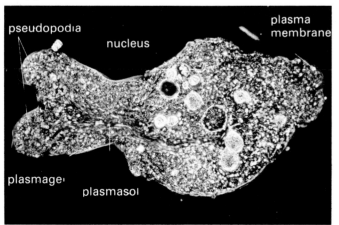

(b) *Spirogyra*

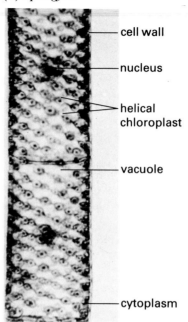

1.2.1. The importance of surface area/volume relationships for gas exchange

In all organisms examined so far, gas exchange takes place all over the body surface. The total surface area is an important factor in determining the amount of gas exchange. The amount of gases passing in and out of the organism depends on its surface area, but the extent of the needs of the organism depends on its volume. This is because the metabolic processes which require or produce gases take place throughout the living tissues.

The shapes in figure 3 represent seven cubes with side lengths varying from 1 to 7 cm. In figure 4, the surface area, volume and surface area/volume ratio are shown. Study figures 3 and 4.

SAQ 4 Use the data in figure 4 to draw a line graph comparing surface area and volume for the seven cubes.

SAQ 5 From your graph, compare the rate of change of surface area and of volume with increasing size of cube.

SAQ 6 How many cm^2 of surface are there for each cm^3 of substance in each cube?

3 Cubes of increasing size

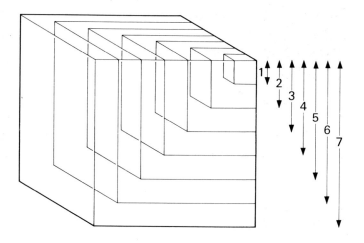

4 Comparison of surface area, volume and surface area/volume ratio for seven cubes

	Cube number						
	1	2	3	4	5	6	7
Surface area	6	24	54	96	150	216	294
Volume	1	8	27	64	125	216	343
Surface area/volume ratio	6	3	2	1.5	1.2	1.0	0.86

SAQ 7 What is the significance of this for living organisms in terms of their using their body surface as a surface for gas exchange?

The shape of the body can have a significant effect on the surface area/volume ratio.

SAQ 8 Calculate the surface area/volume ratio for the two shapes shown in figure 5.

5 Shapes A and B

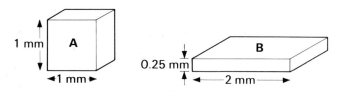

SAQ 9 From your answer to the previous question, make a general statement about how the shape of an organism could affect its body surface area and hence the possible surface area for gas exchange necessary for its metabolism.

Figure 6 shows another animal and plant — the flatworm *Planaria* and a moss.

6 *Planaria* and a moss

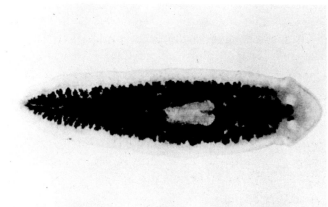

Planaria is aquatic and lives in fresh water. Mosses usually live on land in moist regions.

7 Cross-sections through the body of *Planaria* and a moss

Planaria

A moss

Figure 7 shows a section through the body of *Planaria* and a moss. From this, you can see that *Planaria* has a very flattened body. The moss has a much divided branching body composed of flattened leaves, a stem and a branching underground system of rhizoids.

When compared with *Amoeba* and *Spirogyra, Planaria* and a moss are relatively large organisms. However, because of their shapes, the surface area/volume ratio is high, and diffusion of gases through the body surface is sufficient to provide for their gas exchange needs.

1.2.2. The movement of substances across surfaces

The molecules in gases (and liquids) are constantly moving at random. These movements have no noticeable effect if the gas is evenly distributed throughout an area. However, if there is a difference in concentration of the gas within the area, a net movement of gas will occur, causing the molecules to become evenly distributed.

Thus, if a gas is introduced at one end of a container as in figure 8(*a*), the random movements of the molecules will eventually cause a net movement of the gas so that it comes to occupy the whole of the space evenly as in figure 8(*b*).

8   Movement of molecules

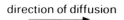

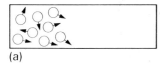 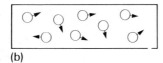

(a)   (b)

Such net movements are known as **diffusion**. Diffusion can also take place across membranes so long as the membrane is permeable to the molecules.

SAQ 10 Define diffusion.

It is by diffusion that oxygen and carbon dioxide move across the body surfaces of *Amoeba, Spirogyra, Planaria* and a moss.

SAQ 11 How is it possible for oxygen to continuously diffuse into *Amoeba* and *Planaria?*

1.2.3. Respiratory surfaces

All the organisms examined so far have been aquatic or semi-aquatic and gas exchange takes place over the whole body surface.

The surface of an organism which is used for gas exchange is known as its **respiratory surface.** In all organisms considered so far, the respiratory surface is the body surface.

All respiratory surfaces have three things in common:
— they have a large surface area in relation to the volume of the organism;
— they are thin and permeable to oxygen and carbon dioxide;
— they are moist to increase the rate of diffusion of gases

1.3 Respiratory surfaces and transport systems in animals

The earthworm is a larger animal than either *Amoeba* or *Planaria*. It is a terrestrial animal which lives in burrows in the soil. Gas exchange takes place all over its body surface, which is kept moist with mucus supplied from glands in the skin. Oxygen from the air dissolves in this film of moisture and diffuses into the cells of the epidermis (skin). The earthworm is very susceptible to desiccation (drying out) and can only survive in a moist or humid environment.

9   An earthworm

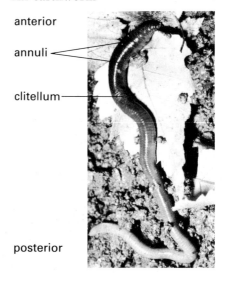

anterior

annuli

clitellum

posterior

The earthworm is a much larger animal than *Planaria* and is not appreciably flattened. It seems unlikely, therefore, that diffusion alone would be sufficient to fulfil its gas exchange needs.

Look at the transverse section of an earthworm in figure 10.

10   TS through an earthworm

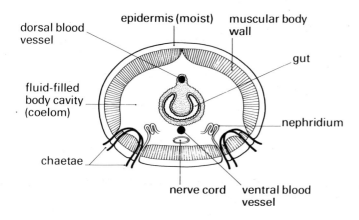

SAQ 12 What does an earthworm have that could speed up the transport of gases to and from the respiratory surface?

Figure 10 shows only the major blood vessels. Microscopical examination of the epidermis of an earthworm reveals that there is an extensive network of fine blood vessels (capillaries) in intimate contact with the respiratory surface. See figure 11.

11   TS skin of an earthworm (HP detail)

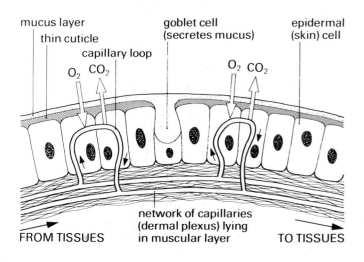

In an earthworm, the movement of gas molecules across the respiratory surface takes place by diffusion, but once across it, gases are transported in the blood system.

In earthworms and in other larger and/or more complex animals, different parts of the body become specialised for separate functions. For instance, in the earthworm the nerve cord is associated with communication and the nephridia (see figure 10) with excretion.

It is as a result of increased size and specialisation that a blood transport system is required to carry oxygen and other materials to all parts of the body and to remove waste products.

Transport of substances in the blood system occurs by mass flow. In mass flow, unlike diffusion, all the molecules are swept along in the same direction. This is brought about by a pressure difference. Pressure in the blood system is produced by the pumping action of the heart or hearts — there are five in the earthworm.

Figure 12 shows part of the lungs of a human. The walls of the small, grape-like structures act as the respiratory surface.

12   Part of human lungs

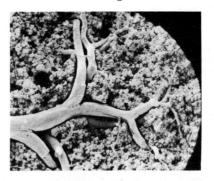

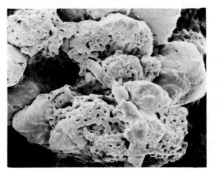

SAQ 13 The twig-like structures shown in figure 12 are not air tubes but are very important in the transport of gases. What do you think they are and what might be their function?

In these larger animals, such as earthworms and humans, the respiratory surface has a fourth important characteristic. In addition to having a large surface area and being moist and permeable to respiratory gases, it is in intimate contact with the blood system.

1.4 Respiratory surfaces and transport systems in plants

In the previous section you saw how, for many animals, an internal transport system is necessary for carrying gases around the body to and from the respiratory surface.

Although higher plants have an internal transport system, it is not involved in the transport of gases. Higher plants have a diffuse branched shape compared with the compact shape of most animals. Hence, they have a large surface area in relation to volume. Thus, no part of the plant is very far away from the external environment and the source of oxygen.

The aerial parts of plants are covered with pores (stomata or lenticels). These link to a series of intercellular spaces within the plant. The walls of the cells lining these spaces act as the respiratory surface. See figure 13.

13   Scanning EM of intercellular spaces and cell surfaces around a stoma of a leaf

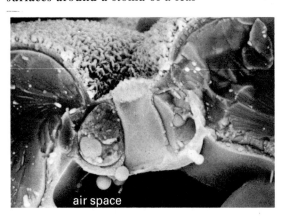
air space

In the roots, the epidermal cells and the root hairs in the root tip region, act as a respiratory surface.

SAQ 14 Compare the respiratory surfaces and the way in which oxygen passes from the respiratory surface to the body cells in a human and a grass plant.

1.5 Uptake of food and water by living organisms

In addition to the exchange of gases, living organisms must take up nutrients such as organic foods, minerals and water.

1.5.1. Food and water uptake by animals

Animals take up complex organic food which must usually be digested in the gut before being absorbed into the body.

Study the organisms in figure 14. The area of food and water uptake is indicated by a heavy line.

14   Food and water uptake in four organisms

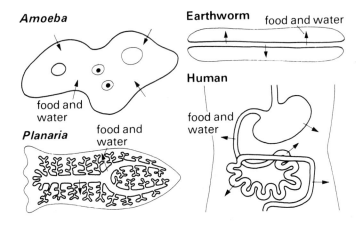

SAQ 15 What feature does the food and water uptake surfaces in these four organisms have in common?

Like respiratory surfaces, the food and water-absorbing surfaces of organisms are relatively thin, moist and have a large surface area in relation to volume. These features all increase the rate at which food can be absorbed.

The mechanism of absorption varies according to the type of food. It may involve diffusion or active transport. Further details of food uptake are included in the unit *Energy and life*.

You can read more about different animal guts in the following short book.

Guts by John Morton, Studies in Biology No. 7.

1.5.2. Food and water uptake by plants

Plant 'food' comprises a gaseous component, carbon dioxide, usually absorbed from the air, together with mineral salts and water which are usually absorbed from the soil.

Figure 15 shows the main areas of uptake of carbon dioxide, water and minerals in plants.

15 Uptake of materials in three plants

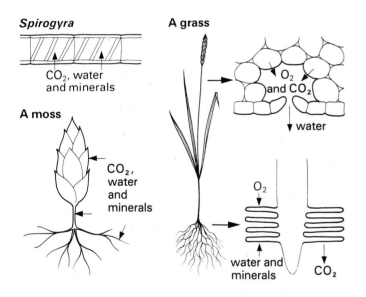

SAQ 16 Name the regions associated with uptake of carbon dioxide, water and minerals in the three plants shown in figure 15.

1.6 Elimination of materials by living organisms

Animals produce more wastes than plants, as explained in the introduction. Figure 16 shows the main regions for elimination of water and other wastes in animals and plants.

16 Sites of waste elimination in four organisms

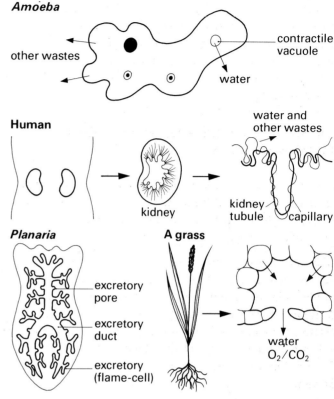

SAQ 17 Name the regions associated with elimination for each of the four organisms shown.

SAQ 18 With what are the kidney tubules in man, and the leaf cell walls in plants, closely associated which enables them to eliminate wastes from *all* parts of the body?

SAQ 19 What do you think is the excretory surface for *Spirogyra* and a moss?

SAQ 20 What is the excretory surface for earthworms? See section 1.3 and figure 10.

1.7 Internal surfaces for exchange of substances between organism and environment

In section 1.2.1, you started to consider the

relationship between surface area and volume with respect to respiratory surfaces. Such relationships are also important for other surfaces of exchange.

SAQ 21 What do you notice about the location of the surfaces for absorption of food and water and elimination of waste by *Planaria*, earthworms, humans and grasses as compared with *Amoeba*, *Spirogyra* and a moss? Refer back to figures 14–16.

The advantage of an internal surface is that it can be much larger and therefore allow a much greater movement of substances across it.

SAQ 22 Devise a way of estimating the surface area of your body.

The ileum, the part of the gut mainly concerned with the absorption of food is a cylinder about 600 cm long and 3 cm diameter in humans.

SAQ 23 Calculate the internal surface area of the ileum using the above information. The area of the curved surface of a cylinder is $2\pi rh$ (π = 3.14). Convert your answer to m^2 and correct it to one decimal place.

The effective surface area for absorption in the ileum is increased over fifty-fold due to the presence of finger-like projections called villi on its inner surface. See figure 17(*a*). The absorptive surface is increased even more, about three-fold, by microvilli on the surface of the lining epithelial cells. See figure 17(*b*).

17 The ileum wall (*a*) internal surface of ileum wall

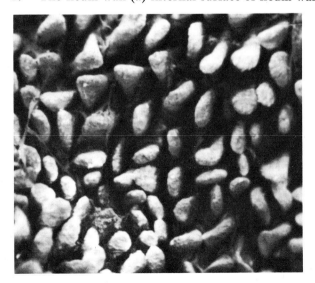

(*b*) surface of epithelial cell lining ileum wall

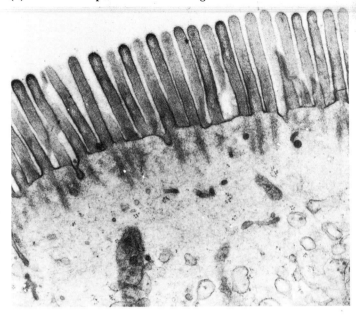

The total absorptive surface of the ileum is equivalent to one quarter of a football pitch.

SAQ 24 From your calculations and the information above, how much greater is the surface area for absorption of food than the surface area of your body?

The respiratory surface of the organisms considered so far in this section have been external, i.e. the body wall. The respiratory surfaces of higher organisms, e.g. insects, fish, mammals and higher plants are found inside the body.

Part of the respiratory surface of a human is shown in figure 12.

The total surface area of the respiratory surface of a human is equivalent to an area the size of a tennis court.

One great advantage of an internal respiratory surface is that its total surface area can be much greater than the area of the external body surface.

SAQ 25 Why is this an advantage?

SAQ 26 What is the other main advantage to terrestrial organisms of possessing an internal respiratory surface? Remember what the three main characteristics of a respiratory surface are.

1.8 Ventilation mechanisms

The respiratory surface must receive a constant supply of fresh air (or water in the case of aquatic organisms). At the same time, used air must be removed.

For organisms such as *Amoeba, Spirogyra, Planaria,* a moss and earthworm, no special mechanism is required to maintain this supply.

For other organisms, including insects, fish and mammals, a special mechanism is required. This is known as a **ventilation mechanism**.

SAQ 27 Why is a ventilation mechanism required in humans but not in *Amoeba?*

1.9 Summary assignment 1

Use the questions and answers to self test 1 as a basis for your notes on this section.

Show this work to your tutor.

Self test 1, page 119 covers section 1 of this unit.

Section 2 Structures involved in gas exchange in animals and plants

2.1 Introduction and objectives

In this section you will be looking more closely at the location of the respiratory surface in four types of organism — insects, fish, mammals and flowering plants. The properties of these sites as surfaces for gas exchange will also be considered.

At the end of this section you should be able to do the following.

(a) State the location of the respiratory surface in an insect, a fish, a mammal and a flowering plant.

(b) Explain how the respiratory surfaces in these organisms are adapted for gas exchange.

(c) State how structure is related to function in the tracheae and tracheoles of an insect.

(d) Describe the structure of the gills of a fish.

(e) State how structure is related to function in the trachea, bronchi and alveoli of mammalian lungs.

2.2 Location and nature of respiratory surfaces

2.2.1 Insects

Figure 18 shows the structures associated with gas exchange in a terrestrial insect.

The tracheae are lined with cuticle. This is the same material that covers the external surface of the insect and acts as the external skeleton or **exoskeleton.** They divide into narrower tubes called **tracheoles,** which are not lined with cuticle. The tracheoles are blind-ending and their tips are filled with a watery fluid.

18   The gas exchange system of an insect

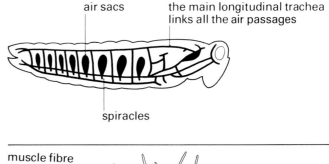

air sacs   the main longitudinal trachea links all the air passages

spiracles

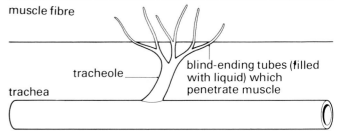

muscle fibre

tracheole   blind-ending tubes (filled with liquid) which penetrate muscle

trachea

SAQ 28 Suggest a reason why the tracheae are lined with cuticle.

Tracheole walls are thin and moist to facilitate gas exchange. The tracheoles form a network of fine tubules penetrating the whole of the body of the insect. They act as the respiratory surface. Thus, the respiratory surface has a very large area and no cell in the body is far away from it.

Since the tips of the tracheoles are normally filled with fluid, gases must diffuse through this as well as the tubule walls. Diffusion is slower through a liquid than through air. This could be a problem when an insect is very active and a faster rate of gas exchange is required. In fact, however, the problem does not arise.

2.2.2 Fish

The respiratory surface of fish comprises the gills. Your investigation in practical A should give you a basic understanding of the structure and function of the gills.

Practical A: The structure of the gills in a fish

Materials

One bony fish (e.g. herring), dissection kit and board, microscope, slides, coverslips, crystallising dish of water

Procedure

(*a*) Place the fish on a dissection board and open its mouth.

(*b*) Trace the route taken by water when the fish breathes. Do this by gently inserting a seeker through the mouth and **pharynx** (throat) and push it until it emerges beneath the **operculum** (gill cover).

(*c*) Lift the operculum and identify the gills beneath it. The position of your seeker should indicate the route of water over the gills.

(*d*) Examine the four gills. Each consists of a double row of filaments attached to a gill arch — see figure 19.

19　One gill of a bony fish

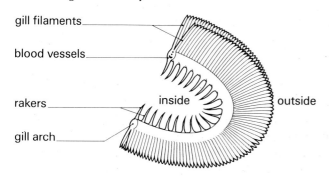

Study the structure of the gill arches and the gill filaments by observation, using a microscope where appropriate, and by feeling them.

Some fish, e.g. herrings, have a third row of structures on the gill arches known as rakers. These project inwards into the pharynx. They act to strain off particles which might damage the gills. In the herring and some other fish, they also strain off small organisms as part of a filter-feeding mechanism.

In some fish, there appears to be a fifth gill in the tissues of the pharynx. This is a non-functional structure called the **pseudobranch.**

In living fish, each row of filaments is separated from its partner and each pair forms a V-shape — see figure 20.

20　Horizontal section through one gill

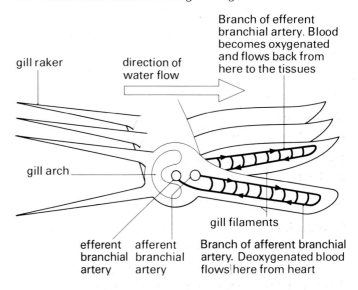

(*e*) Remove the operculum and make a labelled diagram of your dissection to show the gills in position.

(*f*) Remove one gill. Place it in a crystallising dish of water. Observe the appearance of the gill filaments in air and in water. Make a drawing of the gill. Indicate the direction in which water flows over the gills. Does water flow in the same or the opposite direction to the flow of oxygenated blood in the efferent branchial arteries? — see figure 20.

(*g*) Remove a small portion of a filament and examine it under the microscope. You should see the surface folded into small projections which are the gill plates. What do you think is the function of the gill plates?

(h) Do the gills fulfil the characteristics of a respiratory surface? Give reasons for your answer.

Show this work to your tutor.

2.2.3 Mammals

Most mammals are terrestrial animals and all obtain their supplies of oxygen from the air. The organs of gaseous exchange in mammals are the lungs.

The lungs resemble a sponge in that they are made up of many tiny air sacs called **alveoli**. These connect together by a series of tubes which eventually join up to the **trachea** or wind-pipe and finally to the external environment. The walls of the air sacs act as the respiratory surface. The lungs are usually pink or red in colour due to their very rich blood supply. Each air sac is surrounded by a dense network of capillaries.

In practical B you will investigate the position and some aspects of the nature of the respiratory surface.

Practical B: Dissection of the thoracic cavity of a small mammal

---

Materials

One freshly-killed small mammal, waxed dissecting dish or board, dissecting kit, binocular microscope, pins or awls, beaker of water (about 50 cm³), a piece of flexible tubing about 30 cm long and 5 mm in diameter, *Dissection Guide III, The Rat* by H.G.Q. Rowett, 7 cm glass tube (3–5 mm external diameter, with tapering end), 15 cm cotton, U-tube (1–3 mm bore, arms about 20 cm) with coloured oil, 2 cm connecting tubing, syringe barrel with plunger

Procedure

(a) Dissect the mammal to expose the contents of the abdomen — see figure 4 in Rowett. Identify the major organs in the abdomen.

(b) Remove the alimentary canal — see figure 12 (Rowett). Wash away any excess blood.

(c) Examine the diaphragm — see figure 20 (Rowett). Test the tension of the diaphragm with a blunt instrument. Does it feel as if it is under tension?

Follow the instructions in figures 21 and 22 (Rowett). Draw the diaphragm in position, using figure 22 as a guide.

The activities outlined in (d)–(i) are best performed on a rat. A mouse is too small.

(d) Cut into the neck and expose about 1 cm of the trachea. Cut the trachea transversely. Insert a thin glass tube into the posterior section and tie it firmly in position with cotton.

(e) Connect the glass tube to the U-tube with connecting tubing. Mark the fluid levels in each arm of the U-tube.

(f) Pull the diaphragm down into the abdominal cavity. Notice any changes in the fluid levels in the U-tube.

(g) Push the diaphragm up into the thoracic cavity. Again notice any changes in the fluid levels in the U-tube. What do your observation in (f) and (g) indicate about the effects of the diaphragm on the pressure in the thoracic cavity?

(h) Make a small hole in the thorax and move the diaphragm in and out again. Notice what happens to the fluid levels in the U-tube. How does a hole in the thoracic cavity affect the diaphragm's ability to change the pressure within the cavity? What do you think is the significance of these observations in terms of the breathing mechanism? Record your answer as annotations to your diagram.

(i) Remove the U-tube.

(j) Open up and examine the thoracic cavity using Rowett, figures 23–26.

Identify the heart and associated blood vessels, the lungs and the **intercostal muscles** between the ribs. Notice the **pleura** which covers the surface of each lung.

(k) Expose the trachea by following the instructions in figures 27 and 28 (Rowett). The trachea divides into two bronchi, one of which enters each lung.

Touch the trachea to feel the incomplete rings of cartilage in its walls. What sort of material is cartilage? What do you think is its function here?

Figure 21 is a transverse section through the trachea. What do you notice about the surface of the cells lining the tube? Suggest a function for this surface.

Suggest a function for the mucus-secreting cells seen at intervals in the section.

21 TS through trachea.

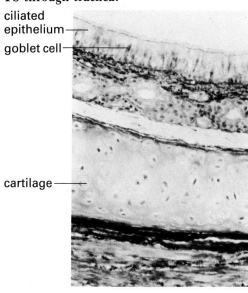

ciliated epithelium
goblet cell
cartilage

(l) Attach the syringe barrel to the trachea. Insert the piston and push it inwards to inflate the lungs. Remove the syringe suddenly and note the elastic behaviour of the lungs in returning to their original size and shape.

(m) Make a labelled drawing of your dissection to show the following: trachea, bronchi, heart and lungs and associated blood vessels, diaphragm, pleural cavity, ribs and intercostal muscles.

(n) Cut off a small piece of lung and drop it into a beaker of water. Explain why it floats.

In texture, lung tissue is similar to foam rubber. What does this indicate about (i) the surface area, and (ii) the thinness of the internal surface of the lungs?

(o) Gently press the cut surface and notice the liquid that oozes out. The inner surface of the lungs is coated with a liquid with a low surface tension.

Figure 22 shows you some differences in the behaviour of liquids of high and low surface tension.

22 Liquids and surface tension

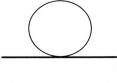

1 cm³ of liquid with a high surface tension, e.g. pure water. The liquid forms a discrete drop because the molecules on the surface are strongly attracted to each other.

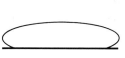

1cm³ of liquid with a low surface tension, e.g. a dilute solution of washing-up liquid. The liquid spreads out over the surface, because the molecules on the surface exert little attraction for each other.

Study the diagrams carefully and then decide: (i) why the liquid in the lungs does not drain down into the bottom of the lungs; (ii) why the presence of this liquid makes it easier to inflate the lung tissue.

(p) Do the lungs fulfil the characteristics of a respiratory surface? Give reasons for your answer and include as annotations on your diagram.

Show this work to your tutor.

2.2.4 Extension: Breathing

More information about the liquid in the lungs can be found in *Breathing Made Easy* (New Scientist, 7 February 1980).

2.2.5 Flowering plants

Living plant tissues contain a network of intercellular spaces. Sometimes, these spaces are relatively small as in the stems and root of most terrestrial plants. In the leaves, however, the spaces are much larger. They are often equivalent in size to the cells themselves.

The spaces are usually air-filled. The cell walls surrounding the spaces are covered by a layer of moisture. Figure 23 shows the internal structure of a leaf in transverse section. Notice the prominent air spaces.

23 Scanning EM of TS through leaf

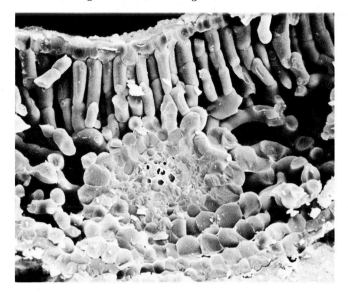

Oxygen and carbon dioxide diffuse through this network of spaces between the external environment and the living plant cells. The site at which these gases pass from the network of air spaces across moist cell walls and membranes into the cell is the respiratory surface of a plant.

SAQ 29 To what extent do you consider the respiratory surface of a plant fulfils the three major characteristics of a respiratory surface?

2.3 Summary assignment 2

Draw simplified diagrams based on figure 8, your drawing from dissection practicals A and B and figure 23.

On each diagram, name the respiratory surface and state to what extent it conforms to the characteristics of a respiratory surface listed in section 1.

Add annotations to show how the structures of the following are related to function: tracheae and tracheoles in insects, bronchi and alveoli in mammals.

Show this work to your tutor.

Self test 2, page 120, covers section 2 of this unit.

Section 3 Movement of gases between the environment and the respiratory surface

3.1 Introduction and objectives

In section 1, you saw that organisms with an internal respiratory surface must have a mechanism for conveying gases between the external environment and the internal respiratory surface. In this section, you will look at the way in which this is done in an insect, a fish, a mammal and a flowering plant.

At the end of this section, you should be able to do the following.

(*a*) Describe the ventilation mechanism in insects with reference to diffusion and pumping movements.

(*b*) Describe the ventilation mechanism in a fish with reference to movements of the mouth, nostrils, pharynx, operculum and gill slits.

(*c*) Draw a diagram to show the relationship between the gills and the blood supply in a fish.

(*d*) Describe the ventilation mechanism in a mammal with reference to the thoracic cavity, diaphragm and intercostal muscles.

(*e*) Draw a diagram to show the relationship between the lungs and the blood supply in a mammal.

(*f*) Describe how breathing is controlled in a mammal.

(*g*) Explain the meaning of the respiratory cycle.

(*h*) Describe the route and the mechanism for movement of gases in a plant between the environment and the individual plant cells.

(*i*) State how concentration gradients are maintained in an insect, a fish, a mammal and a flowering plant.

(*j*) Describe the principles of the counter-current mechanism and show how they apply to gas exchange in a fish.

(*k*) Describe methods for measuring oxygen consumption using (i) a spirometer, and (ii) a respirometer.

(*l*) Extension: Evaluate the evidence about the incidence of lung cancer in people who smoke.

3.2 Movement of gases in insects

In section 2.2.1, you learnt that the respiratory surface of an insect comprised the walls of a system of fine-branching tubes called tracheoles. These connect up to tubes called tracheae. The tracheae connect to the external environment by a series of pores in the, otherwise, impermeable cuticle. These pores are know as **spiracles.** They are found along either side of the body. The spiracles are guarded by valves which open at intervals to let gases in and out of the body

The restriction of sites for entry and exit of gases to a series of small holes which can open and close has an important advantage for insects.

SAQ 30 What do you think this advantage is? (Remember that the majority of insects are terrestrial.)

Practical C: Investigating the gas exchange system in a locust

---

Materials

A living adult locust, male or female, specimen tube or boiling tube approximately 25 mm in diameter and 150 mm long with cork, plug of muslin or loosely-woven material, short piece of plastic tubing or drinking straw, stop-clock or stop-watch, mounted dissection lens or binocular microscope.

Procedure

(a) Carefully place the locust in the specimen tube. Plug the tube with muslin.

(b) Examine the locust under the lens or binocular microscope and look for the spiracles over the body surface.

(c) Notice the position, structure and behaviour of the spiracles. Make annotated diagrams of your observations.

(d) Observe any movements of the abdomen. Record your observations.

(e) Breathe into the tube several times using the tubing or straw provided. Immediately stopper the tube with the cork. Observe the animal closely and note any changes in the movements of the locust.

Remove the cork after making your observations.

(f) Devise a simple quantitative test to investigate the effects of your breathing on the locust.

Discussion of results

1 What might be the function of any abdominal movements you saw?

2 How did these movements change after breathing into the tube? Suggest a reason for this change.

3 Describe the quantitative test you devised. Comment on your methods and results.

Show this work to your tutor.

3.2.1 The mechanism of gas movement in insects

The network of tracheae and tracheoles form a system of air-filled tubes within the body of the insect. At the inner ends of these tubes, oxygen is used up and carbon dioxide is produced by the respiring cells. This creates concentration gradients of the two gases — see figure 24.

SAQ 31 From your study of figure 24, state the mechanism and direction of movement for oxygen and carbon dioxide.

24 Movement of gases in an insect

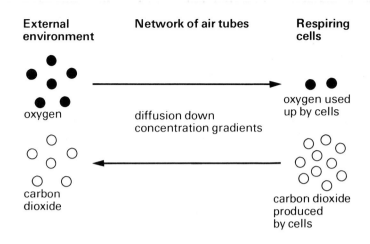

In larger insects and in all active insects, diffusion alone is insufficient to ensure an adequate rate of gas exchange. The rate of movement of gases is increased by pumping movements of muscles of the abdomen. This draws air in and out of the system of tubes by mass flow.

An investigation was carried out in which a live grasshopper was placed in a glass tube. An airtight rubber diaphragm was used to separate the front part of the chamber containing the insect's head and thorax from the back part of the chamber containing the insect's abdomen.

Each part of the chamber was attached to a capillary tube containing a drop of coloured fluid. The position of the drop was noted. See figure 25.

25 Apparatus for investigating gas movement in a grasshopper

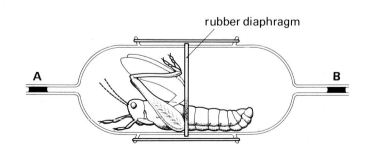

The grasshopper was left for some time. The position of the drops was re-examined. It was found that drop **A** had moved towards the insect and drop **B** had moved away from the insect.

SAQ 32 What does this tell you about air pressure within the two chambers? What does this imply about the volume of air in the two chambers?

SAQ 33 What does this suggest about gas movements within the body of the insect and between the insect and its environment?

These and other studies have indicated that during ventilation in an insect, air is drawn in mainly through the four anterior pairs of spiracles and passed out mainly through the six posterior pairs of spiracles.

3.2.2 Measuring gas exchange

In practical C, you devised a simple test to measure changes in the respiration rate of a locust. In order to measure volumes of oxygen used or carbon dioxide produced, an apparatus called a **respirometer** is used. There are various types of respirometer. One model is shown in figure 26. Examine it carefully.

26   A respirometer

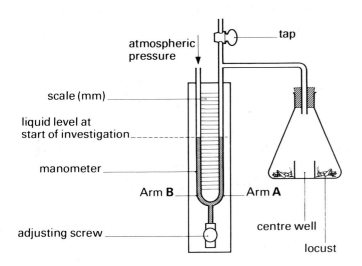

The part of the respirometer labelled manometer comprises a U-shaped tube of coloured fluid. It acts as a pressure gauge.

Initially, the pressure on the fluid in arms **A** and **B** is the same. It is atmospheric pressure. If the volume of gas in the flask decreases, the pressure in **A** will decrease below atmospheric pressure and the fluid will rise up in arm **A** and fall in **B**.

SAQ 34 If the volume of gas in the flask increased, what would happen to
(*a*) the pressure in the flask,
(*b*) the fluid in arm **A**,
(*c*) the fluid in arm **B**?

SAQ 35 What could you deduce about oxygen uptake compared with carbon dioxide production if the liquid level rose
(*a*) in arm **A**, (*b*) in arm B?

In the apparatus as shown, any oxygen removed from the air in the flask during respiration is more or less replaced by carbon dioxide. If carbon dioxide could be prevented from entering the air in the flask, the amount of oxygen used could be measured by the decrease in volume (pressure) in **A**.

SAQ 36 What could you add to the centre well in the flask which would remove the carbon dioxide produced from the atmosphere?

SAQ 37 What assumptions have been made for the respirometer in figure 26 about the pressure on the fluid in arm **B**? Are these assumptions justified?

In addition to changes in atmospheric pressure, temperature changes may affect the apparatus.

SAQ 38 Suggest at least three ways in which temperature might affect the apparatus. Which of these could significantly affect the accuracy of the manometer reading?

To compensate for changing atmospheric pressure during the experiment, arm **B** of the manometer is often connected to a similar flask to arm **A**. In this way, the pressure of the air in the second flask on the fluid in arm **A** would remain constant, despite any changes in the external atmospheric pressure.

The additon of a second flask would also compensate

for the major inaccuracies due to temperature changes.

Practical D: Measuring the oxygen uptake in a locust

The respirometer in this practical is a much-simplified version of the one described above. Nevertheless, the basic principles are the same.

Materials

Living locust in boiling tube (25 mm diameter × 150 mm length), tube graduated in 0.01 cm³ (a graduated pipette with tip cut off may be used), cork or rubber bung for boiling tube with hole that exactly fits the graduated tube, small piece of plastic (about 15 mm long) to fit over end of graduated tube, 6 cm³ marker fluid (1% aqueous methylene blue), cotton wool plug, soda-lime pellets, beaker of water at room temperature, stop-clock or stop-watch with a second hand, thermometer (0–100 °C), dropping pipette, retort stand and clamp to secure apparatus

Procedure

(a) Weigh the boiling tube and cork or rubber bung.

(b) Weigh the boiling tube containing your locust. Calculate the weight of the locust to the nearest 0.1 g.

(c) Carefully set up the apparatus as shown in figure 27.

Leave the tube in the beaker for three minutes before adding the marker fluid.

(d) Record the change in the volume of air in the tube at minute intervals, for a period of ten minutes.

(e) Draw up a table to show
(i) volume of air in the tube per minute,
(ii) volume of oxygen used up during each minute interval,
(iii) cumulative volume of oxygen used up after each minute.

27 Simplified respirometer

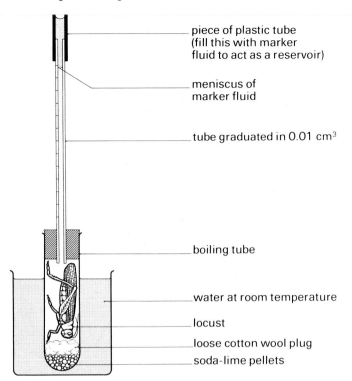

piece of plastic tube (fill this with marker fluid to act as a reservoir)

meniscus of marker fluid

tube graduated in 0.01 cm³

boiling tube

water at room temperature

locust

loose cotton wool plug

soda-lime pellets

(f) Plot a graph of the cumulative change in volume against time.

Discussion of results

1 Explain how this respirometer works.

2 How could you correct for changes in atmospheric pressure and temperature?

3 Using the graph, estimate the oxygen consumption of your locust at room temperature. Is it constant over the ten-minute period? Comment on your answer.

4 Calculate the rate of oxygen consumption at room temperature. Comment on your answer.

5 Explain any precautions you took.

6 In what ways could this experiment be improved?

Show this work to your tutor.

3.3 Movement of gases in fish

Fish obtain their oxygen from water. Oxygen is relatively insoluble in water. At best, water contains about 0.7% oxygen compared to about 20% oxygen in air.

Fish gills, however, remove about 80% of the dissolved oxygen from water, while mammalian lungs can remove only about 25% of the oxygen from air.

There are two factors which seem to be responsible for this efficient oxygen uptake in fish. One is that there is a continuous flow of water over the gills. This is brought about by a ventilation mechanism. The second factor is concerned with the structure of the gills and the blood circulation through them. Both of these factors are now examined in some detail.

Practical E: Ventilation in a fish

Materials

Hand lens, *Kryptopterus bichirrhus* (glass cat-fish or gold-fish), small fish net, 400 cm³ beaker filled with tank water

Procedure

(a) Examine the fish in the fish tank. Locate the operculum — the skin-covered bony plate which protects the gills.

(b) Carefully remove the fish from the tank using the small net. Place the fish in the beaker of water.

(c) Note any movements of the mouth and operculum. Do they occur simultaneously or out of phase?

(d) Make brief notes on your observations.

Show this work to your tutor.

3.3.1 Ventilation movements in a fish

The mouth (**buccal cavity**) and the cavity behind the operculum (**opercular cavity**) are involved in the movements. See figure 28.

28   Structures involved in ventilation mechanism

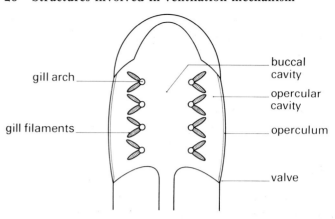

The buccal cavity and opercular cavity can be regarded as two pumps, a pressure pump in front of the gills and a suction pump behind the gills. These pumps work slightly out of phase with each other.

The mechanism of inspiration and expiration is illustrated in figure 29. Study the diagrams carefully.

29   The mechanism of ventilation in a fish

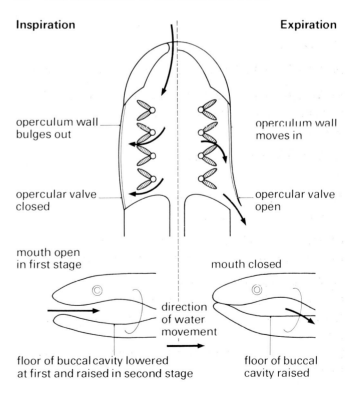

SAQ 39 The following passage has several important words missing. Using what you have learnt from figure 29, select and list the best word(s) to fill in the blanks.

You may like to work in a small group for this question or compare your answers with those of others in the class when you have finished.

During (1)   (drawing water in), the (2)   of the (3)   is lowered, thus (4)   pressure (5)   enters through the opened mouth. The mouth then closes and the floor of the buccal cavity is raised, thus (6)   the pressure within the cavity. This (7)   water out (8)   the (9)   into the (10)   . The (11)   bulges (12)   , but the opercular valve, which can allow (13)   to the outside, (14)   shut.

During expiration ((15)   ), the opercular wall moves (16)   . This (17)   pressure in the (18)   . The opercular valve (19)   and water passes out of the fish.

This mechanism causes a (20)   flow of (21) over the (22)   . Thus, a (23)   supply of (24)   is brought to the gill surface and carbon dioxide is (25)   .

The ventilation mechanism in fishes can respond to changes in the oxygen requirements. For example, the breathing rate speeds up if activity increases or if the water is deficient in oxygen.

3.3.2 Blood circulation through the gills

As water flows over the gills which act as the respiratory surface, oxygen diffuses from the water into the blood stream due to concentration gradients. Carbon dioxide diffuses in the opposite direction from the blood stream to the water.

In the following practical, you will dissect a dogfish to show the blood vessels which supply the gills.

Practical F: Dissection of the blood vessels associated with the gills in a dogfish

This practical is divided into three parts. In part 1, you will expose the internal surface of the pharynx. In part 2 you will dissect the vessels which carry blood containing carbon dioxide to the gill surface. These are called the **afferent branchial arteries.** In part 3 you will dissect the vessels carrying oxygenated blood from the gills. These are called the **efferent branchial arteries** and **epibranchial arteries.**

Materials

Preserved dogfish, dissecting kit, dissecting board and four awls, hammer

Procedure

Part 1 Exposing the inside of the pharynx

(*a*) Cut through the right side of the animal from the angle of the jaw to the posterior limit of the pectoral fin, dorsal to the fin base. Make sure you cut into the cavity of the gut and through the middle of each gill bar — see figure 30.

30   Right side of a fish showing position of first cut

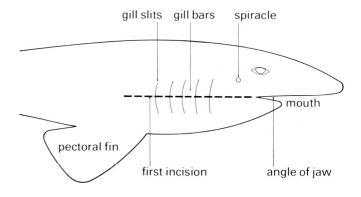

(*b*) Continuing from the end of your first cut, make a transverse cut right across the animal ventrally, to the left pectoral fin — see figure 31.

31 Ventral surface of fish showing position of second cut

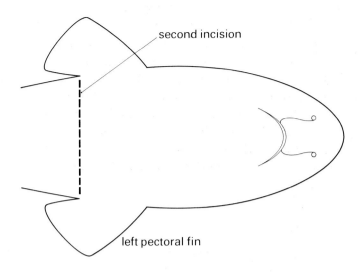

second incision

left pectoral fin

32 The dogfish pharynx opened up

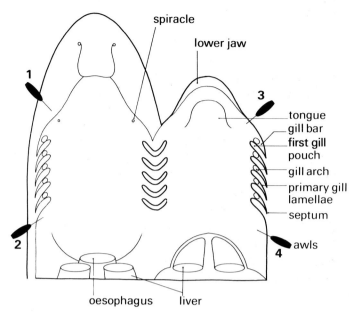

spiracle

lower jaw

1

3

tongue
gill bar
first gill pouch
gill arch
primary gill lamellae
septum

2

4 awls

oesophagus   liver

(c) Use two awls (**1** and **2** — see figure 32) to pin out the right side of the animal, placing them well clear of the gill pouches. Make sure that they are firmly inserted into the dissecting board.

(d) Open out the fish by pulling out the freed lower jaw and ventral part of the pharynx over to your right. To free this region completely, you will have to cut through the oesophagus and the liver. Fix the fish firmly in position using two more awls (**3** and **4** — see figure 32).

(e) Wash out the contents of the gut and clear out the gill pouches. Your dissection should now look similar to figure 32.

Questions after Part 1
1 (a) How many gill pouches are there in a dogfish?

(b) Does each pouch have gill filaments on both sides?

Part 2: Dissection of the vessels bringing blood to the gills

(a) Cut through the mucous membrane of the pharynx floor — as indicated in figure 33. Strip off this section of membrane in one swift movement, starting at the front end.

(b) On the pharynx floor in the region of the fourth and fifth gill pouches, cut through the exposed tissue until you meet firm cartilage. This is the basibranchial cartilage. Refer to figure 33.

(c) Scrape outwards from the mid-line to expose the whole extent of the basibranchial cartilage; do this quite boldly and quickly.

33 The branchial cartilages of the pharynx floor

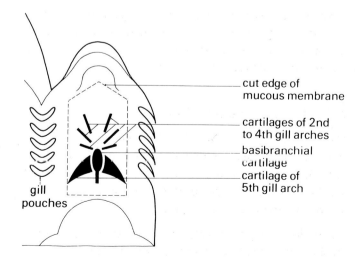

cut edge of mucous membrane

cartilages of 2nd to 4th gill arches

basibranchial cartilage

cartilage of 5th gill arch

gill pouches

(d) Continue scraping forwards and laterally until you can see the cartilages of the second and fourth gill arches and the fifth ceratobranchial of both sides. The scraped area should now resemble figure 33.

(e) Carefully remove the basibranchial and both the cartilages of the fifth gill arch. To avoid damaging the underlying heart, you should lift each section with forceps as you cut it.

(f) Trim the cut edge of the pericardium taking particular care at the posterior margin as the sinus venosus closely adheres to the pericardium. (See figure 34.)

Do not trim away too much of the wall at the anterior end of the pericardial cavity, or you will damage the fifth afferent branchial arteries which arise here from the ventral aorta. (See figure 34.)

(g) Remove the cartilage of the second gill arch on the left side.

(h) Clear the connective tissue along the mid-line until you expose the ventral aorta.

(i) Trace the aorta forwards until you reach the right and left innominate arteries. (See figure 34.)

(j) Free the left innominate artery from connective tissue and trace it as far as you can. The pillar muscles are an obstacle to clearing.

(k) Separate the first pillar muscle from connective tissue and from the innominate and when it is entirely free, cut through it as low down as possible and remove it. This should be done with scissors in a single operation. Try to leave a tidy stump.

(l) Dissect the innominate out as far as its fork into the first and second afferent branchial arteries. Clear the bases of the first and second afferent arteries.

(m) Remove the cartilage of the second gill arch. The third afferent branchial artery lies immediately beneath it.

(n) Free the third afferent branchial artery from connective tissue.

(o) Locate then free the second pillar muscle and remove it with a single scissor cut to leave a tidy

stump, taking care to avoid damaging the second afferent artery.

34   Diagram of the heart and ventral aorta

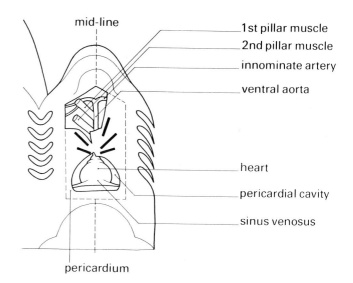

(p) Remove the cartilage of the third gill arch to expose the fourth afferent branchial artery.

(q) Free the fourth afferent branchial artery from connective tissue.

(r) Remove the third and fourth pillar muscles; the fifth afferent branchial artery lies just posterior to the fourth pillar muscle. This is the most difficult of the blood vessels to dissect out neatly.

(s) Now trace the third afferent branchial artery as far as possible. First, you will need to trace it to the beginning of the gill bar along which its course lies. Once this is done it is not too difficult to dissect the artery along the arch provided you keep your scalpel close to the anterior border of the blood vessel and cut upwards all the time. By doing this, you will free the artery from the cartilages of the third gill arch which lie anterior to the artery (see figure 35).

(Note: If your first attempt to trace an afferent artery is unsuccessful, bear in mind where you ran into difficulties and try to trace one of the other arteries. It does not matter which one you finally succeed in tracing so long as you modify the next part of the investigation to fit in with your dissection.)

35 Blood vessels bringing blood to the gills

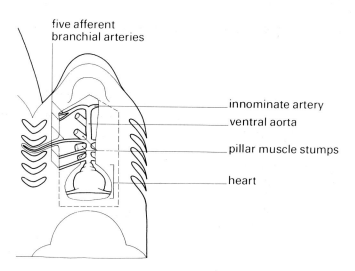

five afferent branchial arteries

innominate artery

ventral aorta

pillar muscle stumps

heart

Questions after Part 2

1 Outline the pathway of blood from the heart to the first gill arch.

2 Will these vessels be rich in oxygen or carbon dioxide?

Part 3: Dissecting the vessels carrying blood away from the gills

(*a*) Cut through the mucous membrane of the pharynx roof, as indicated in figure 36. Strip off this section of the membrane as for the pharynx floor.

(*b*) Locate the cartilages of the four gill arches on the animal's left side by scraping the exposed area until they appear (see figure 36). When you have found them look for the epibranchial arteries. The first artery is tight against the anterior surface of the first pharyngobranchial cartilage, and the remaining three lie clear from their related cartilages (about 3 mm anterior to them).

(*c*) Remove the pharyngobranchial cartilages. The first pharyngobranchial of the left side may join with the corresponding cartilage of the other side, in which case you should cut a small part of the right cartilage away.

(*d*) Locate and clean the dorsal aorta.

(*e*) Trace the epibranchial arteries from the dorsal aorta to the gill bars — see figure 36.

(*f*) Follow the course of the second epibranchial artery into the gill bar. Identify the cartilages of the second bar and carefully remove them.

(*g*) Remove any muscle tissue that obscures the view. Peel the anterior part of the mucous membrane of the second bar forward. (See figure 37(*a*).)

(*h*) Lift up the flap of mucous membrane that you peeled forward to reveal the efferent branchial artery.

36 Blood vessels carrying blood away from the gills

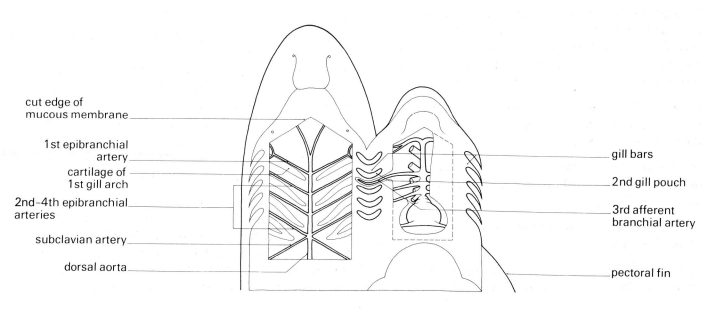

cut edge of mucous membrane

1st epibranchial artery

cartilage of 1st gill arch

2nd–4th epibranchial arteries

subclavian artery

dorsal aorta

gill bars

2nd gill pouch

3rd afferent branchial artery

pectoral fin

37 Exposing the efferent branchial loop

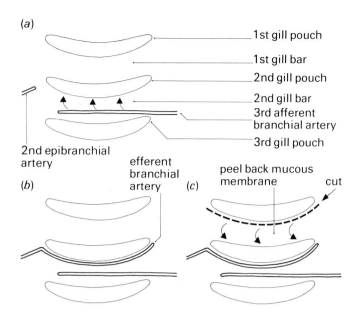

(a)

1st gill pouch
1st gill bar
2nd gill pouch
2nd gill bar
3rd afferent branchial artery
3rd gill pouch

2nd epibranchial artery

efferent branchial artery

peel back mucous membrane

cut

(b)

(c)

Trim the mucous membrane down to the blood vessels — see figure 37(b).

(i) Trace the efferent branchial artery which forms a loop around the second gill pouch. Make a cut in the mucous membrane of the first bar and pull the posterior half of the mucous membrane back until you can see the complete efferent branchial artery — see figure 37(c).

(j) Trim the mucous membrane down to the level of the blood vessel. The dissection is now completed and it should look something like figure 38.

Questions after Part 3
1 Outline the pathway of oxygenated blood to the dorsal aorta.

2 During the whole dissection, you have had to remove muscle and cartilage tissue to display the blood vessels. Suggest functions for these tissues.

Show this work to your tutor.

3.3.3 The flow of blood and water during gas exchange

In the previous practical, you saw the route taken by water through the gill region and the route taken by blood as it passes through the gills. However, it was not possible to see the movements of water and blood themselves.

You can see these movements in another organism — the water louse, *Asellus,* since its body is relatively transparent.

38 Diagram of the finished dissection

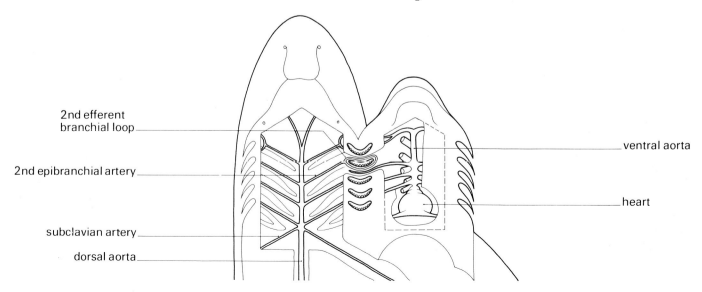

2nd efferent branchial loop

2nd epibranchial artery

subclavian artery

dorsal aorta

ventral aorta

heart

Practical G: Investigating water and blood flow in *Asellus*

Materials

Glass plate about 10 cm², 4 glass slides, wide-mouthed pipette, 2–3 light-coloured *Asellus*, microscope (monocular)

Procedure

(*a*) Mount an *Asellus* on its back in a drop of water, as shown in figure 39, so that it is held firmly but not squashed.

39   Mounting an *Asellus*

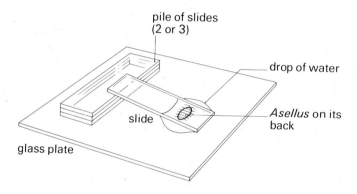

(*b*) Examine under the microscope. Look for movements of materials within any of the limbs.

(*c*) Push gently but firmly downwards on the animal. Examine the posterior end and watch for a colourless plate-like structure to appear on either side. See figure 40.

If the structure is not clearly visible with your *Asellus*, try another one.

(*d*) Look for any movements within this structure. What do you see moving? How do the movements occur? In what direction does movement occur?

(*e*) Do you notice any movements in the water surrounding the plate? How does the direction of this movement compare with the direction of the internal movements?

40   Posterior end of *Asellus*

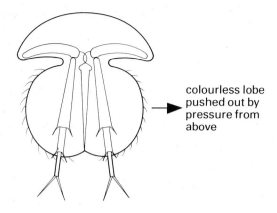

colourless lobe pushed out by pressure from above

(*f*) Write a report of your observations. In your report, suggest a function for the plates you observed and what the movements represent.

Show this work to your tutor.

3.3.4 The counter-current mechanism

In the previous practical you probably discovered that, in the respiratory surface of *Asellus*, the movement of blood in capillaries occurs in the opposite direction to the movement of water over the surface.

Study figure 41 which shows the principles of this exchange system in which blood and water flow in opposite directions. This is known as a **counter-current flow**.

41   Movement of water and blood in the gill region

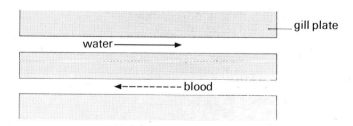

With this arrangement, as blood flows over the gill plates and becomes more saturated with oxygen, it meets water that has had progressively less oxygen removed from it. This ensures the maintenance of a concentration gradient between water and the blood over the gill surface.

The changes in percentage concentration of oxygen in water and blood over the gill surface with counter-current flow are shown in figure 42.

42   Oxygen saturation in water and blood with counter-current flow

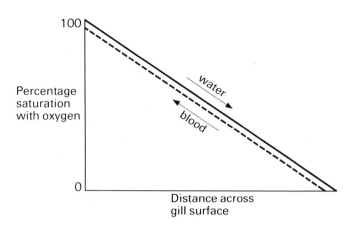

If water and blood flow in the same direction over the gill surface, this is called **parallel flow**. The exchange of oxygen between water and blood in such circumstances is shown in figure 43.

43   Oxygen saturation in water and blood with parallel flow

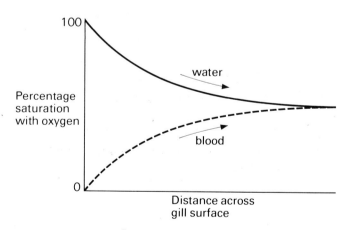

SAQ 40 Explain why counter-current flow produces a more efficient gas exchange system than parallel flow.

Figure 44 shows how the counter-current mechanism for exchange applies to gas exchange in a bony fish. Study this figure carefully.

44   Counter-current mechanism in a bony fish (a) the pharynx, (b) a single gill, (c) the gill surface

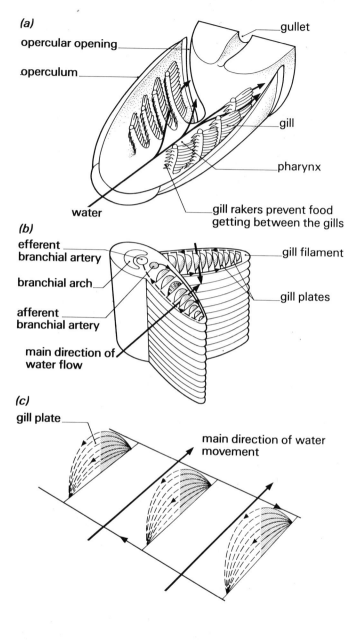

AV 1: The counter-current principle

Materials

VCR and monitor
ABAL video sequence: *The counter-current principle*
Worksheets

Procedure

(a) View the video sequence.

(b) Read through the worksheets and answer as many questions as possible

(c) View the sequence again to check your answers.

Show this work to your tutor.

SAQ 41 The following passage has several important words missing. Using what you have learned from figure 44, select and list the best word(s) to fill in the blanks.

You may like to work in a small group for this question or compare your answers with those of others in the class when you have finished.

During ventilation (1)   passes from the (2)   through the (3)   and out into the external environment. As water passes through the gill slits, it flows over the (4)   and the (5)   which act as the respiratory surface.

(6)   blood flows in the (7)   and it branches outwards along the septum of each gill. (8)   in the gill plates (9)   these branches with the efferent branchial loop and its tributaries which carry (10)   blood back to the (11)   along the (12)   edges of the gill filaments.

As blood flows through the capillaries, water flows over the surface of the gill plates in the (13) direction. It is in the region of these capillaries that (14)   of oxygen and carbon dioxide occurs between the blood and the water. The (15) mechanism of exchange ensures that at every point along the capillaries the (16)   of oxygen is greater in the water than the blood and the (17)   of carbon dioxide is (18)   in the blood than in the water. Hence, along the whole length of these capillaries, oxygen diffuses from the (19)   into the (20)   and carbon dioxide diffuses from the (21)   into the (22)

In dogfish, the counter-flow mechanism is not fully operational. This is because the main flow of water tends to pass over the gill plates rather than between them.

In bony fish, the mechanism of gas exchange in the gills is so efficient that 80% of oxygen is extracted from the water.

3.4 Movement of gases in mammals

Ventilation (or breathing) in a mammal is brought about by the alternate contraction and relaxation of the intercostal muscles and diaphragm. Inward movement of air is called **inspiration** (inhalation). Each inspiration is followed by an **expiration** (exhalation) during which air is forced out of the lungs.

The following investigations will help you understand the mechanisms of breathing in a mammal and show how air is altered when it enters the lungs.

3.4.1 The structure of the human thorax

The organs associated with ventilation in mammals are found in the thorax. In practical B, you examined the thorax of a rat or mouse.

Figure 45 shows the structure of the human thorax. Study it carefully.

SAQ 42 Name the structures labelled **1–14**.

Practical H: Investigating the role of the intercostal muscles and the diaphragm in breathing

---

In this practical, you will use your own body and models to investigate the role of the intercostal muscles and diaphragm in breathing.

Materials

Cardboard model of ribs, sternum and backbone, bell-jar model of the thorax.

Procedure

(a) Place your hands on your ribs and breathe in

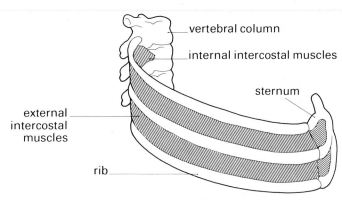

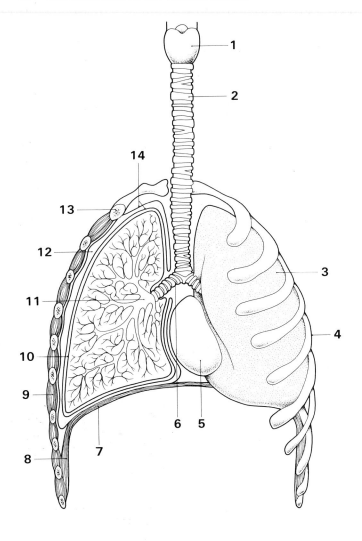

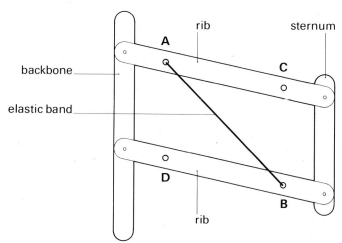

deeply. In which direction do your ribs move during (i) inspiration, (ii) expiration?

(*b*) The movements of the rib-cage are brought about by two sets of intercostal muscles. These are shown in figure 46. Study the diagram carefully before going on to use the model.

(*c*) Now examine your model which should look like figure 47.

(*d*) Place an elastic band between points **A** and **B**, as in figure 47.

Which set of muscles does this represent? What will happen to the ribs when these muscles contract? Is this associated with inspiration or expiration? Note

your findings.

(*e*) Place the elastic band between points **C** and **D**. Which set of muscles does this represent? What will happen to the ribs when these muscles contract? Is this associated with inspiration or expiration? Note your findings.

(*f*) Take a bell-jar model — see figure 48 — and move the rubber sheet up and down. Note your findings.

Discussion of results

1 How does contraction of (*a*) the external intercostal muscles and (*b*) the internal intercostal muscles affect

48   The bell-jar model of the thorax

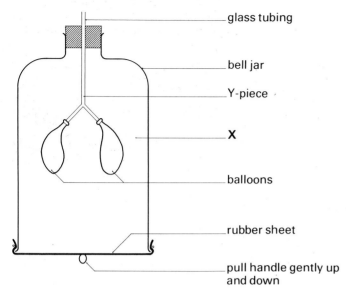

- glass tubing
- bell jar
- Y-piece
- **X**
- balloons
- rubber sheet
- pull handle gently up and down

the volume of the thoracic cavity?

2 Explain the effect on the balloons of moving the rubber sheet in the bell-jar model.

3 Which parts of the thoracic cavity of a mammal are represented in the bell-jar model by:
(*a*) glass tubing;
(*b*) the Y-piece;
(*c*) the balloons;
(*d*) the bell jar;
(*e*) the rubber sheet?

4 The two partially annotated diagrams in figure 49 show the role of the ribs and intercostal muscles and the diaphragm during inspiration and expiration. Study these diagrams carefully and, as a result of your investigations with the models, list the words that would complete the blanks in the labels.

5 For what reasons connected with (*a*) structure and (*b*) function is the glass bell-jar a poor representation of the thorax?

6 Why is the rubber sheet a poor model of the diaphragm (*a*) in terms of structure and position; (*b*) in terms of changes in shape which occur during breathing?

7 (*a*) What does **X** represent in figure 48? (*b*) Why is it inaccurate?

49   The role of the diaphragm and ribs during breathing

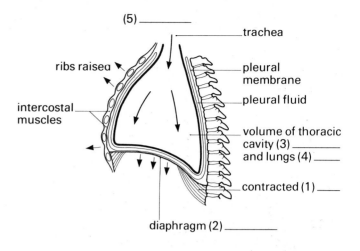

- (5) _____
- trachea
- ribs raised
- pleural membrane
- intercostal muscles
- pleural fluid
- volume of thoracic cavity (3) _____ and lungs (4) _____
- contracted (1) _____
- diaphragm (2) _____

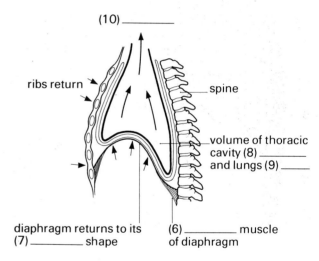

- (10) _____
- ribs return
- spine
- volume of thoracic cavity (8) _____ and lungs (9) _____
- diaphragm returns to its (7) _____ shape
- (6) _____ muscle of diaphragm

8 What type of molecular movement occurs during ventilation of the lungs?

9 Imagine that there is a hole in the wall of the bell jar. How would this affect ventilation in the balloons? Give a reason for your answer.

10 Refer back to the diagram of the structure of the human thorax — figure 45. It shows that the thorax wall and lungs are separated by the pleural membranes. The membranes are separated from each other by the pleural fluid.

State two possible functions of pleural fluid.

Show this work to your tutor.

3.4.2 Past examination question

Answer the following past examination question.

Explain the following terms by reference, where appropriate, to an insect, a fish, a mammal and a germinating seed:
(*a*) respiratory surface; (*b*) respiratory movements; (*c*) respiratory quotients.*
(London, Paper 1, January 1974)

*Respiratory quotients are discussed in the unit *Energy and life.*

Show this work to your tutor.

3.4.3 The respiratory cycle

A respiratory cycle involves one inspiration followed by one expiration. Under normal circumstances, an adult takes in and then expires about 0.5 dm³ of air during one respiratory cycle. This volume of air is known as the **tidal volume.**

Lungs are able to to take in and expel a larger volume than the tidal volume. This enables the respiratory apparatus to adapt to changing needs as, for example, during exercise. You can get some idea of your extra lung capacity by breathing in as deeply as you can. This extra capacity is your **inspiratory reserve volume,** which is about 3 dm³ greater than your tidal volume.

At the end of your next normal expiration, expel as much air as you can from your lungs. This extra expiratory capacity is the **expiratory reserve volume,** which is about 1 dm³. After such a maximum expiration, about 1.5 dm³ of air remains in the lungs. This is the **residual volume.**

SAQ 43 What would happen to the lungs if all the air was removed from them during expiration?

The total of the inspiratory reserve volume (i.e. maximum intake) and the expiratory reserve volume (i.e. maximum expiration) is called the **vital capacity.**

The rate of respiration (ventilation rate) is equal to **tidal volume × frequency of inspiration** (usually calculated for a one-minute period.)

All these volumes (tidal, inspiratory reserve, etc.) can be measured by a spirometer.

A spirometer consists of an airtight chamber which is suspended freely over water. It is counter-balanced so that gas passed in or drawn out of the chamber makes it rise or fall — see figure 50.

50 A spirometer and kymograph in use

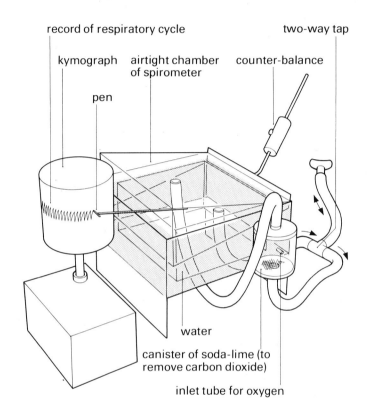

A pen, attached to the chamber, writes on a slowly-rotating drum (the kymograph) so that a permanent record of the respiratory cycle can be made.

As the subject breathes in, the volume of air in the airtight chamber decreases. This causes the chamber to fall and the pen to make a downward movement on the kymograph drum — see figure 51.

The recording on the kymograph in figure 51 is of the subject's tidal volume.

SAQ 44 Is the subject about to breathe in or out?

The spirometer can be used to make a number of measurements on gas exchange in humans, such as measuring a respiratory cycle or the rate of oxygen consumption.

51 Spirometer trace

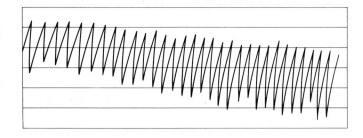

Practical I: Using a spirometer to measure the respiratory cycle and oxygen consumption

---

The spirometer must only be used if a tutor is present. It is best to work in small groups for this investigation.

Materials

Spirometer and kymograph, soda-lime for canister, dilute TCP solution to rinse mouthpiece, 3 pieces of kymograph paper, stop-watch with second hand, 250 cm³ conical flask, right-angled piece of glass tubing, right angled piece of glass tubing with tap attached see figure 52, rubber tubing for attaching glass tubing to water tap and spirometer

Procedure

Part 1: The respiratory cycle

The spirometer should be set up for you — check with your tutor.
(*a*) Check that the soda-lime canister is in place and contains sufficient soda-lime.

(*b*) Fix a piece of kymograph paper onto the drum.

(*c*) With the pen at its highest point, let the drum make one complete revolution, moving the pen every ten seconds so that it makes a vertical mark on the drum. This will provide you with a time scale.

(*d*) To calibrate the spirometer, adjust the chamber to its lowest position. Allow the kymograph pen to mark the drum for one complete revolution. Introduce 250 cm³ air into the chamber by attaching a 250 cm³ flask to the spirometer and a water tap, as shown in figure 52.

52 Method for introducing a known volume of air into a spirometer

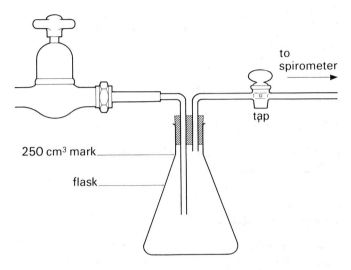

Displace the 250 cm³ air in the flask by water. Allow the kymograph pen to mark the drum for one complete revolution at its new position. Empty the flask and repeat the procedure to calibrate the other two pieces of paper.

(*e*) Rinse the mouthpiece in dilute TCP solution.

(*f*) The subject should now sit down with the mouthpiece and noseclip in position. Position the pen so that it will mark the drum about half-way up. Allow the subject to get used to breathing this way, then switch on the kymograph drum.

(*g*) Record the subject's breathing movements for one revolution of the drum.

(*h*) Remove the paper from the drum. Replace it with a new piece.

(*i*) Instruct the subject to alter his/her breathing so that you may record the following: tidal volume, expiratory reserve volume, inspiratory reserve volume, vital capacity. Switch off the drum when you have finished.

(*j*) Calculate the volumes listed above in dm³.

(*k*) Assuming the total lung capacity is about 6 dm³, calculate the residual volume for your subject.

Not all of the air in the tidal volume is available for gas exchange. Some of it remains in the trachea and bronchial tubes where no gaseous exchange occurs. During normal breathing, only about 350 cm³ of each tidal volume gets into the alveoli where gas exchange is possible.

This relatively small volume mixes with the relatively large residual volume already present in the alveoli. The composition of the air in the alveoli thus remains fairly constant during resting conditions.

Part 2: Measuring the rate of oxygen consumption

As carbon dioxide is removed from the chamber by the soda-lime, it will rise and fall with each breath. It will also gradually subside as the volume of oxygen decreases.

This will appear on the kymograph tracing as a downwards movement from left to right — see figure 53.

53 Kymograph tracings of breathing

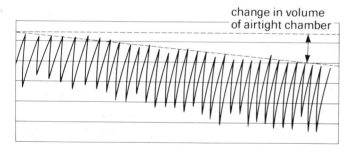

change in volume of airtight chamber

(*a*) Using the first kymograph trace obtained, calculate; (i) the resting subject's oxygen consumption for a five-minute period; (ii) the ventilation rate for the resting subject.

(*b*) Place a third piece of paper on the drum.

(*c*) Ask the subject to perform some exercise (such as running upstairs) for 2–3 minutes. You *must* discuss the nature of the exercise with your tutor beforehand.

(*d*) Record his/her respiratory cycle for five minutes after exercise.

Questions

1 Calculate (*a*) oxygen consumption, (*b*) ventilation rate, for five minutes after exercise.

2 Explain the differences in (*a*) respiratory cycle, (*b*) ventilation rate, (*c*) amount of oxygen used by a resting subject and one who has recently exercised.

Show this work to your tutor.

3.4.4 The composition of inspired and expired air

To determine how the composition of air is changed during breathing, it is necessary to analyse the contents of inspired and expired air.

Known volumes of each type of air are obtained. If a solution which absorbs carbon dioxide is introduced into each of these samples, their total volumes will be reduced. This will allow the proportions of carbon dioxide in them to be calculated.

SAQ 45 What solution could be used to absorb carbon dioxide?

Subsequent introduction of a solution which absorbs oxygen will further reduce the volumes of the samples. It is then possible to calculate the proportions of oxygen in the sample.

SAQ 46 What solution could be used to absorb oxygen?

Figure 54 shows measurements taken from such an investigation.

SAQ 47 Copy out and complete figure 54 by filling in the gaps.

3.4.5 Gas exchange across the alveolar surface

During breathing, about a quarter of the oxygen of inspired air is removed before expiration. The carbon dioxide content of expired air is over 100 times that of inspired air.

These changes are due to movement of the gases by diffusion between the alveoli of the lungs and the blood capillaries of the lungs.

54 The composition of inspired and expired air

	Inspired air	Expired air
Volume 1 Total volume of air (cm^3)	200	150
Volume 2 Air less carbon dioxide (cm^3)	199.04	143.8
Volume 3 Volume of carbon dioxide in air sample (cm^3)		
Volume 4 Air less carbon dioxide and oxygen (cm^3)	157.04	119.2
Volume 5 Volume of oxygen present in the sample (cm^3)		

% carbon dioxide present in
original air sample

$$= \frac{\text{vol. of } CO_2}{\text{total vol. air}} \times 100$$

% oxygen present in original
air sample

$$= \frac{\text{vol. of } O_2}{\text{total vol air}} \times 100$$

Figure 55 shows the amount of oxygen and carbon dioxide in the blood as it enters and leaves the lungs in a mammal.

55 Gas composition of blood in lungs

Gas	Volumes of each gas carried by 100 cm^3 of blood	
	Entering the lungs in the pulmonary artery	Leaving the lungs in the pulmonary vein
Nitrogen	0.9	0.9
Oxygen	10.6	19.0
Carbon dioxide	58.0	50.0

SAQ 48 Copy figure 56 into your notebook and annotate it to indicate what happens to oxygen, carbon dioxide and nitrogen in the lungs, using the data in figure 55.

Nitrogen has been completed for you.

56 Gas exchange in an alveolus

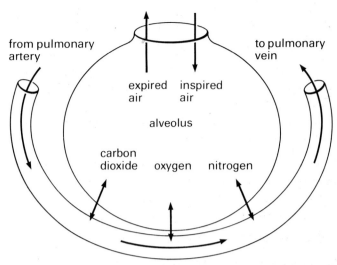

N_2. This diffuses in both directions, to and from the alveolar air and the blood. Nitrogen is not used by the tissues, so blood in all vessels will have the same N_2 content.

SAQ 49 What type of molecular movement accounts for gas exchange at the alveolar surface?

3.4.6 The control of breathing

If a subject is made to breathe air which contains abnormally high quantities of carbon dioxide, his/her ventilation rate will increase. This can be shown by connecting the subject to a spirometer from which the soda-lime canister has been removed. The air in the spirometer chamber will gradually become richer in carbon dioxide. Soon the subject's ventilation rate and tidal volumes will increase as the body tries to remove excess carbon dioxide.

You must never do this. It is very dangerous.

SAQ 50 What control experiment could you set up to show that changes in the pattern of breathing are due to accumulation of carbon dioxide and not decrease in oxygen?

The human body is sensitive to changes in the level of carbon dioxide. These changes are detected by receptors in the brain and receptors in artery walls.

Chemoreceptors in the respiratory centre of the medulla of the hind-brain respond to an increase in acidity in the cerebrospinal fluid in the brain. These changes correspond to any changes in acidity in the blood due to increased carbon dioxide levels.

Chemoreceptor cells in the walls of the carotid and aortic arteries are sensitive to changes in carbon dioxide levels. These clusters of cells are known as the **carotid** and **aortic bodies** respectively. Nerve impulses are sent from these bodies to the brain.

Information received by the brain from these receptors in the medulla, carotid and aortic bodies results in nerve impulses passing to the thorax to increase the rate of breathing. See figure 57.

The receptors in the brain appear to play a greater role in the regulation of breathing.

57   Control of breathing

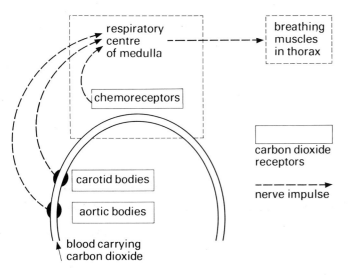

3.5 Extension: Lung cancer and smoking

The delicate surface of the lungs is in constant contact with the air, and there is evidence that certain chemicals in the air can harm the lungs.

There is much evidence indicating a connection between smoking and lung cancer and other respiratory diseases. Investigations on this subject can have important consequences for health. Since it is an area in which research is still in progress, there are many unanswered or incompletely answered questions.

You can find out more about smoking, lung cancer and related problems from the following resources which your tutor may provide. Alternatively, find other references from libraries.

TACADE-ASH Fact Sheets
Your tutor may also show you films on the subject.

Use these and other resources to try to answer the following questions:

1 How much is known about the causes of lung cancer?

2 What is the evidence for the connection between lung cancer and smoking?

3 Why do people smoke?

4 Evaluate the evidence for smoking being a cause of other disruptions to health in addition to lung cancer.

5 What are the risks of smoking and taking oral contraceptives?

6 What are the effects on pregnancy and childbirth to women who smoke?

Show this work to your tutor.

3.6 Movement of gases in plants

The systems of intercellular spaces within the plant are in direct communication with the external environment via pores. These pores are known as stomata (singular: stoma) in the leaves and young stems and lenticels in woody stems.

Figures 58 and 59 show details of these two structures. Study the photographs carefully.

SAQ 51 What do you notice about the thickness of the cell wall in the guard cells surrounding the stomatal pore?

SAQ 52 Which is larger, a stoma or a lenticel? Give reasons for your answer.

SAQ 53 How does the nature of the pore differ in stomata and lenticels?

SAQ 54 Since stomata communicate with the moist internal respiratory surface via intercellular spaces,

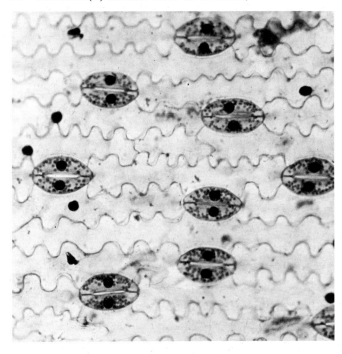

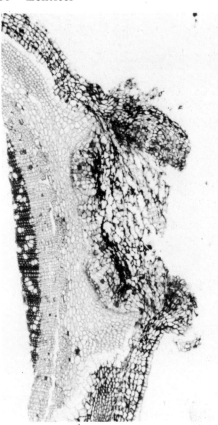

(*b*) VS of stoma

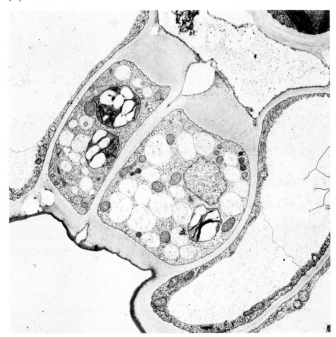

what other substance beside carbon dioxide and oxygen might also pass out through the stomata?

Unlike lenticels, stomatal pores can change the size of their opening.

SAQ 55 Suggest an advantage conferred by this ability to alter in size.

During the day, oxygen is produced within plant cells and carbon dioxide is used up. Therefore, the oxygen concentration in the cells is higher than the oxygen concentration in the intercellular spaces. The carbon dioxide concentration is higher in the intercellular spaces than the cells. As a result of these concentration gradients, oxygen diffuses out of the cells and carbon dioxide diffuses into the cells.

A concentration gradient now exists between gases in the intercellular spaces of the plant and the external environment. Oxygen continues to diffuse through the intercellular spaces to the outside, while carbon dioxide diffuses inwards in the opposite direction.

SAQ 56 What happens to movement of gases at night?

The system of intercellular spaces extends throughout the plant, and it is probable that most of the cells in the root obtain oxygen from, and excrete carbon dioxide into, the intercellular spaces. However, the outermost cells of the root, and especially the root hairs, are also able to obtain oxygen in solution from the soil water. Similarly, carbon dioxide may diffuse out of the root hairs into the soil water.

Unlike insects, fish and mammals, there is no special ventilation mechanism for conveying gases to and from the respiratory surface in plants.

Unlike fish and mammals, the internal transport system in plants does not play a significant role in the transport of gases around the plant. Plants are, however, similar to insects in this respect. This raises the question: how is it that the gas exchange requirements of plants can be met by diffusion alone, even in very large plants?

A number of factors shed light on this question:

1 The branching shape of plants compared with the compact shape of animals means that no part of the body is far away from the external environment.

2 As a general rule, the metabolic rate and, therefore, gas exchange demand of plants, is much lower than that of active animals.

3 The existence of the air-filled intercellular spaces is important.

The degree of movement of molecules is very much greater in the gaseous state than in the liquid state. As a result, gas molecules such as oxygen can diffuse much more rapidly through air than they can through liquids (about 300 000 times faster, in fact).

It has been shown that in a potato, which has a very slow rate of respiration, the oxygen concentration would fall to zero in cells 1 mm beneath the skin if oxygen had to diffuse through the cells from the outside to reach the interior. Cells deeper within the potato would receive no oxygen and would be unable to respire aerobically. However, analyses have shown that even in the centre of the potato, the oxygen concentration is never less than about half that at the surface. This is because the oxygen molecules are able to diffuse rapidly through the air-filled spaces between the cells.

4 The processes involving gas exchange in plants are to some extent complementary. During daylight, at least, some of the oxygen consumed in respiration is replaced by photosynthesis and some of the carbon dioxide produced by respiration is consumed in photosynthesis.

5 Much of the tissue in the largest land plants, the trees, is dead.

3.7 Summary assignment 3

1 Using very simple diagrams, indicate the route of gas movement between the environment and the respiratory surface in an insect, a fish, a mammal and a flowering plant. Label the structures involved. State whether movement would be described as diffusion or mass flow.

2 Copy and annotate figure 60 to explain how mass flow of water occurs over the gills of a fish.

60 Flow of water over the gills of a fish

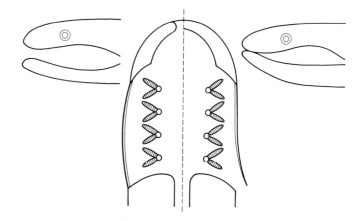

3 Copy and annotate figure 61 to explain how mass flow of air occurs through the alveoli of a mammal.

61 Mass flow of air through the alveoli of a mammal

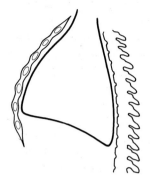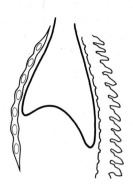

4 Draw a very simplified outline of a human. Indicate the position of the brain, heart, thoracic cavity, aorta and carotid artery (use a text-book to locate the latter). By means of arrows and annotations, explain how breathing rate is controlled.

5 Describe a spirometer and a respirometer. State what each can be used for.

6 Figure 62 is a spirometer trace.

Copy it and label the following: tidal volume, inspiratory reserve volume, expiratory reserve volume, residual volume and vital capacity.

62 Spirometer trace

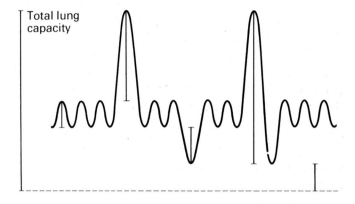

Total lung capacity

Show this work to your tutor.

Self test 3, page 120, covers section 3 of this unit.

Section 4 Exchange of water and minerals in plants

4.1 Introduction and objectives

In this section, the structure of roots will be investigated. A study will then be made of the route and mechanism of exchange of water and minerals within roots and leaves.

At the end of this section, you should be able to do the following.

(a) Describe an investigation showing that roots are involved in water uptake.

(b) Describe the structure of a root.

(c) Identify tissues and cells in a root.

(d) State the source of water for plants.

(e) Outline the route and mechanism of uptake of water from the soil to the xylem across the root.

(f) Describe the endodermis.

(g) Outline the effect of the endodermis on the uptake of water.

(h) Outline the evidence for the active uptake of ions into plant roots.

(i) Explain the term transpiration and describe how it is measured.

(j) Describe the route and mechanism of water movement in a leaf.

(k) State the role of stomata in transpiration.

(l) State the factors affecting stomatal movement.

(m) Describe two hypotheses for the mechanism of stomatal movement and evaluate the evidence for each.

(n) List the factors that affect transpiration.

(o) Name three xerophytic plants and show how each is adapted to dry habitats.

4.2 The effect of roots on water uptake in plants

The role of roots in water uptake can be investigated quite simply. Figure 63 illustrates the apparatus and method that was used in such an investigation.

63 Investigating the role of roots in water uptake

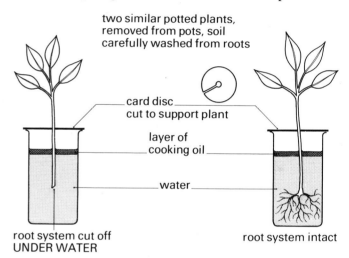

The two sets of apparatus were set up under identical conditions of temperature, light and humidity and were weighed at hourly intervals. The results obtained are given in figure 64.

64 Mass loss in plants with and without roots

Time (h)	Mass (g)	
	Intact plant	Plant with roots removed
0	488.1	452.3
1	478.0	446.0
2	468.1	439.8
3	459.1	433.8
4	449.0	427.3
5	439.5	421.2
6	430.0	415.1

SAQ 57 Plot these results as a graph.

SAQ 58 Calculate the mass of water loss for the two sets of apparatus.

SAQ 59 Was the rate of loss in mass constant?

SAQ 60 In using this apparatus as a means of measuring water uptake, two assumptions are being made. What are they? Do you think it is reasonable to make these assumptions?

SAQ 61 Does the presence of roots affect the rate of water uptake?

SAQ 62 What is the purpose of the oil film?

SAQ 63 When cutting off the root system, it is necessary to keep the stem submerged. Why is this so?

4.3 The anatomy of roots

Figure 65 shows some of the main features of root anatomy.

The part of the root largely responsible for water uptake in terrestrial plants is the zone of root hairs a few millimetres behind the root tip. This zone usually extends along the root for about 2 cm. The epidermis in this zone is referred to as the **piliferous layer** (Latin: *pilus* — hair, *ferre* — to carry).

Plants of specialised habitats may use different surfaces for water uptake. In aquatic plants for instance, water is absorbed over all submerged parts of the plant.

Study figure 65 carefully and answer the following questions.

SAQ 64 Suggest one way in which the piliferous layer is well adapted for water uptake.

SAQ 65 Name the regions through which water must move during its passage from the root hairs to the xylem where long-distance transport occurs.

The root grows as a result of cell multiplication and growth in the root-tip region. Associated with this growth, old root hairs die and new ones form near to the extending root tip.

SAQ 66 As the root grows through the soil, new root hairs are brought into contact with new regions of the soil. How may this increase water absorption?

65   Root anatomy

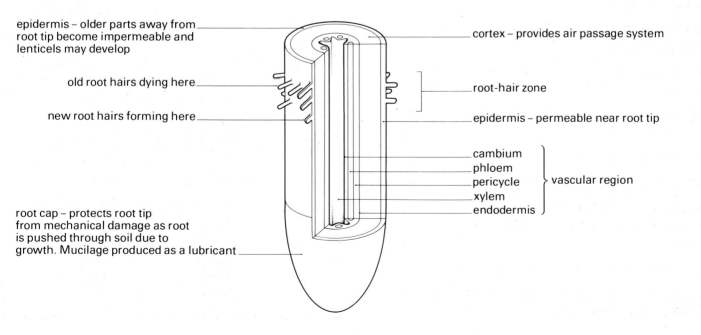

4.3.1 Drawing plant sections

When drawing sections of plant (or animal) tissues, two distinct styles of record should be made. **Low power tissue plans** and **accurate high power drawings.**

The purpose of a LP plan is to show regions, rather like a map, of different tissues without any attempt to show individual cells. See figures 66 and 67.

66 LP photograph of marrow stem (TS)

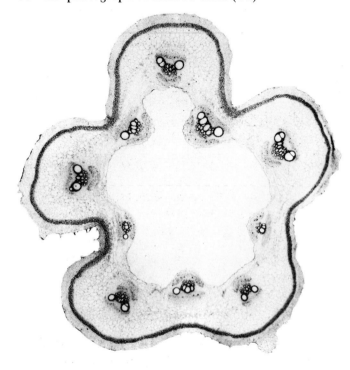

However, to recognise tissues, you must first be able to identify the cells that make them up. To do this, you need higher magnifications to see more details of the section. These characteristic details of cells should be recorded as accurate HP drawings. See figures 68 and 69.

The following instructions should be followed whenever drawing sections of plant (or animal) tissues.

Low power tissue plans

(*a*) Using LP and HP, search the section to identify the types of cell present.

67 LP tissue plan of marrow stem (TS)

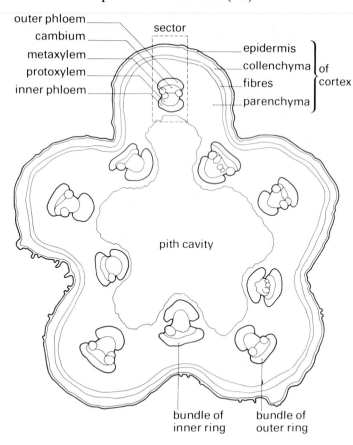

outer phloem
cambium
metaxylem
protoxylem
inner phloem
sector
epidermis
collenchyma
fibres
parenchyma
of cortex
pith cavity
bundle of inner ring
bundle of outer ring

68 HP photograph of part of a buttercup root (TS)

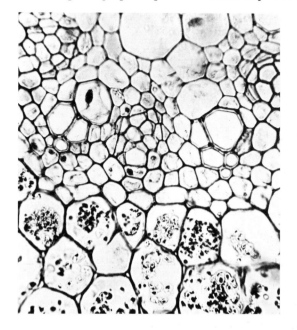

Cortex cells

intercellular space   granules

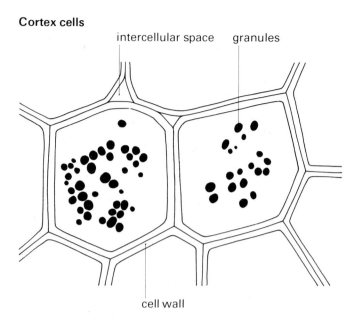

cell wall

Xylem cells

thick lignified wall   protoxylem vessel element

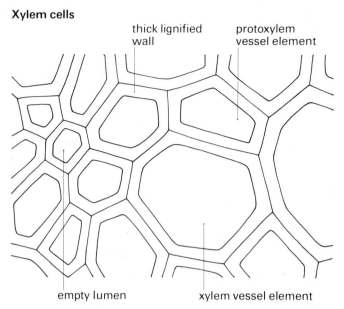

empty lumen   xylem vessel element

(*b*) If parts of the section are incomplete or unclear, look at several sections to get a clear picture of the overall structure.

(*c*) Draw, very lightly, the overall proportions and positions of the tissue regions.

(*d*) Use single lines to show different tissue areas.

(*e*) Label and annotate your plan.

Accurate high power drawings

(*a*) Search the section, using LP and HP, and decide on all the characteristic features of the cell type you are studying.

(*b*) Find two or three representative cells that include all the relevant detail and make your drawing from these.

(*c*) Use a sharp pencil and plain paper.

(*d*) Make your drawing large. The smallest cells should not be less than 1 cm across.

(*e*) All lines should be even, distinct and continuous, *not sketchy*, as shown in figure 70.

(*f*) Cells walls should be represented by a double line. The distance between the two lines will depend on the thickness of the cell walls.

(*g*) Cell contents, such as protoplasm vacuoles, nuclei, etc., should be carefully drawn in when visible, as shown in figure 69.

(*h*) Do not use shading or colour.

When drawing cells, it will help to *very lightly* sketch the cells to establish the correct proportions and positions of the structures. Then, more boldly, draw the cells and *lightly* rub out the guide lines.

70   Drawing cells

thick cell wall (lignified)   empty lumen (no protoplast, cell dead)

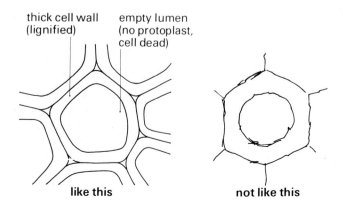

like this   **not like this**

(*i*) Use reference books to help you identify the cells and their characteristic features.

(*j*) Label your drawing and annotate by adding any relevant information.

Practical J: Investigating root structure

Materials

Prepared slide of a dicotyledon (dicot) root in the region of the root hairs, prepared slide of monocotyledon (monocot) root, microscope and lamp

Procedure

(*a*) Examine the dicotyledon root and identify the features shown in figure 71.

71   TS through one-year-old dicotyledon root

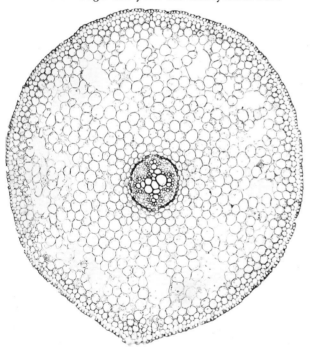

(*b*) Count the number of arms radiating from the central region in your slide. In dicots, this number usually varies from two to eight. Such roots are described as **diarch** (2 arms), **triarch** (3 arms), etc.

(*c*) Make a low power map of the tissues in your section. Label your diagram fully.

(*d*) Examine the root hairs and endodermis under high power. Make a representative drawing of a root hair and 2-3 endodermis cells.

(*e*) Examine the monocotyledon root under low power and high power. Note any differences especially in the vascular region. Record these differences.

Show this work to your tutor.

4.3.2 Passage of water through the root

Figure 72(*a*) shows diagrammatically the regions through which water must flow from the soil to the xylem.

72   Route of water movement through root from soil to xylem (*a*) TS through root cells, (*b*) TS of above region showing cell walls and intercellular spaces only, (*c*) TS of above region showing cytoplasm only

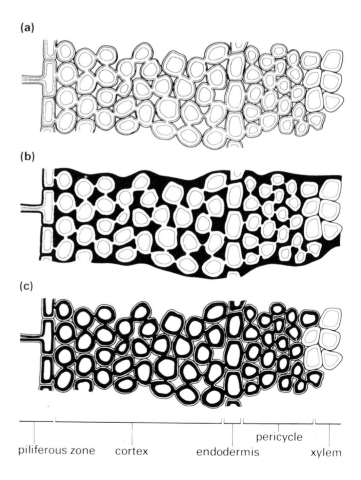

(a)

(b)

(c)

piliferous zone   cortex   endodermis   pericycle   xylem

Figure 72(*b*) shows the same regions, but only cell walls and intercellular spaces are drawn in. Notice that these regions form a complex interconnecting network from the soil to the xylem. This network is known as the **apoplast.**

Figure 72(*c*) shows the same region again, but this time only the cytoplasm is drawn in. Owing to the cytoplasmic connections between cells known as plasmodesmata, there is a continuous network of cytoplasm from root hairs to xylem. This network is called the **symplast.**

Water can diffuse freely through cellulose cell walls, intercellular spaces and cytoplasm. The only cells whose walls contain impermeable materials are those of the endodermis.

4.3.3 The endodermis

The endodermis forms a cylinder of cells around the vascular region. The endodermal cells become impregnated with corky material. This forms a band known as the **Casparian strip** after its discoverer, Caspari. Figure 73 shows an endodermis cell.

73 Whole endodermis cell

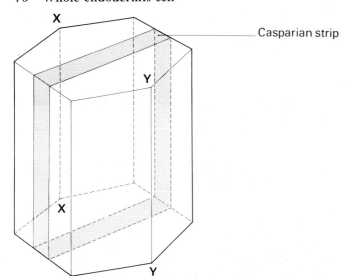

SAQ 67 Which of the diagrams in figure 74 represents a TS of the above endodermal cell?

SAQ 68 If water molecules diffused from **XX** to **YY,** through which of the following routes could it pass?
(*a*) Through the cell walls only.

(*b*) Through the cytoplasm only.
(*c*) Through the cell walls and cytoplasm.

Explain your answer.

The exact significance of your answer to SAQ 68 is not known. It could be that some active control on the inward movement of water and ions occurs in the endodermis cytoplasm,

4.3.4 Movement of water

Water can pass by diffusion from the soil into the root hairs from where it moves through the apoplast towards the centre of the root. The only point at which water cannot pass through the apoplast is in the region of the endodermis. Here, the Casparian strip presents a barrier. Therefore, the water must move through the symplast in this region.

Some water may also move over the whole distance through the symplast, crossing the root from the hairs to the xylem.

A water concentration gradient is maintained between the soil and the inside of the root. Water continually enters the soil due to rain, etc., while water is continually removed from the inside of the root by an upward movement in the xylem stream.

Finally, some water may pass across the root from cell to cell via the vacuoles. This movement occurs down a concentration gradient by osmosis.

74 TS endodermis cell

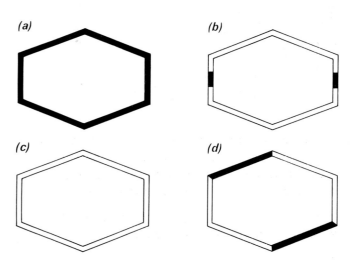

Water required by individual cells of the root is obtained directly from the apoplast. In very dry conditions, water from the cell vacuoles is used as a resource but is replaced when water becomes available again.

4.4 Movement of ions into roots

Plants obtain their ions from the soil solution. Ions enter the roots in solution through the first few centimetres behind the tip. This includes the region of the root hairs and also the region of extension growth.

The soil solution can penetrate the apoplast of the roots as far inwards as the endodermis. This effectively means that the cortical cells are all bathed in soil solution. They may accumulate ions from this solution into their cytoplasm and/or into their vacuoles.

Ions can move inwards from cortex to xylem within the symplast. This may take place by diffusion, aided by cytoplasmic streaming. There is a declining concentration gradient of ions from the outside to the inside of the root.

When they reach the endodermis, ions must cross the endodermis in solution in the symplast. This is due to the impermeable Casparian strip in the endodermal cell walls.

Ions may enter the xylem by release from the symplast of the pericycle cells. Or, they may enter the apoplast immediately they pass through the endodermis and may be carried passively into the xylem cells.

SAQ 69 Suggest two points at which active transport of ions might occur in roots.

Investigations on ion uptake in plants have shown the following:
1 ions are selectively absorbed,
2 ions are absorbed against a concentration gradient,
3 absorption is temperature dependent,
4 absorption is related to respiration.

These finding all suggest that an active mechanism is, at least, partially involved in ion uptake.

SAQ 70 Figure 75 shows the results of four different investigations into ion uptake in plants. For each graph, state which of the above statements (1–4) apply to each investigation.

4.5 Loss of water from the aerial parts of the plant

Plants lose water by evaporation from their aerial parts, especially the leaves. Much of this water loss by evaporation takes place through the stomata. The loss of water from the plant by evaporation is called **transpiration.** Any apparatus used to measure water uptake and transpiration by cut shoots is called a **potometer.**

Practical K: Investigating the rate of water uptake and loss

Materials

Capillary tube 10 cm, mm scale for capillary tube or strip of graph paper, three potted *Impatiens balsamina* ('Busy Lizzy') plants of similar size, water (boiled and cooled) to half fill sink, translucent plastic tubing, retort stand, clamp, scissors, single-edged razor blade, petroleum jelly (Vaseline), fine wire, methylene blue, 500 cm^3 beaker, stop-clock or stop-watch with second hand

Procedure

(*a*) About half fill a sink with water and place in it the capillary tube with the plastic tubing attached. Make sure that there are no air bubbles trapped in the tubes.

(*b*) Using scissors, cut off one of the plants just above the soil. Transfer it quickly to the sink.

(*c*) *Keeping the stem under water,* cut it a second time, using a sharp razor blade and making a slanting cut, so that it is the right diameter to fit tightly into the plastic tubing.

(*d*) *Under water,* insert the cut end of the stem into the plastic tubing, making as tight a fit as possible. If necessary, gently twist a piece of thin wire around the tube.

(*e*) Place a finger over the end of the capillary tube and carefully remove the apparatus and plant from the sink and immerse the end of the capillary in the beaker of water which has been boiled and allowed to cool.

(*f*) Support the apparatus with a suitable stand and clamp as shown in figure 76. Dry any wet leaves,

smear petroleum jelly around the connection to ensure an airtight fit, and leave the whole apparatus to settle down for five minutes.

(*g*) The rate of water uptake can be measured by introducing an air bubble into the end of the capillary tube. To do this, loosen the clamp and carefully raise the potometer until the end of the tube is just out of the water. Allow an air bubble to enter and lower the apparatus back into the beaker. The rate of movement of the bubble can be measured using a suitable scale attached to the capillary tube.

75 Results of experiments on ion absorption in plants.
(*a*) **Uptake of Na$^+$ from solutions of NaCl at two different concentrations and two different temperatures**
(*b*) **Sugar consumption and uptake of potassium in different concentrations of oxygen.**

(*c*) **Uptake of potassium and bromide ions in oxygen and nitrogen.**
(*d*) **Diagram showing the relative concentrations of different ions in pond water (clear boxes) and in the sap of the green alga *Nitella* (shaded boxes).**

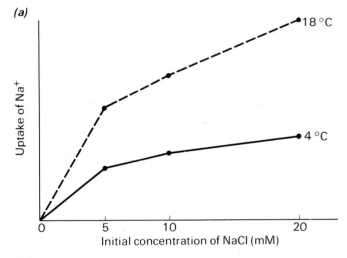

(a)

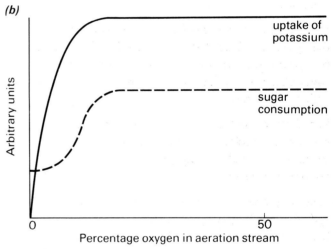

(b)

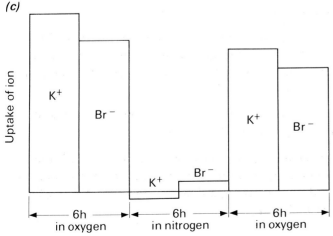

(c)

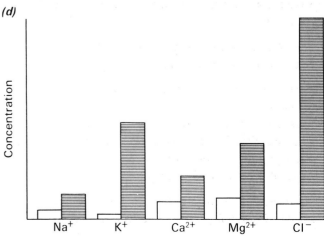

(d)

76 A simple potometer set up

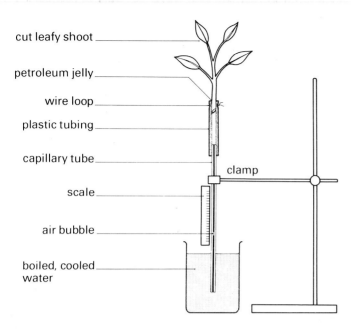

cut leafy shoot

petroleum jelly

wire loop

plastic tubing

capillary tube

clamp

scale

air bubble

boiled, cooled water

When the bubble reaches the upper end of the scale, pinch the plastic tube gently and release slowly to expel the bubble and restart. The addition of a few drops of methylene blue to the water makes the air bubble easier to see.

(*h*) Investigate the rate of transpiration under laboratory conditions as follows: Use a ruler or a scale made from graph paper to measure the rate of movement of the air bubble. On the basis of your preliminary observations of the rate of movement of the bubble, decide on an appropriate time interval and take a series of ten readings. Plot the results graphically.

(*i*) Smearing petroleum jelly (Vaseline) over the surface of the leaves will produce a waterproof coat. Using this technique, investigate the transpiration rate with either the lower surfaces of the leaves smeared, or the upper surfaces of the leaves smeared. You will need to use a new plant for the second part of this investigation.

(*j*) When you have completed this investigation, measure the transpiration rate when *both* leaf surfaces are smeared. This will give you an indication of the effect of leaves on the transpiration rate. Present all your results graphically.

Discussion of results

1 The potometer actually measures water uptake. Do you consider it is valid to use it for measuring transpiration?

2 What is the effect on water uptake of preventing transpiration from (*a*) the upper surfaces of the leaves, (*b*) the lower surfaces of the leaves?

Suggest a hypothesis to explain your observations

3 Suggest ways in which this experiment could be made more accurate.

Show this work to your tutor.

4.5.1 Movement of water through the leaf

Water enters the leaf via the long-distance water transport system, the xylem. The xylem cells in the terminal veins of this system are surrounded by parenchyma cells of the mesophyll — see figure 77.

77 Movement of water through the leaf

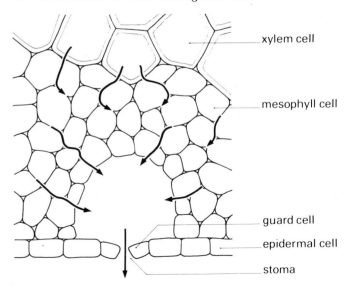

xylem cell

mesophyll cell

guard cell

epidermal cell

stoma

There are three routes by which water can move from the xylem cells into the rest of the leaf. These are:
(*a*) through the apoplast;
(*b*) though the symplast;
(*c*) from vacuole to vacuole.

The mechanism of movement in routes (*a*) and (*b*) is diffusion. Osmosis is involved in (*c*).

As figure 77 shows, the system of intercellular spaces within the leaf connect with the external environment via the stomatal pores. When moist surfaces are exposed to the air, evaporation occurs. It is from the cell walls surrounding the intercellular spaces that transpiration occurs. Thus, there is a continuous movement of water from the xylem, across the mesophyll cells of the leaf, to the external environment.

As water moves through the leaf in the apoplast or symplast, it may be withdrawn into the cell vacuoles. At times of water shortage, it may pass from the vacuoles into the cytoplasm.

Movements of the guard cells surrounding the stomatal pores can alter the size of the pore and, hence, control the amount of water lost by transpiration. This is important in terms of water conservation.

4.5.2 The control of transpiration by the stomata

Much of the water loss by transpiration occurs through the stomata. The size of the stomatal opening is not constant but is regulated by changes in the shape of the guard cells which surround it. These changes are the result of water flowing in and out of the guard cells. This is shown in figure 78. The cells on the left are flaccid and the pore is fairly small. The cells on the right are turgid and the opening is much larger.

The guard cells are unlike other epidermal cells in that they contain chloroplasts. A second important characteristic is that their walls are thickened on the surface adjacent to the pore. See figure 78.

When the cells take up water, they become **turgid.** The walls stretch. However, they cannot stretch in the thickened region. Therefore, the cells assume a curved sausage shape. This causes the pore between them to increase in size.

A similar effect can be demonstrated by inflating a sausage-shaped balloon which has a piece of sticky tape stuck on one side — see figure 79.

79   Balloon representing guard cell

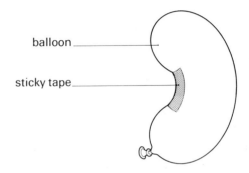

When the cells lose water, they become **flaccid.** The cells become less curved. The thickened walls come together and the pore closes.

4.5.3 The mechanism of stomatal movement

There are three factors which have an important effect on stomatal opening. These are carbon dioxide, light and water.

78   Guard cells

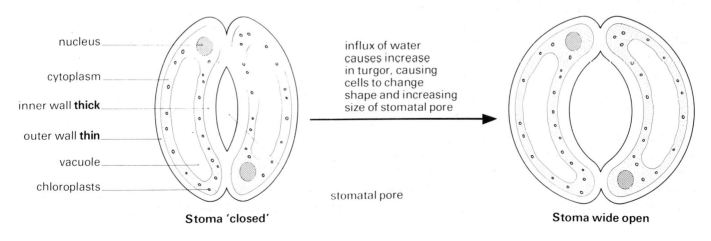

nucleus

cytoplasm

inner wall **thick**

outer wall **thin**

vacuole

chloroplasts

influx of water causes increase in turgor, causing cells to change shape and increasing size of stomatal pore

stomatal pore

Stoma 'closed'

Stoma wide open

Low concentrations of carbon dioxide cause stomatal opening. In high concentrations, carbon dioxide causes closure. Most stomata open in the light and close in the dark. An exception is found in certain succulent plants which open at night and close in the day.

It is known that these succulent plants take in carbon dioxide at night and store it as organic acids. In the daytime the carbon dioxide is released within the plant for photosynthesis.

SAQ 71 Which factor appears to be more important in determining stomatal movement? Explain your answer.

When a slight water shortage develops in the plant, the hormone **abscisic acid** (ABA) is produced and causes the stomata to close. If the water level falls below a certain critical level, the stomata will close without the production of ABA.

Many hypotheses have been put forward to explain how these factors cause the changes in turgidity in the guard cells which bring about stomatal movement. The two main theories will be considered here.

According to the **classical theory,** stomata open when sugar produced during photosynthesis accumulates in the guard cells. This leads to the uptake of water by osmosis, causing the cells to become turgid. At night, it was thought that the conversion of sugar into starch reduces the solute concentration in the guard cells. This results in a loss of water so that the cells become flaccid.

Figure 80 summarizes this theory.

80   Classical hypothesis for the mechanism of stomatal movement

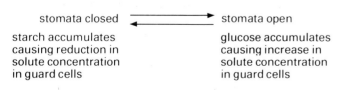

stomata closed — stomata open

starch accumulates causing reduction in solute concentration in guard cells

glucose accumulates causing increase in solute concentration in guard cells

SAQ 72 Copy out and complete figure 80 by writing the following words in the appropriate places above or below the arrow.

light, dark, high CO_2 concentration, low CO_2 concentration.

SAQ 73 Do the observed effects of carbon dioxide and light on stomatal movement conflict with the classical hypothesis?

There are three important factors which contradict the classical hypothesis.

1 Stomata often open at the beginning of the day before enough sugar has accumulated to cause sufficient change in osmotic potential.

2 Many plants close their stomata for a brief period around midday.

3 Some plants do not store starch at all, e.g. some monocotyledons such as onion.

SAQ 74 Suggest a factor which might cause temporary closure of stomata around midday.

An alternative hypothesis of stomatal movement depends on the movement of potassium ions, K^+. It has been shown that when stomata are open, the guard cells contain a high concentration of K^+. When they are closed, the K^+ concentration in guard cells is much lower.

It has been suggested that a K^+ pump exists to move K^+ into the guard cells during the day. This would affect their ability to take up water and hence increase their turgor. It is possible that the pump operates using ATP produced during photosynthesis. At night the K^+ ions would diffuse out of the guard cells down a concentration gradient.

This alternative hypothesis is shown in figure 81.

81   Alternative hypothesis for the mechanism of stomatal movement

stomata closed — stomata open

low K^+ concentration in guard cells

high K^+ concentration in guard cells

SAQ 75 If stomatal opening requires the active pumping of K^+ into the guard cells using ATP, which of the following are likely to be true when the stomata are open?

(a) Carbon dioxide levels are high.

(b) Carbon dioxide levels are low.

(c) Photosynthesis is occurring.

(d) It is light.

(e) It is dark.

SAQ 76 Do the observed effects of carbon dioxide and light on stomatal movement conflict with the alternative hypothesis?

In many plants, there is an internal diurnal rhythm for stomatal movement. Stomata will continue to open and close for several days under constant conditions. Many diurnal rhythms in plants are under the control of the pigment phytochrome, which absorbs blue light. There is some evidence that blue light has an effect on stomatal movements.

You can study more about phytochrome and biological rhythms in the unit *Response to the environment.*

4.5.4 Factors affecting transpiration

The rate of water loss from plants due to transpiration is affected by the degree of opening of stomata. As you learnt in the previous section (4.5.3), this depends on environmental factors such as light, carbon dioxide and water availability.

However, even when stomata are open, the rate of evaporation from the internal surfaces of the plant will be affected by environmental factors. These will be identical to factors affecting evaporation from any surface — including wet clothes hanging on a washing line. Washing dries best in warm, windy conditions when the atmospheric humidity is low.

82 **Environmental conditions affecting transpiration**

Environmental factor	Transpiration rate	
	High	Low
1 Temperature		
2 Air movement		
3 Humidity		
4 Light		
5 CO_2 level		
6 Soil water		

SAQ 77 Copy out and complete figure 82 as a summary of the environmental conditions affecting transpiration.

SAQ 78 Which of the factors in the table (figure 82) affect transpiration by affecting evaporation rate and which affect transpiration by affecting stomatal movement.

Plants which live in dry habitats show a variety of adaptations to their environment. These adaptations may be grouped into three main types:
1 Adaptations to store water, e.g. succulent plants such as stonecrop.

2 Adaptations to obtain more water, e.g. the long taproots of date palms and the extensive fibrous root system of marram grass.

3 Adaptations to reduce transpiration. These usually involve positioning of stomata such that a layer of humid air is trapped around them. This reduces transpiration.

A certain amount of water loss occurs through the epidermis itself. Therefore, a thick waxy cuticle will also reduce transpiration.

Rate of water loss depends on the surface area to volume ratio of the transpiring surface. If this is decreased, water loss will be reduced.

Study figure 83 carefully and then answer the questions below

SAQ 79 How might the position of the stomata in a pine leaf reduce transpiration?

SAQ 80 How might position of stomata and nature of the leaf of marram grass reduce transpiration?

SAQ 81 State one adaptation shown in figure 83 associated with water storage.

SAQ 82 Using information from figure 83, which plants show adaptations to obtain more water?

SAQ 83 List two other ways in which the plants in figure 83 are adapted to a dry enviroment.

Plants which are adapted to dry enviroments are called **xerophytes.**

(a) The Scots pine *(Pinus sylvestris)*
Shoot

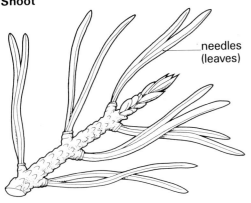

needles
(leaves)

TS leaf – LP plan

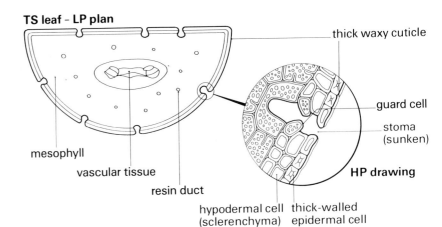

thick waxy cuticle

guard cell

stoma
(sunken)

HP drawing

mesophyll

vascular tissue

resin duct

hypodermal cell   thick-walled
(sclerenchyma)   epidermal cell

(b) Marram grass *(Ammophila arenaria)*

Whole plant
(grows on sand
dunes)

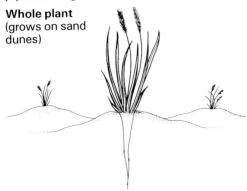

TS leaf – LP plan

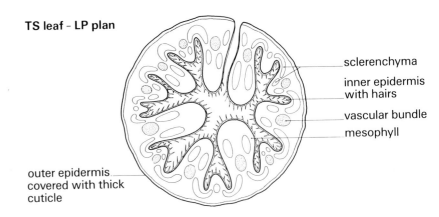

sclerenchyma

inner epidermis
with hairs

vascular bundle

mesophyll

outer epidermis
covered with thick
cuticle

(c) A cactus *(Echinocactus sp.)*
Whole plant

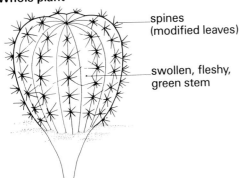

spines
(modified leaves)

swollen, fleshy,
green stem

TS epidermis
and cortex – HP

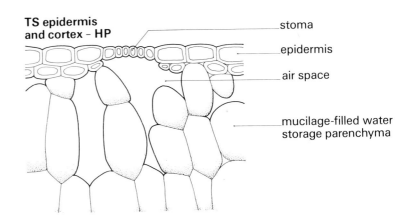

stoma

epidermis

air space

mucilage-filled water
storage parenchyma

4.5.5 Past examination question

Answer the following past examination question.

Explain how you could measure (*a*) the uptake of water by a leafy shoot, and (*b*) the loss of water from a leafy shot. Discuss the possible relationship between the two processes.
(London, Paper 2, January 1971)

Show this work to your tutor.

4.6 References for section 4

How Sap Moves In Trees by M. Zimmerman (Scientific American, March 1963).
Sap in Tree-tops by J. Sutcliffe (New Scientist, 11 June 1981).
Plants and Water by J. Sutcliffe (Edward Arnold, 1979).
Transport Phenomena in Plants by D.A. Baker (Chapman & Hall, 1978).
Cell Membranes and Ion Transport by J.L. Hall and D.A. Baker (Longman, 1977).
Translocation in Plants by M. Richardson, Studies in Biology No. 10 (2nd edition, 1976).
Plants and Mineral Salts by J.F. Sutcliffe and D.A. Baker, Studies in Biology No. 48 (1978).
Transpiration by A.J. Rutter (Oxford University Press, 1972, Oxford Biology Reader No. 24).

4.7 Summary assignment 4

1 Make a large diagram of a TS through a root and a VS through a leaf. Label the main regions. Indicate on your diagram the route(s) of water and ion movement. State which of the following processes are involved in movement along the route: diffusion, osmosis, active transport.

84   Transpiration

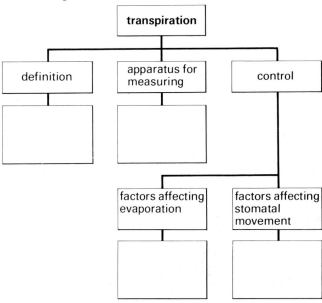

2 Copy the diagram (figure 84), adding the appropriate information in the blank boxes.

Show this work to your tutor.

Self test 4, page 121, covers section 4 of this unit.

Section 5 Transport in animals

5.1 Introduction and objectives

You will already be familiar with the movement of substances over short distances by random motion from an area of high concentration to an area of low concentration.

Apart from this movement by diffusion, substances can move across cell membranes by active transport.

Over large distances, efficient supply of materials is only provided by **mass flow,** the bulk movement of substances from one area to another due to differences in pressure.

In this unit, transport will be considered as 'movement of substances by mass flow *inside* an organism'. According to this definition, ventilation mechanisms would not be considered as part of a transport system as ventilation involves the movement of substances over the *outside* surfaces of the body (see figure 85).

85 Transport and ventilation

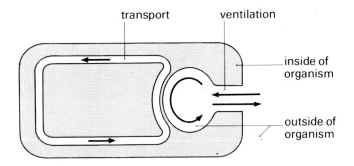

Substances move across the exchange surfaces by diffusion. They also move in and out of cells by diffusion. Once certain factors becoming limiting (e.g. surface area : volume ratio) mass flow of substances in a transport system becomes necessary to link these two areas of diffusion. Transport

systems are therefore intimately linked with increasing cell number (size) and specialised exchange systems. Their main function is to maintain concentration gradients. Other functions have, however, developed with time.

This section considers the range of transport systems found in the animal kingdom and examines their structures and functions.

The minute size of the Protozoa gives them a high surface area in proportion to their volume, enabling them to absorb materials from their surroundings and transport them around their bodies.

In larger organisms, the ratio of surface area to volume is inadequate for diffusion to supply the needs of the organism and so they must either reduce their oxygen and food demands, thus becoming less active, or they must develop an efficient internal transport system. In larger animals, diffusion across the whole surface is replaced by specialised exchange surfaces together with a transport system. In these animals, particularly those which are not aquatic, this system can become quite complex. A blood system is developed which causes the continuous and fairly rapid movement of fluids to all parts of the body.

After completing this section, you should be able to do the following.
(*a*) State the difference between mass flow and diffusion.

(*b*) Describe, compare and state the advantages and limitations of (i) open and closed circulations, (ii) single and double circulations.

(*c*) Explain the relationships between blood, tissue fluid, lymph, plamsa and serum.

(d) Describe the role of the blood system in both earthworm and locust.

(e) Discuss the functions of the blood and explain, in outline, the circulatory system of a fish.

(f) Describe, in outline, circulation in man.

(g) Describe the structure and function of (i) the heart, (ii) the arteries, (iii) veins, (iv) capillaries in a mammal.

(h) Explain the pumping action of the heart and describe the events of the cardiac cycle.

(i) Describe the structure and control of cardiac muscle.

(j) Explain the effects of exercise on (i) the circulatory system, (ii) exchange of gases at the tissues.

(k) List the functions of the lymphatic system.

(l) Discuss the role and nature of respiratory pigments.

(m) Describe how oxygen and carbon dioxide are carried in the blood.

(n) Define an oxygen–haemoglobin dissociation curve.

(o) Describe what happens to oxygen and carbon dioxide in the capillaries of (i) the lungs, (ii) the tissues.

(p) Describe the structure and functions of mammalian blood.

(q) Outline the mechanisms for defence against disease.

Extension:
(r) Describe and explain the physiological adaptations that occur at high altitudes.

(s) Describe one route by which the vertebrate circulatory system may have evolved.

(t) State the safety factors that exist in the human heart.

(u) Describe the development of understanding of the functioning of the lymphatic system.

Practical L: Mass flow in *Elodea* and *Daphnia*

Materials

Elodea plant, *Daphnia* culture, monocular microscope and lamp, cavity slides and coverslips, forceps, Pasteur pipette

Procedure

(a) Mount one *Elodea* leaf, in water, on the cavity slide and cover with a coverslip.

(b) Observe the cells of the leaf under LP and HP.

(c) Look for signs of mass flow and record your observations in the form of annotated diagrams.

(d) Repeat the above procedure for *Daphnia*. Make sure your specimens do not get too hot or dry out.

Discussion of results

1 Describe the pattern of movement (called cyclosis) seen in *Elodea*. Is there any indication of movement *between* cells?

2 What functions do you think these movements could be performing?

3 In *Daphnia,* how is the circulation of fluid maintained?

4 Comment on the function of the rapid backward and forward motion of the legs in *Daphnia* even when at rest.

5 Explain why planarians of a similar size to *Daphnia* do not possess a circulatory system

Show this work to your tutor.

5.2 Open and closed circulatory systems

The simplest kind of transport system circulates the external water medium which, in sponges and some coelenterates, is propelled through channels by cilia or body movements so that food and oxygen reach every part of the body. See figure 86.

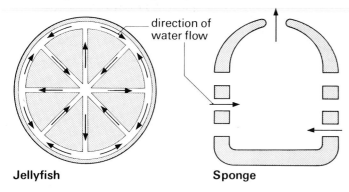

Jellyfish   **Sponge**

Cross-sectional diagrams to show relations of the body cavities in annelids and arthropods

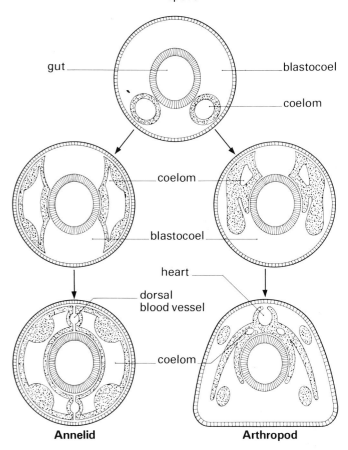

Annelid   **Arthropod**

The majority of animals of any size have more specialised blood systems for transport of materials. In these animals there are two fundamental patterns of blood circulation. These patterns reflect differences seen early in embryonic development.

Figure 87 shows the patterns of early embryonic development in annelids and arthropods. It is the primary body cavity or **blastocoel** that will carry blood later in development. During development, this cavity is obliterated to varying extents by the secondary body cavity or **coelom.**

Embryonic development is considered more fully in the unit *Continuity of life.*

SAQ 84 Which animal group shown in figure 87 develops larger blood spaces?

In insects, the blood system plays little part in conveying respiratory gases.

SAQ 85 How do respiratory gases reach the tissues of an insect?

SAQ 86 Suggest three functions of insect transport systems.

In insects (and other arthropods), as blood is not entirely enclosed within vessels but lies in the body cavity (see figure 88), the body cavity is called the **haemocoel.**

This arrangement is called an **open circulation.** Blood is kept circulating around the haemocoel by a dorsal vessel which has a series of contractile hearts incorporated into it. The hearts contract and force blood forwards and out into the haemocoel. During relaxation, the hearts increase in volume and blood is

88   **The circulatory system of an insect**

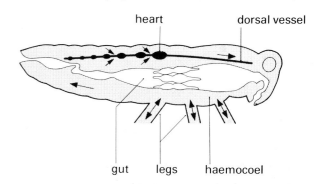

sucked in through paired lateral apertures, called the **ostia.** These have valves that allow blood to move in only one direction, i.e. into the hearts. See figure 89.

89 Arthropod heart

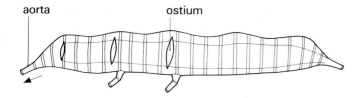

Insect blood is called **haemolymph** and is made up essentially of **plasma** and **haemocytes,** cells capable of phagocytosis. The plasma is predominantly water containing proteins, inorganic salts and substances being transported from one part of the body to another. Other important functions of the blood of insects include transporting hormones, maintaining the body fluids at a constant concentration and assisting in egg-laying and moulting. Blood is used to create a pressure enabling the insect to break out of its old cuticle at moulting and to expand the wings after pupation.

In earthworms, the transport of gases between the gas exchange surface and the respiring cells is brought about by blood contained within a circulatory system consisting of vessels.

Water and other small molecules pass out of the vessels, producing *tissue* or **intercellular fluid** that forms a link between the blood and body cells. This arrangement is called a **closed circulation.**

The movement of gas molecules across the gas exchange surface takes place by diffusion. Once across it, gas transport takes place by mass flow in the bloodstream.

Similarly, at the respiring cells, movement across the cell membranes takes place by diffusion.

Waste gases are transported away by mass flow. (See figure 90.)

This system of transport and exchange is typical of most animals which are larger than the flatworms. The circulatory system of the earthworm (see figure 91) consists basically of a main dorsal blood vessel along the length of the earthworm's back, which acts as the main collecting vessel. The blood is pushed forwards in this vessel by muscular contractions of

90 Diagram to show the relationship between gas exchange surface, blood system and respiring tissues

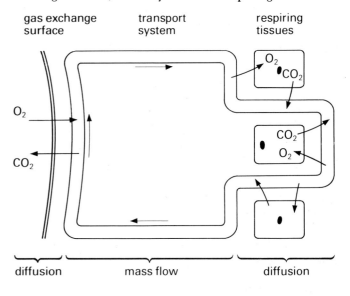

91 Earthworm circulatory system

Transverse section

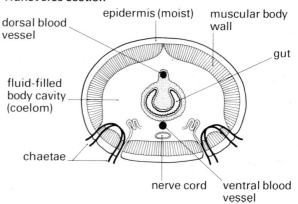

Longitudinal section showing principal blood vessels

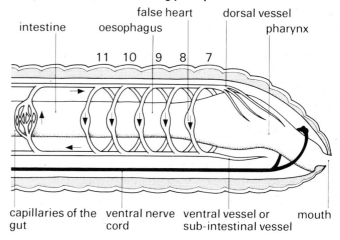

the vessel wall. The major vessel which distributes the blood runs *ventrally* (in the lower position) along the earthworm's body and blood in this vessel is pushed backwards.

The dorsal and ventral vessels are connected by five pairs of muscular transverse vessels which act as hearts, pumping blood through the ventral vessel. Valves in these hearts and the dorsal vessel prevent blood from flowing the wrong way. Blood also flows from the ventral vessel to the dorsal vessel through capillaries in the body wall. The gut is supplied by branches from the ventral vessel. In this way, assimilates are transported to the dorsal vessel and thence around the body.

The supply of oxygen to the tissues is improved by the circulation of blood which increases the rate of oxygen uptake, thus maintaining a steep concentration gradient between the outer environment and the inner body.

Figure 92 compares open and closed circulatory systems.

92   Comparison of open and closed circulations

	Open	Closed
1	Cells actually bathed in blood	Cells bathed in tissue fluid
2	Materials pass from blood to cell across cell membrane	Materials pass from blood into tissue fluid and then across cell membrane into cell
3	Simple hearts pump blood into haemocoels which are blood-filled spaces surrounding organs of the body	Blood flows in a continuous series of vessels to and from a muscular heart. It never leaves the vessels to come in direct contact with the tissues
4	Large blood spaces result in a low blood pressure suitable only for relatively small animals e.g. arthropods and molluscs	Narrow vessels allow high blood pressure to be developed, hence increased efficiency

5.2.1 Past examination question

You will need graph paper for this essay question. Plan your essay first before the final writing. Try to limit yourself to 1 hour for this exercise.

A student investigating the relationship between temperature and the heart-beat rate of the water flea, *Daphnia,* wrote the following report. Study this carefully and then answer the questions (a)–(e).

'I placed a water flea in a test-tube of pond water and put the tube into a water-bath at 5 °C. After five minutes, I removed the water flea from the test-tube, placed it on a cavity slide and quickly counted the heart-beats over a twenty second period by viewing through a microscope. The water flea was then put back into the test-tube of pond water, the water-bath temperature raised 5 °C and the test-tube immersed therein for five minutes, before a further heart count was recorded. This procedure was repeated at 5 °C intervals up to 40 °C. However, during the 30 °C reading, the first water flea died and was replaced by a second animal for the remaining counts.'

93   Table of results

Temperature (°C)	Beats/minute
5	108
10	144
15	180
20	216
25	258
30	300
35	204
40	0

The results are shown in figure 93.

(a) Plot the results obtained.

(b) Assuming the results to be accurate, what can you conclude from the investigation?

(c) List *five* possible sources of error in the experiment.

(d) Give *three* ways in which the method could be improved so as to obtain more accurate quantitative results.

(*e*) Suggest *four* other investigations that might develop from the one described in this question.

(London, Paper 2, January 1974)

Show this work to your tutor

5.2.2 Summary assignment 5

Obtain a copy of figure 94. Label and annotate the diagrams to show the differences between open and closed circulatory systems.

Show this work to your tutor.

94 Diagrams for summmary assignment 5

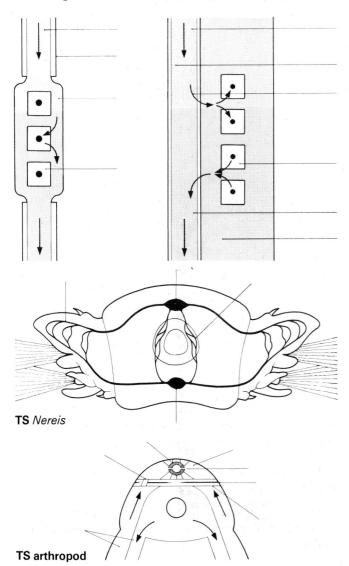

TS *Nereis*

TS arthropod

5.3 Single and double circulatory systems

Among animals that possess a closed circulation, there are differences in the relationship between the organs of the body and the position of the heart in the transport system. The circulatory systems of four vertebrates and a mollusc will be considered to outline the development of a double circulation and its advantages.

Practical M: The circulatory system of a fish

Materials

Small fish net, Petri dish with lid, binocular microscope with light source from below, a specimen of *Kryptopterus bichirrhus* (glass cat-fish)

Procedure

(*a*) Almost fill the Petri dish with water.

(*b*) With a small fish net, carefully remove one fish from the tank and place it on its side in the Petri dish.

(*c*) Make sure there is enough water in the dish to cover the fish.

(*d*) Place the lid on the Petri dish, and then examine the fish using a light source from beneath the fish.

(*e*) With the aid of figure 96, identify the following in the fish:

the heart, the dorsal aorta, the vena cava, gill vessels, capillaries (these are most easily seen in the region near the tail).

(*f*) Make a plan drawing of the circulatory system of your fish.

(*g*) When you have finished with your fish, carefully place it back in the tank.

Discussion of results

1 Describe the possible route that a blood cell in the gill vessels could take on its travels away from and back to the gills.

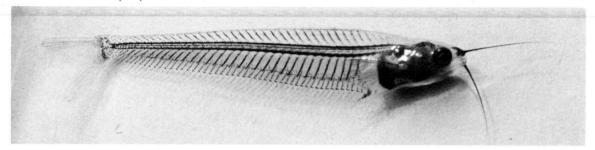

2 How many times would that cell pass through the heart on one circulation (i.e. from gill back to gill)?

3 What do you think the oxygen concentration and blood pressure of blood in the vessels will be just before and after the gills?

Show this work to your tutor.

5.3.1 The problem of a single circulation

Although blood does not leave these vessels, exchange of assimilates and gases can take place between the tissues and the smallest blood vessels, the **capillaries,** via the intercellular or tissue fluid.

In the fish there is a **single circulation.** This means that blood passes through the heart only once during one circulation of the body. The heart firstly pumps blood through the capillaries of the gills, from where it then passes via the main distributing vessel, the **dorsal aorta,** to the capillaries of the rest of the body. Thus, in this type of circulation the blood is pumped through two capillary networks before returning to the heart again. Examine figure 96.

96   Diagram of the circulatory system of a fish

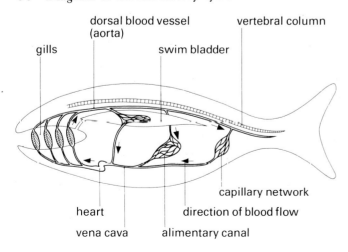

Capillary networks have two major effects on the blood flowing though them. The concentration of respiratory gases is altered and the pressure is considerably reduced. For efficient diffusion at capillary networks, blood pressure has to be relatively high.

SAQ 87 (*a*) Which capillary network in the circulation of the fish receives blood at high pressure?

(*b*) What will be the consequence of this for diffusion at other capillary networks in a *single circulatory system?*

A single circulation is adequate for fishes since they tend to have a low metabolic rate.

SAQ 88 Suggest two ways that a single circulatory system could meet the demands of a higher metabolic rate.

The octopus has developed an interesting circulatory system to overcome this problem of low pressure blood entering capillaries. See figure 97.

97   The central vascular system of the octopus

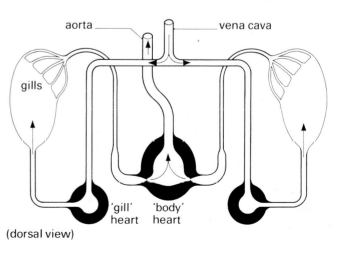

(dorsal view)

The octopus has three hearts, one supplying the body capillaries and a pair supplying the gill capillaries. After flowing through the gills, blood pressure is raised by the 'body' heart.

Another solution is seen in amphibians. Here, unlike in the fish, the blood vessel leaving the heart branches and carries high pressure blood to gas exchange surfaces and the body. Figure 98 compares the circulation of fish and amphibians.

Look carefully at figure 98.

98 Circulation in fish and amphibians

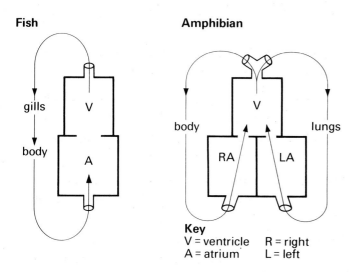

Key
V = ventricle   R = right
A = atrium   L = left

SAQ 89 Although capillary networks receive high pressure blood, what disadvantage does the amphibian system present?

The circulatory system of mammals and birds represents an advance on the amphibian system. The lung and body circulations have been separated by modifications to the heart. The heart has become two pumps joined side by side, one pumping to the lungs and the other pumping to the body — a similar solution to that of the octopus. See figure 99.

As blood flows through the heart twice in one circulation, this arrangement is termed a **double circulatory system.** To emphasise the double nature

99 Circulation in mammals and birds

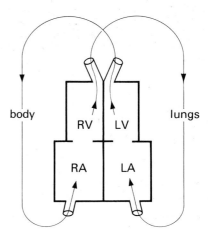

of this system, body and lung circulations have been given different names, **systemic** and **pulmonary** respectively. However, it must be clearly remembered that these two circulations are a continuous network of vessels connected via the heart.

5.3.2 Summary assignment 6

Answer the following essay question. Plan your essay first.

What is meant by (a) an open, (b) a closed, (c) a single and (d) a double blood circulation? Give an example of each. What are the advantages of a double circulation?

(London, Paper 1, Summer 1974)

Show this work to your tutor.

Self test 5, page 123, covers sections 5.2 and 5.3 of this unit.

5.4 The heart

The changes from single to double circulation have been associated with complex changes in the vertebrate heart. This section looks briefly at some of these modifications before studying the mammal heart in detail.

5.4.1 Development of the vertebrate heart

In more 'primitive' vertebrates, the heart is a single 'tube' consisting of four chambers, as shown in figure 100.

100 A 'primitive' vertebrate heart (side view)

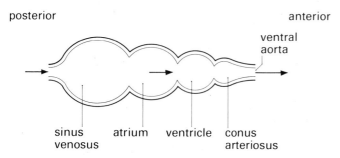

Modifications leading to the fish heart are shown in figure 101.

101 The fish heart (side view)

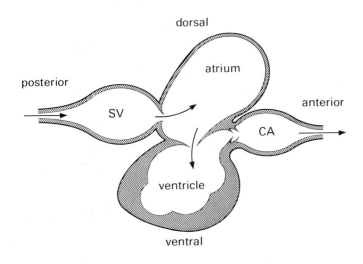

SAQ 90 What modifications to heart structure are illustrated in figure 101?

In the frog heart, see figure 102, the atrium divides into two chambers and moves to lie completely anterior to the ventricle. The **sinus venosus** empties into the right atrium while the **conus arteriosus** is completely modified, helping in keeping oxygenated and deoxygenated blood separate.

Reptile hearts show a further modification. The ventricle also develops a dividing septum although the separation is not complete. See figure 102.

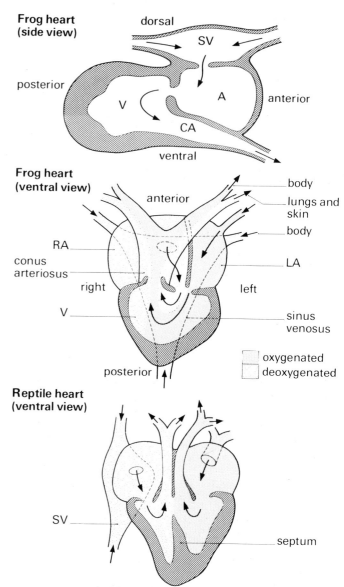

Complete separation of blood occurs in the hearts of birds and mammals. The single four-chambered pump has now become two, two-chambered pumps side by side (see figure 103). The sinus venosus completely disappears and is represented as a patch of cells, the **sinus node,** in the wall of the right atrium. This sinus node is returned to in section 5.4.6.

103 The mammal heart

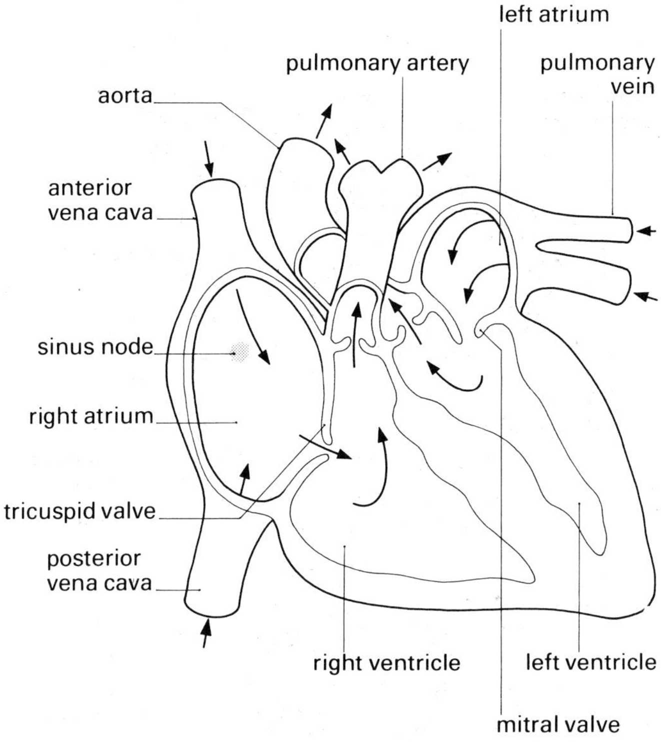

5.4.2 Extension: the evolution of the vertebrate circulatory system

There are certain similarities between the circulatory systems of fish and mammals which suggest that these two groups may have evolved from a common ancestor.

This is discussed in the following article: *Air-breathing Fishes* by K. Johansen (Scientific American reprint, 1968).

Read the article and answer the following questions.

1 Why, according to Johansen, was a lung developed?

2 What was the stimulus for such a development?

3 What structures were adapted to become air-holding chambers?

4 According to this article, from what did the first true land animals evolve?

5 What other changes had to accompany development of a lung for effective air-breathing?

6 Of the Australian and African lungfish, which is better adapted to air-breathing?

7 Draw diagrams to compare the circulatory system of a typical fish, a mouth-breathing fish and a lungfish.

8 How is the lungfish adapted for efficient use of oxygen taken up by the lung?

9 What further adaptations were necessary for lungfish to give rise to true land animals.

Show this work to your tutor.

5.4.3 Structure and function of the mammalian heart

Figure 104 shows a functional diagram of the mammalian heart.

104 Functional diagram of the mammalian heart

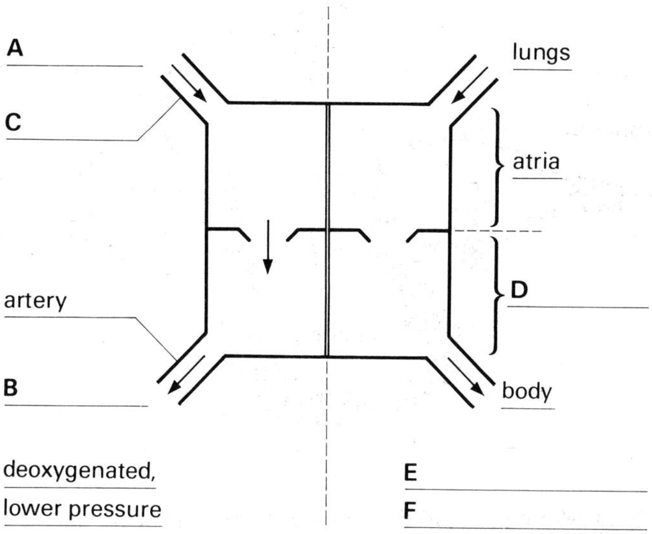

SAQ 91 Copy the diagram and complete the labels **A–F.**

Practical N: Heart dissection

To understand how the mammalian heart acts as a pump, it is necessary to be familiar with its structure.

105 Heart of mammal — external features (ventral view)

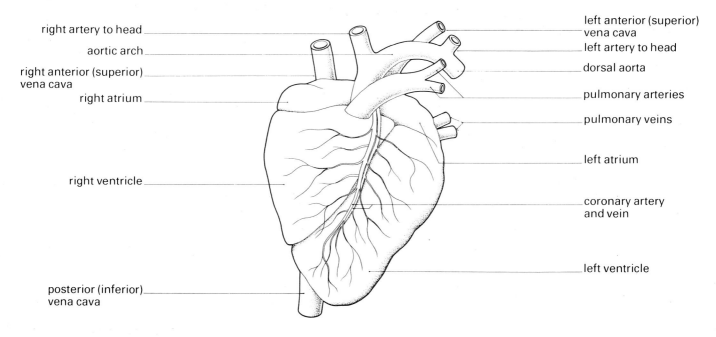

right artery to head

aortic arch

right anterior (superior) vena cava

right atrium

right ventricle

posterior (inferior) vena cava

left anterior (superior) vena cava

left artery to head

dorsal aorta

pulmonary arteries

pulmonary veins

left atrium

coronary artery and vein

left ventricle

Materials

Sheep's heart, dissecting kit and dissecting board

Procedure

External structure

(a) Place the heart on a board so that the major blood vessels are furthest away from you. Identify the ventricles (nearest to you) and the atria (see figure 105).

(b) Examine and feel the thick, rubbery tubes, the arteries. Look inside the arteries and notice the thickness of their walls. Note that the arteries appear to leave the anterior end of the heart although, of course, they originate in the ventricles.

(c) Identify the thinner-walled veins that are connected to the atria. Look inside the veins and compare the thickness of their walls with those of the arteries.

(d) Examine the ventricles, noting that the left ventricle has a thicker wall.

(e) Identify all the features show in figure 105. Make a drawing of the external features of the heart (ventral view).

Internal structure

(a) Open the dorsal aorta by cutting its ventral surface down towards the left ventricle. Follow the dotted line, as shown in figure 106.

106 Opening the aorta

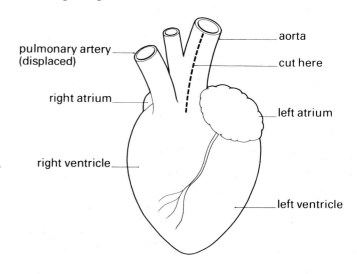

pulmonary artery (displaced)

right atrium

right ventricle

aorta

cut here

left atrium

left ventricle

(*b*) Pull the edges of the aorta apart and examine the semi-lunar valves (see figure 108).

(*c*) Now open up the left atrium. Aim to cut it in two so that you can separate the ventral surface from the dorsal surface. Do this by cutting, as shown by the dotted line in figure 107.

107 Opening up the heart

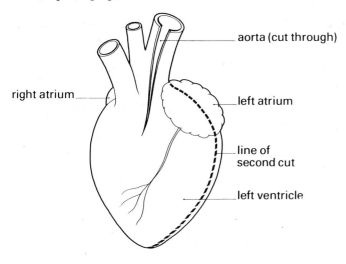

108 Diagram to show the internal structure of the mammalian heart

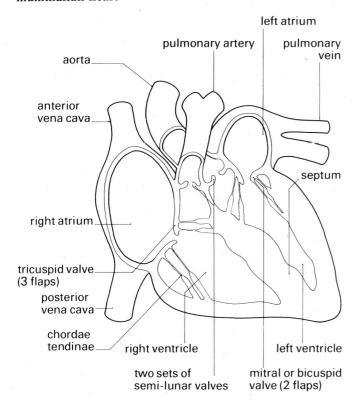

(*d*) Continue your incision around the left ventricle and up through the right ventricle so that both are cut through the dorso-ventral plane.

(*e*) Finally, cut through the right atrium and separate the ventral region of the heart from the dorsal region.

You should be able to identify all the structures shown in figure 108.

(*f*) Make a labelled drawing of your completed dissection.

Discussion of results

1 What is the function of the coronary artery?

2 Why do the ventricles have thicker walls than the atria?

3 Why is the wall of the left ventricle thicker than that of the right?

4 Why should the aorta have a thicker wall than the pulmonary artery?

5 Comment on the output volume of the left and right ventricles.

6 What do you think is the function of the semi-lunar valves?

7 What is the function of the chords attached to the valve flaps between the atria and the ventricles?

Show this work to your tutor.

5.4.4 Heart action

The heart is responsible for maintaining the circulation of blood within the blood vessels. The pumping action of the heart consists of alternate contractions (**systole**) and relaxations (**diastole**).

Figure 109 illustrates the pumping action of the heart. During **ventricular diastole,** the ventricles relax simultaneously while the atria contract (**atrial systole**). Blood is forced through from the atria into the ventricles.

oscilloscope producing a **phonocardiogram.** See figure 110.

110   A phonocardiogram

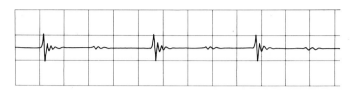

Defects in valve operation give different sounds — see figure 111.

111   Normal and defective valve phonocardiograms

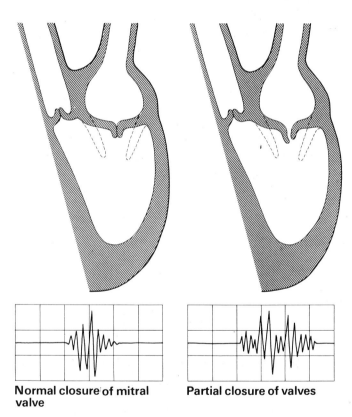

Normal closure of mitral valve   Partial closure of valves

Experienced doctors can diagnose many heart malfunctions by the sounds that the heart makes.

Ventricular contraction forces relatively large volumes of blood through arteries in a short space of time. This expansion of the arteries can be felt as a

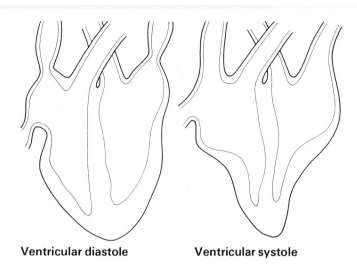

Ventricular diastole   Ventricular systole

This is followed by **ventricular systole,** and **atrial diastole.** The ventricles contract, forcing blood into the arteries, while the atria relax and blood flows into them from the veins.

Notice that in figure 109 the positions of the semi-lunar and cuspid valves have not been drawn in. When the heart beats, these valves play an important role in controlling the flow of blood.

SAQ 92 Obtain a copy of figure 109 and complete it by drawing in the cuspid and semi-lunar valves. Indicate when they are open and when they are closed. By means of arrows, indicate the direction of blood flow through the heart.

SAQ 93 Explain how the semi-lunar and cuspid valves play an important part in controlling the flow of blood.

The series of events between one ventricular contraction and the next is termed the **cardiac cycle.** These events can be investigated by monitoring the beating heart.

Vibrations of structures in the heart produce sounds that can be heard using a **stethoscope.** The 'lubb dubb' sound is caused by the rapid closure of the cuspid and semi-lunar valves. These sounds can be picked up by a microphone placed against the chest and the vibrations shown on a cathode-ray

pulse especially when arteries run over bone. Figure 112 shows the position where the **radial pulse** can be felt.

112 Taking the radial pulse

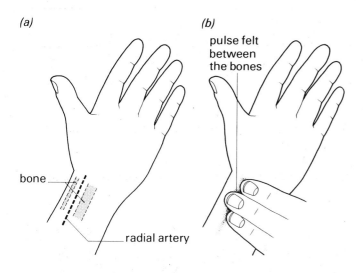

(a)

(b) pulse felt between the bones

bone

radial artery

Figure 113 shows the average resting pulse for 100 individuals.

113 Resting pulse of 100 people

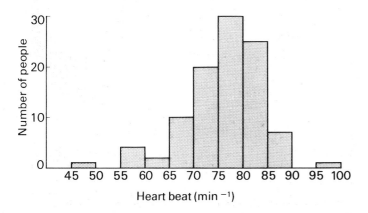

Normal heart rate is said to be 75 beats per minute.

SAQ 94 What does 'normal' mean in this context?

The pressure with which the heart pumps blood around the body can be measured using a **sphygmomanometer.** It is basically an inflatable tourniquet attached to a pressure gauge — see figure 114.

114 Diagram of a sphygmomanometer

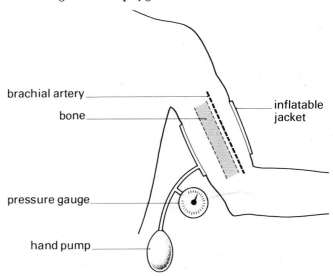

brachial artery

bone

inflatable jacket

pressure gauge

hand pump

When the jacket is inflated, the pressure squeezes the artery closed. By listening for a pulse (see figure 115)

115 Using a sphygmomanometer

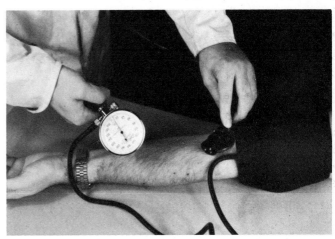

the doctor can find the pressure at which the pulse stops and the artery is closed. The pressure is equal to the fluid pressure developed by the heart.

There are two pressures measured, the blood pressure as the heart is contracting (systolic) and the pressure when the heart is relaxing (diastolic). Blood pressure is shown as systolic/diastolic, e.g. 120/70.

Like any other muscle, cardiac muscle contracts as a result of electrical stimulation. The impulse starts at the top of the right atrium and then travels down the heart to the ventricles.

If electrodes are placed on the chest and connected to an oscilloscope, the electrical changes occurring in the cardiac muscle during heart-beats can be measured. The trace shown on the oscilloscope is called an **electrocardiograph** or ECG. See figure 116.

116   Components of an ECG trace

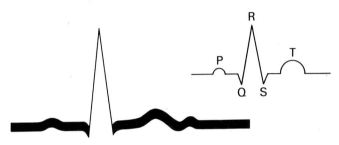

Contracting and relaxing muscle cause different electrical records:
the **P wave** is caused by atrial contraction;
the **QRS complex** is caused by ventricular contraction;
the **T wave** is caused by ventricular relaxation.

SAQ 95 Why should the QRS complex be much larger than the P wave?

Figure 117 show an ECG trace. heart-rate can be calculated from the R–R interval. Use figures 117 and 118 to answer the following questions.

117   ECG trace

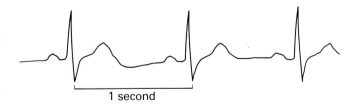

1 second

118   Path of conduction of impulse in cardiac muscle

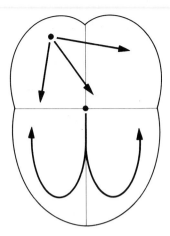

SAQ 96 What was the heart-rate of the subject when the ECG trace was recorded?

SAQ 97 (*a*) State the time taken for each of the following: (i) conduction of impulse across the atria; (ii) conduction of impulse over the ventricles; (iii) period of relaxation of the ventricular muscle; (iv) delay between ventricular relaxation and atrial contraction.
(*b*) Use the PQRST notation to explain your answers to (*a*).

5.4.5 Summary assignment 7

1 The diagrams in figure 119 show the state of the heart during the cardiac cycle. Using these diagrams, copy and complete the table shown in figure 120.

2 Study figure 121 which show three traces recorded during one cardiac cycle.

With reference to events shown on the three traces, state what is happening to the valves and ventricles during periods **A** to **E.**

3 Write preparatory notes for the following past examination question:
What is a heart? Describe the gross structure and action of the mammalian heart.

(London, Paper 1, January 1970)

Show this work to your tutor.

Phase 1 – Isometric relaxation   **Phase 2 – Rapid filling**   **Phase 3 – Diastasis**   **Phase 4 – Atrial systole**

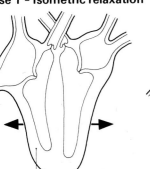
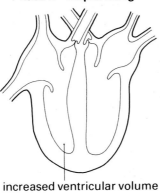

elastic recoil   increased ventricular volume   ventricles fully filled
                                                                                            and stretched

Phase 5 – Ventricular systole
(a) isometric contraction   *(b)* ejection

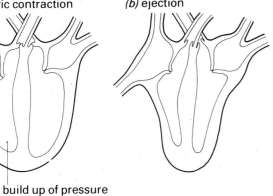

build up of pressure

120   Table summarising the cardiac cycle

Phase in the cycle	Movement of blood	Condition of atria	Condition of ventricles	Condition of cuspid valves	Condition of semi-lunar valves
1 Isometric relaxation					
2 Rapid filling					
3 Diastasis					
4 Atrial systole					
5 Ventricular systole – isometric contraction, ejection					

121 Recordings of heart activity

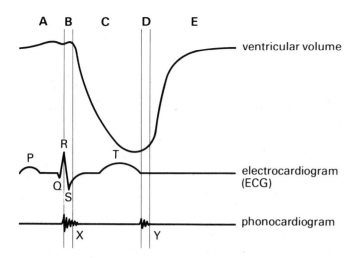

ventricular volume

electrocardiogram (ECG)

phonocardiogram

5.4.6 Cardiac muscle

The heart is composed mainly of cardiac muscle. During life, this muscle undergoes alternate contractions and relaxations which constitute the heart-beat.

The mammalian heart (and the heart of many other animals) can beat when all nerves have been cut away from it, and even when isolated from the body. Cardiac muscle contraction is **myogenic,** which means that the stimulus for contraction arises within the muscle itself.

In contrast, muscles from other parts of the body do not contract when isolated from nerves. These muscles contract only if external stimulation is applied. This type of muscular contraction is known as **neurogenic.**

Cardiac muscle consists of a network of interconnected muscle fibres — see figure 122.

122 The arrangement of cells in cardiac muscle

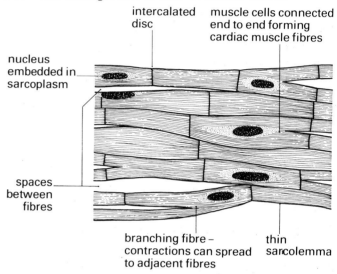

Excitation waves are able to spread quickly in many directions through these muscle fibres.

The heart-beat originates in a patch of cells in the wall of the right atrium. This patch of cells is called

123 Origin and path of excitation waves

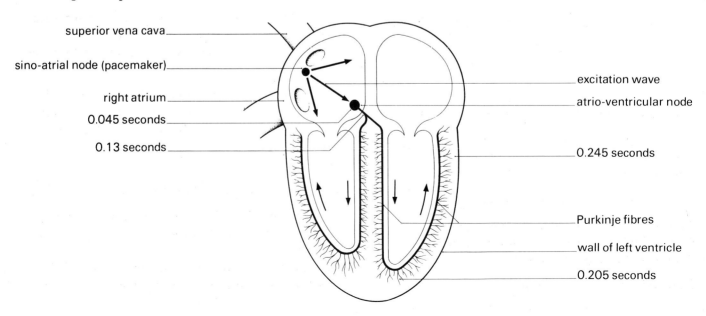

the **sino-atrial node** (SAN), and is shown in figure 123. The SAN is the site of origin of an excitation wave that travels across the whole heart. The SAN is the remnant of the sinus venosus of 'lower' vertebrates (see section 5.4.1).

The SAN acts as a **pacemaker** from which originate successive waves of excitation that determine the rhythm of heart beat.

The excitation wave is delayed for a fraction of a second at a second patch of cells, the **atrio-ventricular node** (AVN), before being conducted along the special conducting muscle fibres (**Purkinje fibres**) to the ventricles.

SAQ 98 What is the importance of the time delay at the AVN?

Look at the timing of conduction by the Purkinje fibres.

SAQ 99 Describe the way in which the ventricles will contract.

The 'inherent' rhythm of the heart is established by the SAN. Nerves from the **sympathetic nervous system** (stimulatory effect) and the **parasympathetic nervous system** (inhibitory effect) run to the SAN. See figure 124.

SAQ 100 With reference to figure 124, explain how the heart rhythm can respond to changing demands of the body.

Self test 6, page 124, covers section 5.4 of this unit.

5.4.7 Extension: Safety factors of the heart

Further information about the heart can be found in: *The Heart* by C.J. Wiggers (Scientific American reprint, 1957).

Read the article and answer the following question.

To what extent is the heart able to continue functioning effectively even with some major disorders of its constituent parts?

Show this work to your tutor.

124   Connection of the heart to the nervous system

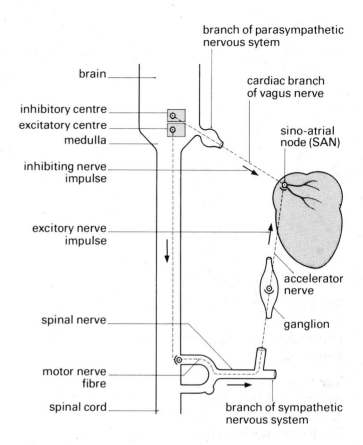

5.5 Circulation in mammals

This section looks at the vessels that transport fluid around the body and the way in which the circulatory system responds to changing needs of the body.

With an understanding of heart function in mind, you can gain an insight into the functioning of the circulatory system by a study of the structure of blood vessels.

5.5.1 The structure of blood vessels

An **artery** can be defined as a vessel that carries blood away from the heart and a **vein** carries blood to the heart. Arteries divide into smaller vessels (**arterioles**) which further divide into thin-walled vessels called **capillaries.** See figures 125 and 126.

125   The structure of arteries and veins

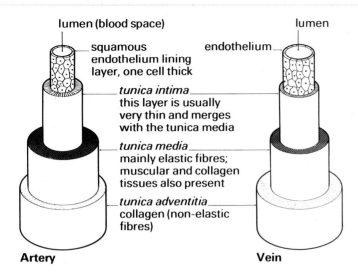

lumen (blood space)

squamous endothelium lining layer, one cell thick

tunica intima — this layer is usually very thin and merges with the tunica media

tunica media — mainly elastic fibres; muscular and collagen tissues also present

tunica adventitia — collagen (non-elastic fibres)

lumen

endothelium

Artery   **Vein**

126   The structure of a capillary

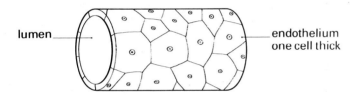

lumen   endothelium one cell thick

Capillary networks bring the blood into close association with the cells of the body. Capillaries join together again and form small vessels called **venules.** Venules then join together to form the larger veins.

The relationship between the vessels and direction of blood flow is shown in figure 127.

127   The relationship between types of blood vessel

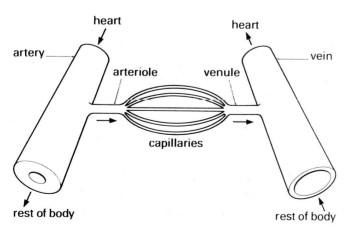

heart

artery

arteriole   venule

capillaries

rest of body

heart

vein

rest of body

Materials

Microscope and lamp, eyepiece micrometer, TS arteries and veins

Procedure

(*a*) Examine the prepared sections under LP and HP.

(*b*) Make labelled, LP plan drawings of each type of vessel.

(*c*) Using a graduated eyepiece, measure:
(i) the thickness of the individual layers in the vessels;
(ii) the thickness of the vessel wall;
(iii) the diameter of the circular lumen of the vessels.

Discussion of results

1 Describe the difference in proportions of the tissue layers found in arteries and veins.

2 Calculate the ratios of wall thickness to lumen diameter for arteries and veins.

3 Explain why size of lumen or wall thickness *alone* is not a reliable indicator of whether a vessel is an artery or a vein.

4 What feature or features of vessels could be used to characterise arteries and veins?

Show this work to your tutor.

SAQ 101 Suggest the functions of the elastic tissue and collagen fibres present in blood vessels.

SAQ 102 In light of your answer to SAQ 101, suggest reasons for the difference in relative proportions of these tissues in arteries and veins.

The heart is the main driving force behind the flow of blood. Figure 128 shows the changes in velocity of blood as it flows through the circulatory system.

SAQ 103 What causes the sharp fluctuations in velocity shown at the left of figure 128?

128 Velocity of blood

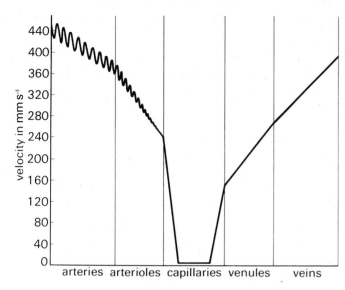

These fluctuations are smoothed out by the time blood reaches the capillaries. The nature of the vessel wall and a process called **elastic recoil** are responsible for this smoothing effect.

Ventricular contraction causes a large volume of fast-moving blood to enter the aorta, some of the energy of contraction is used in stretching the elastic wall of the artery. See figure 129.

129 Elastic recoil in the aorta

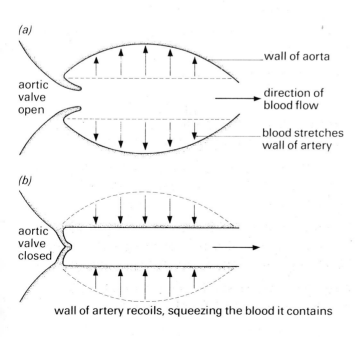

wall of artery recoils, squeezing the blood it contains

When the ventricle is filling and not exerting any pressure on the blood in the artery, the blood velocity does not fall to zero due to the elastic recoil of the artery wall. See figure 129.

After ventricular contraction, the extended elastic tissue returns to its normal state and so forces the blood to continue moving. As these pulses of blood move along the arteries energy is lost in stretching the elastic tissue and the velocity fluctuations decrease until a steady flow occurs.

The small diameter capillaries offer a large resistance to the flow of blood and the velocity in capillary networks is very low.

SAQ 104 Why does the velocity of blood increase in the venules and veins?

As shown in figure 128, the velocity of venous blood is 40 mm s^{-1} *lower* than the arterial velocity. Although the blood is flowing more slowly in the vein, the same *volume* of blood must enter the heart as leaves it.

SAQ 105 Explain this apparent contradiction.

Valves in the walls of veins prevent the back flow of blood away from the heart — see figure 130.

130 Diagram of the valves in veins

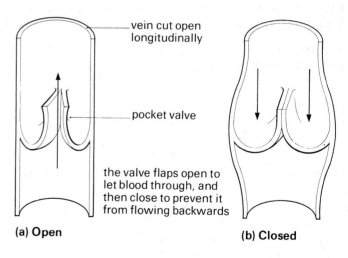

the valve flaps open to let blood through, and then close to prevent it from flowing backwards

(a) Open **(b) Closed**

An important factor in the return of blood to the heart is the contraction of skeletal muscle. During normal movement, contracting muscles often press against veins and force blood towards the heart. Lack of this skeletal muscle contraction can cause fainting, for example in guardsmen during ceremonial parades.

Each organ in the body has its own capillary network, and every living cell is close to this network. Figure 131 shows the relationship between a capillary and the surrounding cells.

131 A capillary network and tissue cells

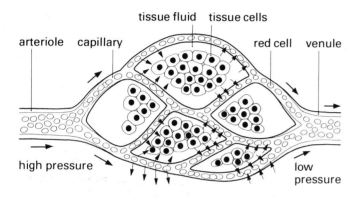

At the arterial end of the capillary, blood is under considerable pressure. This pressure forces fluid and non-cellular components of blood across the capillary wall. This liquid fills the spaces around the cells and is known as **tissue fluid.** Tissue fluid contains some proteins (e.g. hormones), glucose, oxygen (which has diffused from the red blood cells) and other useful materials. These materials can be taken up from tissue fluid into the cells of the tissues.

Some wandering white blood cells (**phagocytes**) can also move between the blood system and the tissue fluid. They do so by forming fine pseudopodia which can pass down narrow channels between the cells of the capillary walls. Red blood cells cannot pass through the capillary wall.

Waste materials diffuse from the tissue cells into the tissue fluid and through the capillary wall back into the circulation.

Figure 132 summarises the events that occur at capillaries.

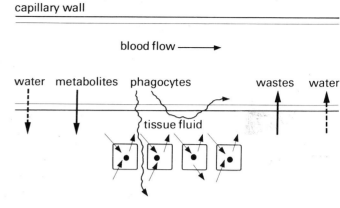

The movement of non-cellular substances across the capillary wall depends on the hydrostatic and osmotic pressures of the blood and tissue fluid.

At the arteriole end of the capillary, the hydrostatic pressure is so high that water and solutes are forced across the wall under pressure.

At the venule end, the hydrostatic pressure falls to half its original value, and water and solutes diffuse back into the blood (see figure 133).

133   Capillary pressures and diffusion

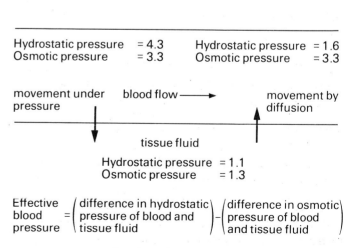

134 Lymph vessels

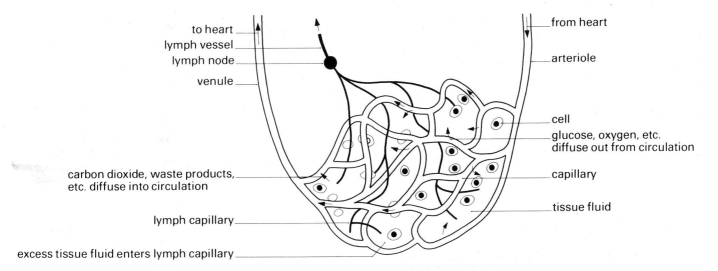

to heart · lymph vessel · lymph node · venule · from heart · arteriole · cell · glucose, oxygen, etc. diffuse out from circulation · capillary · tissue fluid · carbon dioxide, waste products, etc. diffuse into circulation · lymph capillary · excess tissue fluid enters lymph capillary

SAQ 106 (*a*) Using the data and equation in figure 133, calculate the effective blood pressure at the arteriole and venule ends of a capillary.

(*b*) What would be the effect of a decrease in the osmotic or hydrostatic pressure of blood?

Not all the water that leaves the capillary eventually returns. To prevent an increase in volume of the tissue fluid there is an accessory system of vessels to drain away excess fluid. These vessels are collectively known as the **lymphatic system.**

5.5.2 The lymphatic system

Figure 134 shows the relationship between a capillary network, tissue cells and lymph vessels.

Once excess tissue fluid enters these vessels, the fluid is called **lymph.**

The lymph vessels unite to form the lymphatic system. Lymph collected from all over the body is poured back into circulation via the veins at the base of the neck (figure 135).

The fluid pressure in the lymphatic system is very low and, as in the veins, lymph vessels contain valves to maintain a one-way flow of fluid. At points along main lymphatic vessels are swellings or **lymph**

135 The lymphatic system of humans

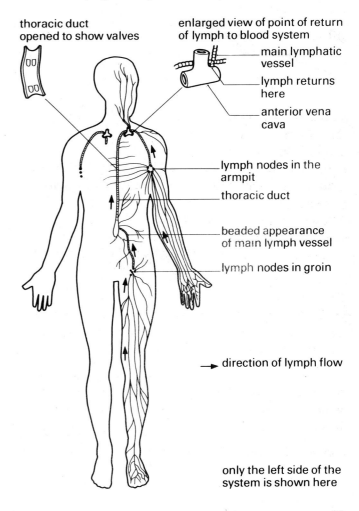

thoracic duct opened to show valves · enlarged view of point of return of lymph to blood system · main lymphatic vessel · lymph returns here · anterior vena cava · lymph nodes in the armpit · thoracic duct · beaded appearance of main lymph vessel · lymph nodes in groin · → direction of lymph flow · only the left side of the system is shown here

73

nodes. Lymph nodes are important in the defence of the body against foreign bodies.

5.5.3 Extension: Investigating the function of the lymphatic system

Read *The Lymphatic System* by H.S. Mayerson (Scientific American reprint, 1963) and answer the following questions.

1 What did Claude Bernard mean by the *milieu interieur?*

2 What is the primary role of the lymphatic system in its maintenance?

3 Why was the lymphatic system an evolutionary necessity?

4 What is the relationship between the thymus and lymph node function?

5 According to E.H. Starling, why is it important that proteins do not leave the blood plasma?

6 What did C.K. Drinker believe to be the primary function of the lymphatic system?

7 What methods was H.S. Mayerson able to use that were not available to Drinker?

8 Which view of lymphatic function was supported by Mayerson's results?

9 What conditions cause increased lymph flow from the lungs and pulmonary oedema?

10 How has the lymphatic system been implicated with hardening of the arteries?

11 What is the cause and effect of lymphoedema?

Show this work to your tutor.

5.5.4 The human circulatory system

Figure 136 is a plan of the circulatory system in man. Copy this diagram into your notebook and answer the questions below.

SAQ 107 Label the vessels 1–15. (Refer to figure 137 to help you do this.)

136 A simplified plan of the heart and circulation in man

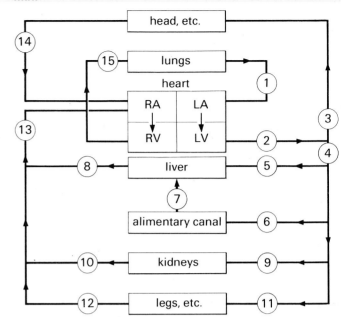

RA and LA = right and left atria
RV and LV = right and left ventricles

SAQ 108 What differences in the composition of blood would you expect in the following pairs of vessels: 6 and 7, 1 and 15, 9 and 10?

5.5.5 Summary assignment 8

1 Construct a table to show the differences between arteries and veins.

2 Use figure 138 to explain the differences between blood, plasma, tissue fluid and lymph.

138 Relationship of body fluids

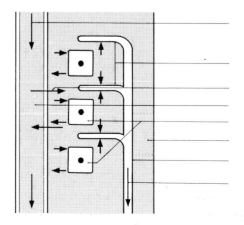

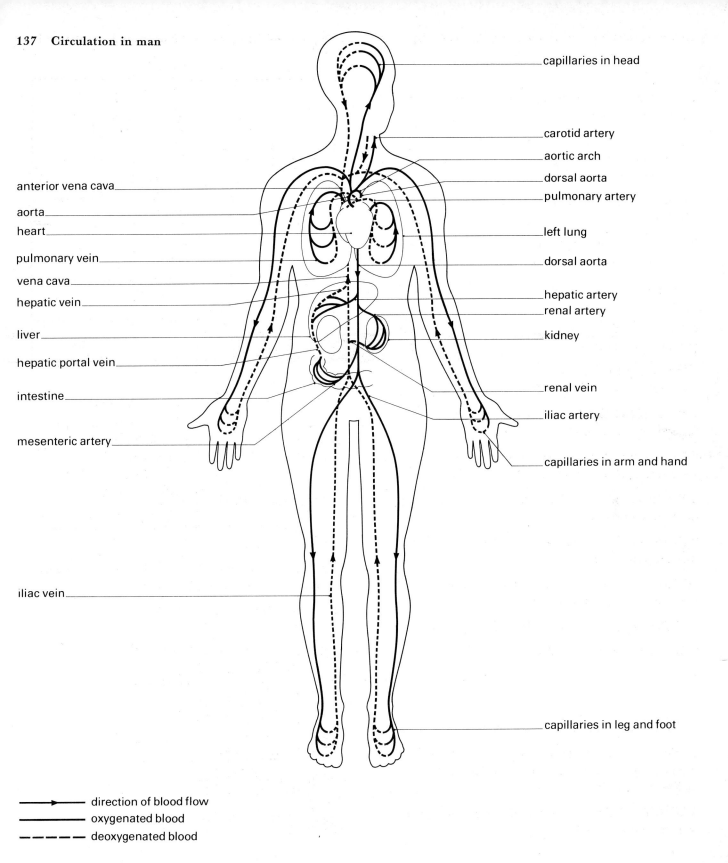

capillaries in head

carotid artery

aortic arch

dorsal aorta

pulmonary artery

anterior vena cava

aorta

heart

left lung

pulmonary vein

dorsal aorta

vena cava

hepatic artery

hepatic vein

renal artery

liver

kidney

hepatic portal vein

intestine

renal vein

mesenteric artery

iliac artery

capillaries in arm and hand

iliac vein

capillaries in leg and foot

→ direction of blood flow

⎯⎯⎯ oxygenated blood

- - - - - deoxygenated blood

3 Your answers to SAQ 107 and 108 summarise the circulatory system in humans.

Show this work to your tutor.

5.5.6 The circulatory system in action

The circulatory system must be able to respond to the changing requirements of the tissues it supplies.

Unlike cardiac muscle, the muscle in blood vessel walls is neurogenic. Under normal circumstances, the muscle fibres of large vessels are kept in a state of partial contraction by a steady flow of nerve impulses.

During exercise, however, this state of partial contraction is altered and changes occur in the muscle of the artery walls.

The muscles in the walls of arteries which supply blood to the limbs become relaxed. These arteries thus become **dilated** (widen) and are able to carry more blood to the limbs.

At the same time, muscles in arteries which supply blood to other organs (e.g. stomach and alimentary canal) become contracted. This **constriction** (narrowing) restricts blood flow to non-essential organs, and allows more to flow to the limbs.

These changes are brought about by the sympathetic nervous system, which also speeds up heart-beat during exercise.

During stress or excitement, adrenalin (a hormone) is released into the blood. Adrenalin also dilates arteries and arterioles and it causes constriction of the veins, and a speeding-up of heart-beat.

A local control of flow is also possible by the existence of **sphincters** (rings of muscle) at the entrance to capillary beds and arterio-venous shunts. See figure 139.

Capillaries are able to respond to changes in the oxygen requirements of the tissues. It is thought that capillaries respond to chemical changes which occur in their surroundings. If respiring tissues produce excessive amounts of waste products (as happens in exercise) these accumulate in and around capillaries.

139   Local control of blood flow

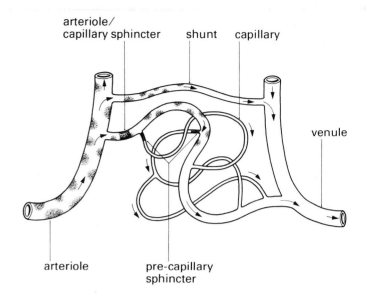

The sphincter muscle at the entrance to the capillary network is sensitive to these waste products. An excess of waste products causes relaxation of the muscle, and more blood flows through the capillaries, removing the waste products. Once their level has returned to normal, the sphincter contracts again.

Capillaries can also respond to changes in body temperature. If body temperature rises, the capillaries dilate (**vasodilation**) and more heat is lost from the skin surface. If body temperature drops, **vasoconstriction** occurs and less heat is lost.

Changes in the internal environment may occur as a result of changes in bodily activity. The body must make adjustments if it is to continue operating efficiently.

SAQ 109 What changes in blood composition will occur as a result of increased activity?

The concentration of respiratory gases present in the body at a given moment is affected by the respiratory and circulatory systems.

SAQ 110 (*a*) How might you expect the respiratory and circulatory systems to respond if blood carbon dioxide is too high and oxygen too low?

(*b*) How will vasodilation and vasoconstriction aid the responses mentioned in part (*a*)?

The respiratory and circulatory systems work together to keep the concentration of respiratory gases constant. Section 3.4.6 considered the functioning of the respiratory system. The control of the circulatory system is very similar.

The **cardiovascular centre** in the medulla of the brain controls the frequency of heart-beat. Chemoreceptors in the carotid and aortic bodies monitor carbon dioxide concentration in the blood and, via nerve fibres and the cardiovascular centre, affect the pacemaker activity of the heart. See figure 140.

140 Diagram to show the control of heart-beat

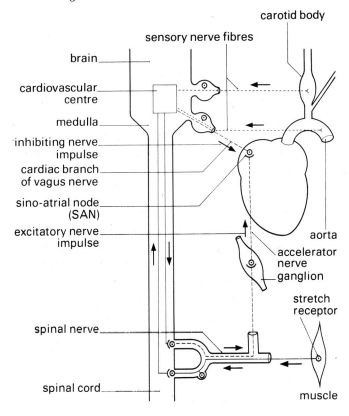

SAQ 111 With reference to figure 140, describe the passage of nerve impulses and the effects they have when the concentration of blood carbon dioxide increases.

The heart is not the only structure to respond to carbon dioxide concentration — accumulation of carbon dioxide in muscles has a direct effect of dilating the supplying arterioles. The cardiovascular centre also sends nerve impulses to peripheral blood vessels that cause general vasoconstriction and an increase in blood pressure.

SAQ 112 What effect will these two changes in vessel diameter have upon the flow of blood through muscles?

Apart from the concentration of respiratory gases, the heart and blood vessels also play an important part in the control of blood pressure. At the base of the *internal* carotid artery there is a swelling, the **carotid sinus,** that contains **stretch receptors.** See figure 141.

141 Carotid body and carotid sinus

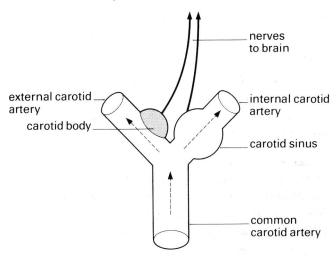

A rise in blood pressure stimulates the stretch receptors and nerve impulses pass to the cardiovascular centre in the brain. Impulses pass from the brain to the heart and peripheral arterioles cause a decrease in heart-rate and vasoconstriction.

Higher centres in the brain can also have an effect on the circulatory system. During periods of excitement or shock, the **cerebral cortex** passes nerve impulses to the **adrenal glands** which respond by secreting the hormone adrenalin into the bloodstream.

Adrenalin increases cardiac frequency and constriction of the peripheral arterioles, an effect identical to stimulation from the cardiovascular centre. Although the nervous and hormonal systems produce identical effects, there is an important difference. The nervous system (cardiovascular centre) adjusts the body to changes that are taking place. The hormonal system (cerebral cortex/adrenalin) adjusts the body to changes that have yet to occur. The hormonal system of control prepares the body for action in emergencies.

5.5.7 Summary assignment 9

1 Construct a diagram to summarise the way in which the body responds to a *decrease* in blood carbon dioxide concentration.

2 Describe the process involved in the control of blood pressure.

3 Describe the chemical and physiological changes that occur in an athlete's body before and during a 100 m race.

Show this work to your tutor.

5.5.8 Past examination questions

1 Describe the changes that occur in the blood of a mammal as it passes through (*a*) the liver, (*b*) the kidneys and (*c*) the lungs.

(London, Paper 1, January 1973)

2 Study figure 142 which indicates the variations in pressure in different parts of the human circulatory system. Answer the following questions.

142 Blood pressures

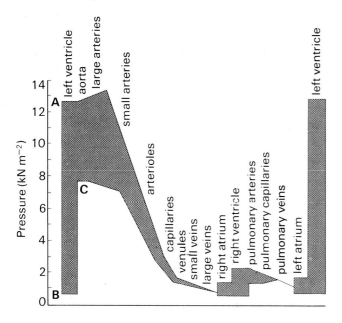

(*a*) Which part of the circulation shows the greatest fluctuations in pressure?

(*b*) Which parts show no fluctuations?

(*c*) Which part of the circulation always maintains a pressure above 7.5 kN m^{-2}?

(*d*) Describe the factors which exert the pressures evident at:
(i) **A,** (ii) **B,** (iii) **C.**

(*e*) Suggest the sector of the circulation which offers the greatest resistance to the flow of blood. How is this indicated by the diagram?

(*f*) Blood flow in the main veins is under relatively low pressure. Describe how the return of blood to the heart is maintained.

(*g*) Account for the different ranges of pressures in the pulmonary and systemic circulations. What are the advantages to the mammal in having a double circulatory system?

(AEB, Paper 2, June 1978)

Show this work to your tutor.

Self test 7, page 125, covers section 5.5 of this unit.

5.6 Blood — the transport medium

So far, all the structures of the transport systems you have studied have been involved in circulating a fluid medium around the animal's body. It is this fluid that transports the substances. The structure and function of this fluid is therefore of great importance.

One of the major functions of blood in most animals is the transport of the respiratory gases, oxygen and carbon dioxide. It is this function which will be considered first.

5.6.1 Transport of respiratory gases

The carriage of oxygen

For efficient transport of respiratory gases, the circulatory fluid should have two basic properties — it should load and unload gases with relative ease and it should carry large quantities of gases.

SAQ 113 Where does this loading and unloading of respiratory gases take place?

Water does not possess these two qualities. At 20 °C and 76 mm Hg, 100 cm³ of water can carry a maximum of 0.6 cm³ of dissolved oxygen.

A simple water vascular system imposes constraints on cellular respiration and hence on the activity of the organism. For increased activity, the **oxygen affinity** (the readiness to accept oxygen) of the vascular fluid needs to increase. The oxygen-carrying properties of vascular fluids in many animals have been greatly improved by the presence of **respiratory pigments.** These are chemicals (coloured when in solution, hence the name pigment) that have a high affinity and capacity for respiratory gases.

SAQ 114 What does 'capacity' mean in this context?

Figure 143 gives a brief survey of the respiratory pigments found in different animal groups.

SAQ 115 (*a*) What is the blood pigment of vertebrates and where is it found?

(*b*) Which group of organisms shown in figure 143 shows the greatest range of blood pigment?

Haemoglobin

A clue to the nature of this chemical comes from its name. *Haemo* — iron-containing, *globin* — globular protein. Haemoglobin is made up of a protein chain connected to an iron-containing **prosthetic group,** a non-protein substance combined with a protein (see figure 144(*a*)). It is the *haem* prosthetic group that is responsible for the carriage of oxygen. The iron atom combines loosely and reversibly with oxygen (see figure 144 (*b*)).

144   The structure of haemoglobin

(a) Haemoglobin chain

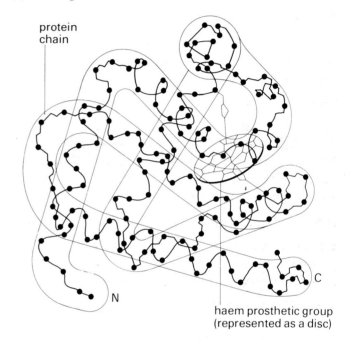

protein chain

haem prosthetic group (represented as a disc)

143   Respiratory pigments

Pigment	Colour	Site	Animal	Oxygen Vol. per cent
haemoglobin	red	corpuscles	mammals	15−30
			birds	20−25
			reptiles	7−12
			amphibians	3−10
			fishes	4−20
		plasma	annelids	1−10
			molluscs	1−6
haemocyanin	blue	plasma	molluscs	
			gastropods	1−3
			cephalopods	3−5
			crustaceans	1−4
chlorocruorin	green	plasma	annelids	9
haemerythrin	red	corpuscles	annelids	2

(b) Haem prosthetic group

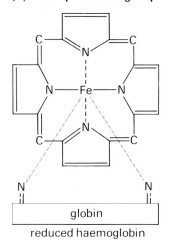
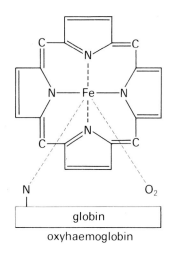

reduced haemoglobin   oxyhaemoglobin

There are different types of haemoglobin, differing in the nature of the protein chain or the number of haemoglobin units. Muscle haemoglobin (**myoglobin**) contains one unit per molecule while blood haemoglobin contains four units. See figure 145.

145 Mammalian haemoglobin

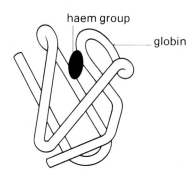

Muscle haemoglobin (myoglobin)
one unit

Blood haemoglobin
four units

One blood haemoglobin molecule can combine with four molecules of oxygen, a process called **association.** The reaction is reversible and **dissociation** liberates the four oxygen molecules. The equation is shown in figure 146. *Hb* is often used as a shorthand version of haemoglobin.

SAQ 116 Why is it important that the reaction between haemoglobin and oxygen is reversible?

EQUILIBRIUM

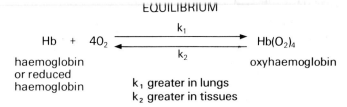

$$Hb + 4O_2 \underset{k_2}{\overset{k_1}{\rightleftharpoons}} Hb(O_2)_4$$

haemoglobin or reduced haemoglobin   oxyhaemoglobin

k_1 greater in lungs
k_2 greater in tissues

Haemoglobin increases the capability of blood to take up oxygen from the lungs. Without it, blood could carry very little oxygen.

SAQ 117 Refer back to page 68 and figure 143. How many times more efficient at carrying oxygen is haemoglobin than water?

In order to understand exactly how haemoglobin takes up oxygen, it is necessary to understand something of gas pressure.

Consider a sealed balloon which has been filled with a mixture of three gases (see figure 147). The total pressure of the gas mixture is 50 kN m^{-2}.

147   A sealed balloon

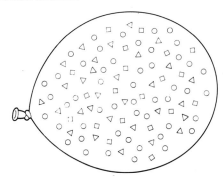

Gas	Molecules	% component of mixture
A	□ □ □	20
B	○ ○ ○	50
C	△ △ △	30

The pressure is due to the molecules of the gas mixture constantly bombarding the wall of the balloon.

SAQ 118 Explain why gas B exerts 25 kN m^{-2} of pressure in the balloon.

This phenomenon is called **partial pressure.** In a mixture of gases, the partial pressure of a gas can be defined as the pressure that that gas would produce if kept in the same volume and if all other gases were removed from the mixture.

SAQ 119 (*a*) What is the partial pressure of gas A?

(*b*) What would be the pressure in the balloon if gases A and B were removed?

The partial pressure (abbreviated to p.p.) gives an indication of the amounts of gases present in a mixture. See figure 148.

148   Partial pressures for gases in air at sea-level

Gas	Partial pressure (kNm^{-2})
oxygen	21.1
carbon dioxide	0.04
nitrogen	79.9

Air pressure (sea-level) = 101.04 kNm^{-2}

An investigation was carried out in which equal samples of blood were exposed for a standard period of time to a number of different air samples. The air samples were all of the same volume and pressure, but had differing partial pressures of oxygen. The blood and air were allowed to reach **equilibrium** where the rate of oxygen association with the haemoglobin is equal to the rate of oxygen dissociation. The haemoglobin samples were therefore carrying their maximum load of oxygen. See figure 149.

149   Blood and air in equilibrium

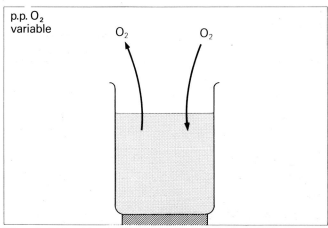

50 cm³ of blood in equilibrium with 1 dm³ air at STP

The blood samples were then analysed to see how much oxygen each had taken up. These amounts were then converted into percentage values known as the **percentage saturation of haemoglobin with oxygen.**

Figure 150 shows the results for the investigation but not the percentage saturation of haemoglobin.

150   Results for the investigation into oxygen uptake by haemoglobin

Partial pressure of O_2 in air (kNm^{-2})	Volume O_2 in blood sample (cm^3)
0	0
1	5
2	11
3	21
4	33.5
5	40.5
6	44
7	46.5
8	47
9	47.5
10	48

SAQ 120 (*a*) A 50 cm³ sample of blood was used for each partial pressure of oxygen. Calculate the volume of oxygen each blood sample contained as a percentage of the blood volume.

(*b*) Remembering which is the dependent and which the independent variable, plot a graph of partial pressure of oxygen in air against *percentage saturation of haemoglobin with oxygen.*

The curve has a characteristic **sigmoidal** or S-shape. This graph is called the **oxygen equilibrium curve of haemoglobin.** Put this title on the curve you have just drawn for SAQ 120.

SAQ 121 Over what approximate range of partial pressures of oxygen is there the greatest *rate of change* in percentage saturation of haemoglobin?

SAQ 122 What will happen to haemoglobin at 5 kN m⁻² if the partial pressure of oxygen is (*a*) increased or (*b*) decreased?

The steepest part of the equilibrium curve coincides with the range or partial pressures of oxygen found in the body. Within this range (1 to 5 kN m^{-2}) there is a large variation in the percentage saturation of haemoglobin.

SAQ 123 Using your graph from SAQ 120:
(*a*) Which partial pressure would you expect at (i) the lungs and (ii) the tissues?

(*b*) What is the change in percentage saturation of haemoglobin over the range 1 to 5 kN m^{-2}?

(*c*) Why is it advantageous for the steepest part of the curve to coincide with the range of normal body partial pressures?

If the partial pressure of oxygen is decreased, haemoglobin liberates oxygen. The curve (answer to SAQ 120) is also often called the oxygen–haemoglobin **dissociation curve**. However, as the curve can also give information about oxygen–haemoglobin association with increasing partial pressure, the more general term of 'equilibrium curve' is used in this unit.

The investigation described on page 81 was repeated but this time blood samples were exposed to two different mixtures of oxygen *and* carbon dioxide. In one mixture, the carbon dioxide was at a partial pressure of 1.0 kN m^{-2} and in the other it was at 1.5 kN m^{-2}. The oxygen equilibrium curves were then plotted on a graph. See figure 151. Notice how these oxygen equilibrium curves differ.

SAQ 124 Describe the effect that carbon dioxide has on oxygen–haemoglobin equilibrium curves.

With reference to figure 152 and the graph from figure 151, answer the following SAQs.

SAQ 125 (*a*) For the time **X,** the state of the blood and tissues is shown in figure 152. Calculate the *decrease* in haemoglobin saturation when blood travels from A to C (use figure 151 as *dissociation* curves).

(*b*) For time **Y,** calculate the *decrease* in haemoglobin saturation between A and C.

(*c*) For time **Z,** calculate the *decrease* in haemoglobin saturation when blood tavels from A to C.

151   Oxygen–haemoglobin equilibrium curves for two partial pressures of carbon dioxide

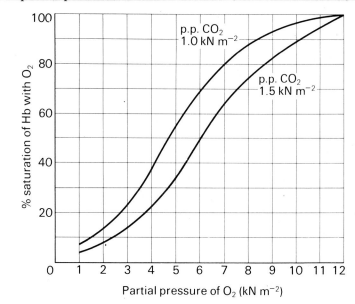

152   Oxygen and carbon dioxide partial pressures for a capillary network

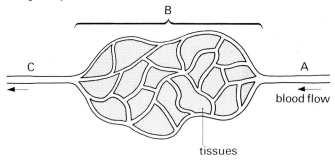

Time	Blood (p.p. O_2)		Tissue (p.p. CO_2)	
X	A = 9	C = 3	A = 1	B = 1
Y	A = 9	C = 3	A = 1.5	B = 1.5
Z	A = 9	C = 3	A = 1	B = 1.5

SAQ 126 What information do your answers to SAQ 125(*a*) and (*b*) give you about the shape of the equilibrium curves in figure 151?

SAQ 127 What is the effect of an *increase* in the partial pressure of carbon dioxide in blood as it enters a capillary network?

SAQ 128 Sketch the graph shown in figure 151 and indicate, using a dotted line, the approximate *dissociation curve* for blood flowing through the capillaries at time **Z.**

SAQ 129 What tissues of the body would you expect to have higher carbon dioxide partial pressures than blood?

SAQ 130 How does decreasing the partial pressure of carbon dioxide in lungs contribute to the efficiency of haemoglobin as an oxygen carrier?

This shift in the oxygen–haemoglobin equilibrium due to changes in carbon dioxide concentration is called the **Bohr effect** (after the scientist who first recorded it).

It has been found that carbon dioxide has no direct effect on haemoglobin but that carbon dioxide dissolving in the plasma changes pH which causes the shift.

SAQ 131 Does an *increase* in dissolved carbon dioxide cause an increase or decrease in (*a*) acidity, (*b*) pH?

A shift to the right of the equilibrium curve is also caused by an increase in temperature.

SAQ 132 From your knowledge of protein structure, how might pH and temperature affect the functioning of haemoglobin?

SAQ 133 Explain how actively respiring tissues, e.g. contracting muscle, can acquire greater amounts of oxygen due to the shift in the equilibrum curve.

Refer now to figure 153. This shows the oxygen equilibrium curves for haemoglobin from three different animals.

SAQ 134 (*a*) Which of these haemoglobins combines most readily with oxygen at low partial pressures?

(*b*) Which one of these three animal would you expect to be aquatic? Explain your answer.

Planorbis (a snail) and *Arenicola* (the lugworm) are two aquatic invertebrates which have haemoglobin in their blood. They both live in environments which contain little oxygen.

Increased partial pressures of carbon dioxide do not affect their equilibrium curves.

SAQ 135 Explain the advantage to these organisms of possessing this 'unresponsive' haemoglobin.

153 Oxygen–haemoglobin equilibrium curves for three animals

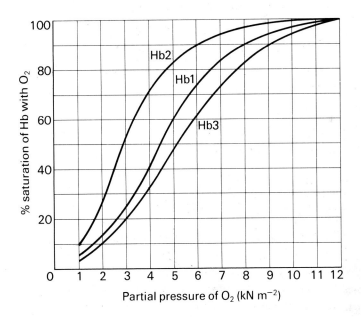

The carriage of carbon dioxide

Carbon dioxide from respiring cells is carried back to the lungs in the blood. It is carried by two different components of the blood.

Some carbon dioxide is carried in the plasma as hydrogen carbonate ions. The carbon dioxide reacts with water to form carbonic acid, which dissociates:

$$H_2O + CO_2 \rightleftharpoons H_2CO_3 \rightleftharpoons H^+ + HCO_3^-$$

carbonic acid   hydrogen carbonate ion

Formation of carbonic acid occurs relatively slowly. In the red blood cells carbon dioxide is transported partly as **carbamino compounds** — these are combinations of carbon dioxide and haemoglobin.

Red cells also carry carbon dioxide as carbonate ions. Carbon dioxide diffuses into the red blood cells where an enzyme, **carbonic anhydrase,** brings about the reaction:

$$H_2O + CO_2 \xrightarrow{\text{carbonic anhydrase}} H_2CO_3$$

carbonic acid

This weak acid easily dissociates:

$$H_2CO_3 \rightleftharpoons H^+ + HCO_3^-$$

The hydrogen carbonate ions diffuse out of the red blood cell into the plasma and the hydrogen ions accumulate inside the red blood cell.

SAQ 136 What effect would an accumulation of H^+ ions have on the oxygen–haemoglobin equilibrium curve?

It is this enzyme reaction in red blood cells that raises the acidity by accumulation of H^+ ions that, in turn, causes the Bohr effect.

Figure 154 summarises the carriage of carbon dioxide by blood.

154   Carbon dioxide transport

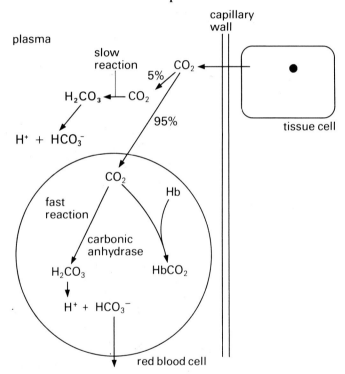

$HbCO_2 \equiv$ carbamino compound

Due to the differences in rate of carbonic acid formation in red blood cells and plasma, 95% of the carbon dioxide is transported by combination with the red blood cells.

Hydrogen carbonate ions do not accumulate in the red blood cells. The red cell membrane is very permeable to negative ions and the hydrogen carbonate diffuses out into the plasma. The cell membrane, however, is relatively impermeable to positive ions and so this constant loss of negative hydrogen carbonate ions would produce a massive internal positive charge that would disrupt the red cell functioning.

To maintain **ionic** and **electrical neutrality**, a normal ratio of positive and negative ions within the cell, chloride ions diffuse into the red cell to take the place of the hydrogen carbonate ions. This process has been called the **chloride shift** — see figure 155.

155   The chloride shift

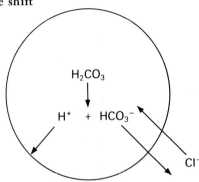

Figure 156 outlines the events leading to release of carbon dioxide into the lungs from the blood.

156   Release of carbon dioxide at the lungs

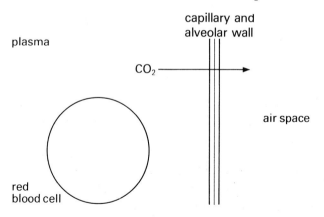

SAQ 137 Copy and complete figure 156.

5.6.2 Extension: Questions

1 (a) What are the principal properties of an efficient blood pigment?

(b) Name *two* blood pigments and state a group of animals in which each pigment may be found.

(c) The graph shown in figure 157 shows the relationship between the percentage oxygen saturation for two blood pigments and the oxygen concentration in the surrounding air.

157   Graph for question 1

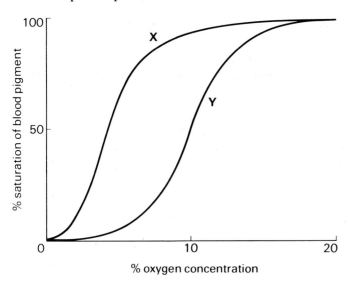

(i) What will be the effect on the saturation of the blood pigments **X** and **Y,** of reducing the external oxygen concentration from 20% to 10%?
(ii) Which of the pigments would be more suitable for a mud-dwelling animal? Briefly give reasons for your answer.

(London, Paper 1, January 1977)

2 The amount of oxygen combining with haemoglobin in the blood depends on the partial pressure of oxygen. In mammals, oxygen enters the body via the lungs and in pregnancy is transferred from the mother's blood to that of the foetus. The relation between oxygen saturation and oxygen partial pressure in a certain species is shown in figure 158.

158   Graph for question 2

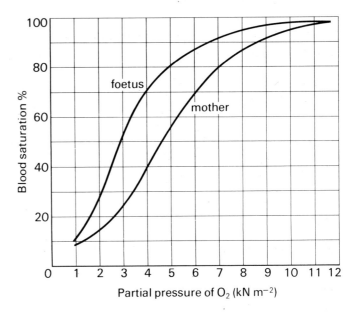

(a) At what partial pressure of oxygen is the oxygen saturation at 50% (i) in the mother, (ii) in the foetus?

(b) What do you suggest would be the oxygen saturation of maternal blood exposed to air (atmospheric partial pressure of O_2 = 18 kN m^{-2})?

(c) Explain how the relation between oxygen saturation and partial pressure facilitates the carriage of oxygen in the mother from the lungs to her tissues.

(d) How does the difference in the oxygen loading between maternal and foetal blood help the transfer of oxygen from the mother to the foetus?

(AEB, Paper 1, June 1978)

3 The figures set out in the table (figure 159) represent the rates of release of carbon dioxide from a solution of sodium bicarbonate resulting from its mixture with acid phosphate buffer solution (a)

159   Data for question 3

Time (s)	0	5	10	15	30	45	60	90	100	160	220
Bicarbonate + buffer solution alone	0	0	0.1	0.2	0.3	0.4	0.5	0.6	0.7	0.8	0.8
Bicarbonate + buffer solution + blood	0	0.1	0.7	0.8	1.2	1.3	1.4	1.5	1.5	1.5	1.5

alone, and (b) in the presence of diluted blood. It is assumed that the temperature is constant throughout both experiments and that the carbon dioxide evolved is measured at atmospheric pressure. (The figures in rows 2 and 3 of the table represent the volumes of carbon dioxide, in millilitres, measured at the corresponding time intervals from zero.)

(a) Plot these figures on a graph.

(b) From the graph, deduce the effect of blood on the release of carbon dioxide.

(c) What might be the explanation of the effect?

(d) What further experiment might be carried out to test this explanation?

Show this work to your tutor.

5.6.3 The structure of blood

If blood is spun for a few minutes in a high-speed centrifuge, two layers separate in the tube. The lower fraction at the bottom of the tube is a dark red cellular layer; the upper fraction a pale yellow fluid fraction. The fluid layer, called **plasma** is made up of water, ions, metabolites and soluble proteins.

Serum is the name given to plasma from which the soluble protein **fibrinogen** (a protein involved in blood clotting) has been removed.

The cellular fraction contains **erythrocytes** (red cells), **leucocytes** (white cells) and **thrombocytes** (platelets). See figure 160.

The cellular component develops from stem cells in bone marrow or lymph nodes. Refer to figure 161 as you complete the following practical.

161 Cellular compoments of blood

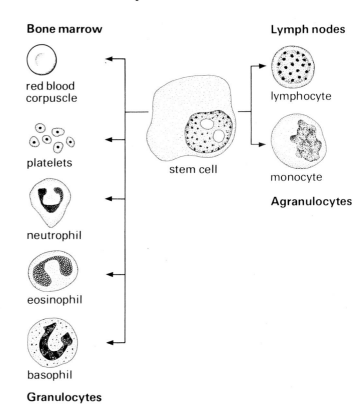

160 Blood components

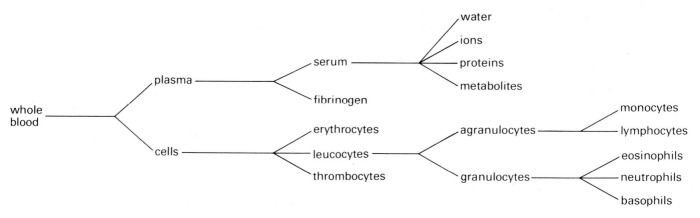

Practical P: Blood cells

Materials

Microscope and lamp, microscope slides and coverslips, Leishman's stain, buffered distilled water, human blood (☠).

Procedure

(*a*) Place one drop of blood on a microscope slide and add a coverslip.

(*b*) Examine the blood sample under the microscope and record your observations in the form of annotated drawings.

(*c*) Place one drop of blood onto a microscope slide towards one end of the slide, as shown in figure 162(*a*).

(*d*) Make a blood smear by using a second microscope slide, as shown in figure 162(*b*) and (*c*).

162   Making a blood smear

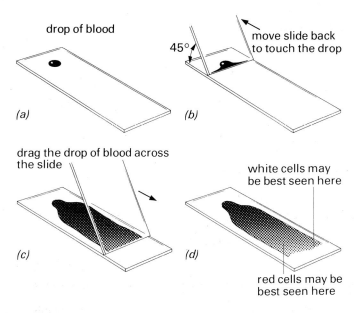

drop of blood

45°

move slide back to touch the drop

(a)

(b)

drag the drop of blood across the slide

white cells may be best seen here

red cells may be best seen here

(c)

(d)

(*e*) Leave the blood smear for three or four minutes until it is dry.

(*f*) Add one or two drops of Leishman's stain and one or two drops of buffered distilled water.

(*g*) Leave the slide for five minutes and wash off the surplus stain under a gently-running tap.

(*h*) Shake off the surplus water and leave the slide to dry.

(*i*) Examine the slide under LP and HP and record the different types of cells you can see.

Show the work to your tutor

5.6.4 The functions of blood

Blood is the medium of transport in the circulatory system. Blood transports respiratory gases to and from the tissues and the lungs, and it also transports other materials throughout the body. Blood also distributes heat. In addition to its function as a transport medium, blood plays an active part in combating and preventing the entry of disease-causing agents such as bacteria.

The following video sequence looks more closely at the defensive functions of blood.

AV 2: Defence against disease

Materials

VCR and monitor
ABAL video sequence: *Defence against disease*
Worksheets

Procedure

(*a*) View the video sequence.

(*b*) Read through the worksheets and answer as many questions as possible.

(*c*) View the sequence again to check your answers.

Show this work to your tutor.

5.6.5 Summary assignment 10

1 Figure 163 shows how one student started her patterned notes for section 5.6.1.

Either finish off these notes or start your own notes with the structure you think best.

163 Patterned notes for section 5.6.1

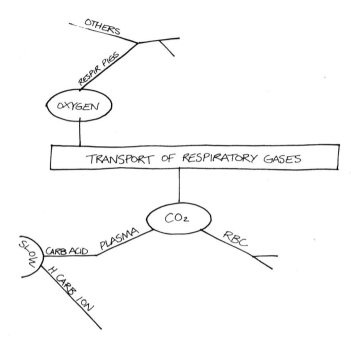

2 Copy figures 160 and 161 and annotate your diagrams to summarise the structure and functions of blood.

Show this work to your tutor.

Self test 8, page 126, covers section 5.6 of this unit.

5.6.6 Extension: Adaptations to high altitude

As altitude increases, the partial pressure of oxygen decreases. Air at high altitudes has less oxygen per unit volume than air at sea-level.

When a person who normally lives at sea-level moves to a region of high altitude, several physiological changes occur in his or her body.

A clear explanation of these is given in the following publications, which you should read before answering the AEB past examination question given below.

Revised Nuffield Biology (1975). Text 2. *Living Things in Action*. Longmans (pages 100 and 101).

The Physiology of High Altitude by R.H. Hock (Scientific American reprint, 1970).

(*a*) Graph 1 (figure 164) shows the percentage of haemoglobin associated with oxygen to form oxy-haemoglobin over a range of partial pressures of oxygen. Graph 2 (figure 164) shows the relationship between altitude and partial pressures of oxygen.

Note that chemical details of glycolysis and Krebs' TCA cycle are *not* required in any part of this answer.

(i) Using the information given on both graphs, explain why most people who are not acclimatised to

164 Graphs 1 and 2

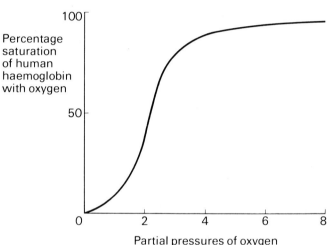

living at high altitudes will lose consciousness at altitudes between 6000 and 8000 metres.

(ii) Permanent human habitations occur up to approximately 7000 metres and people who are acclimatised to high altitudes can survive for a few hours when breathing air at approximately 9000 metres.

Suggest *three* adjustments which probably occur in the physiology of such acclimatised people.

(iii) Explain the physiological reasons for each of the adjustments you have suggested.

(*b*) The following data refer to Olympic Games held at the sites stated — see figure 165.

(i) Carefully explain why unacclimatised athletes were relatively unsuccessful during the 10 000 m race at the Mexico Olympic Games.

(ii) Some unsuccessful athletes collapsed and were given oxygen. Clearly explain the role of this oxygen with specific reference to the athletes' livers.

(iii) By referring only to general principles, explain the role of oxygen in energy release in mitochondria.

(iv) Describe a quantitative experiment which you have carried out to compare the composition of inspired and expired air in any named *living* organism.

(AEB, Paper 2, June 1979)

Show this work to your tutor.

165   Result of the 10 000 m race

Tokyo 1964 (200 m above sea-level)		Mexico 1968 (2242 m above sea-level)	
1. M. Mills	USA	1. N. Tamu	Kenya**
2. M. Gammoudi	Tunisia**	2. M. Wolds	Ethiopia**
3. R. Clarke	Australia	3. M. Gammoudi	Tunisia**
4. M. Wolds	Ethiopia**	4. J. Martinez	Mexico**
5. L. Ivanov	Russia	5. N. Sviridov	Russia*
6. K. Tsuduroya	Japan	6. R. Clarke	Australia*
7. M. Halberg	New Zealand	7. R. Hill	UK*
8. A. Cook	Australia	8. W. Masresha	Ethiopia**

** Indicates athletes who had lived most of their life at high altitudes.
 * Indicates athletes who trained at high altitudes for an extended period prior to the games.

Section 6 Transport in plants

6.1 Introduction and objectives

The most successful land plants: those which are the largest, which inhabit the greatest numbers of different habitats and produce the greatest numbers of individuals, all possess well-developed internal transport systems.

Some terrestrial plants, the mosses and liverworts, do not possess an internal transport system, which seems to indicate that this is not a criterion for life on land. Plants like these are very likely to have been among the earliest forms to colonise land in moist places. Such plants are still totally dependent on being covered by a film of water for sexual reproduction to occur.

It is significant that mosses and liverworts are never very large — their thin permeable bodies do not provide enough strength to enable stems to grow tall and stand upright. The lack of a transport system in the stems of mosses limits water conduction to a short distance, thus restricting the size to which they can grow.

However, a transport system is not essential for a plant to grow large. Some brown seaweeds, the giant kelps, may reach lengths of 100 m but do not possess specialised conducting tissues.

The surrounding water provides such aquatic plants with essential materials and, at the same time, supports their large bodies.

In terrestrial plants, the tissues associated with transport also play a role in support. In order to grow large and to be able to colonise a vast variety of habitats, a transport system does seem to be essential.

The development of transport systems in plants can be associated with two of the major features of life on dry land, i.e. the necessity for some means of support and the ability to resist drying out.

A system of vessels for the conduction of water and dissolved nutrients is called a **vascular system.** Plants with such a system are referred to as **vascular plants.** The vascular system facilitates the efficient transport of water and nutrients throughout the plant, overcoming the need for each cell to obtain them directly from the environment. At the same time, the vascular tissue of plants helps to support their mass.

This section of the unit investigates the different roles of the stem in the 'long-distance' transport of water and nutrients.

After completing this section, you should be able to do the following.

(*a*) Describe, by means of annotated diagrams:
the structure of xylem tissue;
the structure of phloem tissue;
the anatomy of a typical dicotyledon and monocotyledon stem.

(*b*) Explain the cohesion–tension theory and list three observations which seem to support it.

(*c*) Describe the pathway of transport of water and mineral salts from the root to the leaf.

(*d*) Describe two phenomena which suggest the existence of root pressure and discuss the probable contributions of root pressure and transpiration.

(*e*) Describe, in outline, ringing experiments using radioactive isotopes and give conclusions that can be drawn from the results.

(*f*) Describe a method for obtaining samples of phloem sap and list three of the main components of phloem sap.

(*g*) Describe three hypotheses of phloem transport, including reference to supporting and conflicting evidence.

(*h*) Extension: Evaluate results from experiments into the mechanism of translocation.

6.2 Stem structure of flowering plants

To fully understand the transport system in plants, it is necessary to be able to recognise and describe the cellular components of plant stems.

In this section, you will be looking at transverse sections of **monocotyledons** and **dicotyledons.** Monocotyledons and dicotyledons are two divisions of flowering plants. They get their names according to the number of seed leaves or **cotyledons** that their embryos form.

Pratical Q: Investigating the structure of monocotyledon and dicotyledon stems

Materials

Microscope and lamp, LS and TS monocotyledon stem, LS and TS dicotyledon stem

Procedure

(*a*) Using LP and HP magnifications, locate and identify the cell types show in figures 166 and 167 in your stem sections (TS).

166　TS portion of young dicotyledon stem

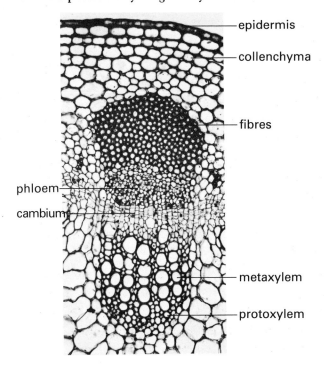

- epidermis
- collenchyma
- fibres
- phloem
- cambium
- metaxylem
- protoxylem

167　TS portion of young monocotyledon stem

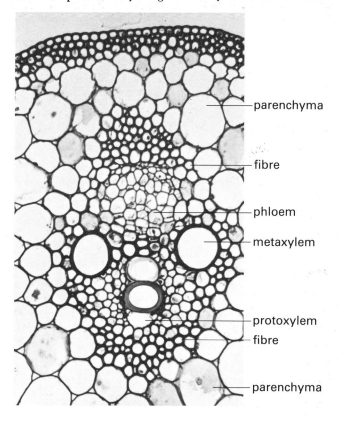

- parenchyma
- fibre
- phloem
- metaxylem
- protoxylem
- fibre
- parenchyma

(*b*) Make LP tissue plans for both stems in TS.

(*c*) Make HP drawings of all the cell types present in both types of stem.

(*d*) Make LP tissue plans and HP drawings of monocotyledon and dicotyledon stems in LS.

Discussion of results

With reference to your drawings and tissue plans, comment on the differences between *young* monocotyledon and dicotyledon stems.

Show this work to your tutor.

6.3 The transport of water

In section 4 you saw that plants lose water to their surroundings by evaporation through the stomata of leaves and gain water from soil via their roots. In this section, you will study the vascular system connecting leaves and roots and the theories proposed to explain movement of water over long distances through the plant.

Practical R: Investigating water uptake by a stem

For this investigation you are provided with a stem of *Impatiens balsamina* (Busy Lizzy) which has been cut under water and placed in an aqueous solution of methylene blue for twenty-four hours. The dyed water should have travelled well up into the stem enabling you to investigate the tissues responsible for water transport.

Materials

Microscope and lamp, cut *Impatiens* stem in methylene blue solution, sharp, single-edged razor blade, fine paint-brush, slides and coverslips, Pasteur pipette, Petri dish or watch glass.

Procedure

(*a*) Cut the *Impatiens* stem about half-way up at right angles to its long axis. The blue dye should be visible at places in the stem. If not, make another cut nearer to the end of the stem.

(*b*) Hold the stem in one hand, as shown in figure 168. Moisten the cut surface with a little water from a pipette.

168   Cutting stem sections

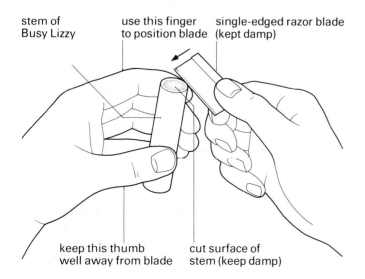

stem of Busy Lizzy

use this finger to position blade

single-edged razor blade (kept damp)

keep this thumb well away from blade

cut surface of stem (keep damp)

(*c*) Have a Petri dish or watch glass containing water ready. Wet the razor blade and cut thin sections from the stem. KEEP YOUR THUMB WELL DOWN THE STEM AND AWAY FROM THE CUTTING EDGE OF THE BLADE.

(*d*) With a little practice you should be able to cut sections only a few cells thick. Cut as may sections as you wish, transferring them to the Petri dish with a fine brush. Remember to keep the cut surface and the blade wet. The sections do not have to be complete, but they should be as thin as possible.

(*e*) Select a thin section and mount it on a clean slide in a few drops of water. Cover with a clean coverslip, dry off any excess water and examine under the low power of you microscope.

(*f*) Using a sharp pencil, make a large, annotated LP tissue plan of your section on plain drawing paper. If the section is not complete, you may need to build up a drawing from several sections.

(*g*) Mark on your tissue plan the position of the cells that contain blue dye.

Discussion of results

1 Describe any differences in structure of cells that contain the dye and those that do not.

2 What evidence is there that water is conducted by specialised tissues?

3 Describe the distribution of water-conducting tissues.

4 As an investigation into water transport, what assumption is being made about the dye?

Show this work to your tutor.

6.3.1 Water-conducting tissue

The vascular system of a plant is composed of **xylem,** the principal water-conducting tissue, and **phloem,** the food-conducting tissue. As components of the vascular system, xylem and phloem are called the **vascular tissue.** The term xylem is derived from the Greek — *xylos* — meaning wood. The wood of trees is composed of xylem cells.

In most plants, phloem and xylem tissues are associated together making up a **vascular strand.** These strands extend through the stem, leaves and roots. In stems and leaves, the tissues are grouped into bundles called the **vascular bundles.**

Many of the cells of xylem tissue are long and narrow with their walls impregnated by a complex organic material called **lignin.** Made from various derivatives of phenylpropane and often associated with cellulose, this substance makes up the greater part of the wood in plants. It is the presence of lignin, which stains easily, that will enable you to determine the position of xylem tissue in the following practicals.

Practical S: Observing lignified tissue of the stem

The walls of some types of plant cell become impregnated with lignin. This is a hard substance which has a high tensile strength and makes the cell wall impermeable to water.

Materials

Microscope and lamp, stem of *Vicia faba* (broad bean), petiole of fresh celery (in water), sharp, single-edged razor blade, fine paint-brush, slides and coverslips, Pasteur pipette, Petri dish or watch glass, phloroglucinol, ☠ conc. hydrochloric acid, plant sections in macerating fluid (☠ CAUSTIC!), mounted needles, forceps

Procedure

(*a*) Cut off a portion of celery petiole and approximately 2 cm of *Vicia faba* stem and prepare thin transverse sections, as described in practical R.

(*b*) Mount thin sections of celery petiole and *Vicia faba* stem in a few drops of water on clean slides. Add two to three drops of phloroglucinol to the sections. Leave them for three to four minutes, drain off the reagent and add a drop of concentrated hydrochloric acid (CARE!). Drain off any liquid and add two or three drops of water. Cover each section with a clean coverslip.

(*c*) Examine under the microscope, first under low power, then under high power. Lignified tissue will be stained red or purple.

(*d*) Using a sharp pencil, make a large annotated low power plan of each section.

(*e*) Make high power drawings of small groups of cells (not more than six) from the lignified tissues.

Only limited information about the structure of cells can be obtained from transverse sections. In order to examine whole cells, **macerated** tissues must be used. (Maceration is the separation of tissues into their individual cells, and can be achieved by either chemical or mechanical means.)

(*f*) Using forceps, remove a piece of stem from the macerating fluid and rinse it thoroughly, but gently, in water. Place it on a clean slide and tease the tissue into a pulp using mounted needles. If this produces too great a bulk of tissue, remove some.

(*g*) Stain for lignin as before and examine under the microscope.

(*h*) Make high power drawings of a representative selection of lignified cells.

Discussion of results

1 Which tissues in your sections are lignified?

2 Suggest two features of vascular tissue which make them ideal for water transport.

3 Bearing in mind the properties of lignin, what other function might lignified tissues aid in addition to water transport?

4 From your observations, comment on the way lignin is deposited around the cells.

5 Suggest a tissue found in the vascular bundle which is responsible for the production of new vascular tissue. Explain your answer.

Show this work to your tutor.

6.3.2 The structure of xylem

Xylem is a complex tissue, for it consists of many different types of cell, living and non-living. The cells responsible for the conduction of water are non-living and are the **xylem vessel elements** and **tracheids.**

Xylem also contains specialised supporting elements, the **fibres.** In addition, there is the presence of *living* parenchymatous cells which are concerned with various vital activities such as food storage.

Vessels

Xylem vessels are formed from a chain of elongated cells joined end-to-end. Each of these cells is called a **vessel element.** When mature, the protoplasmic contents of the vessel elements die, and the cross walls break down leaving long tubes with an empty lumen. See figure 169.

169   Xylem vessel elements showing lignification

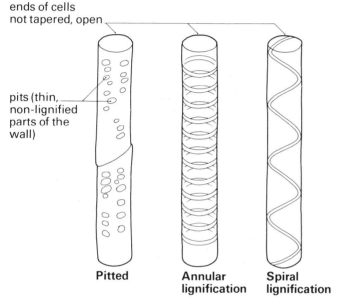

In trees, vessel elements range in diameter from 20 μm to 400 μm. In vines, their diameter may reach 700 μm. Xylem vessels can extend several metres in length. Some vessel elements have thinner, unlignified areas in their side walls called **pits.**

SAQ 138 Suggest a function of the pits in the pitted vessel elements.

Tracheids

Like vessels, tracheids are dead when mature. They are long, narrow cells with tapering ends. Unlike xylem vessel elements, their tapering end walls do not break down but possess numerous pits. See figure 170.

94

170   Tracheids

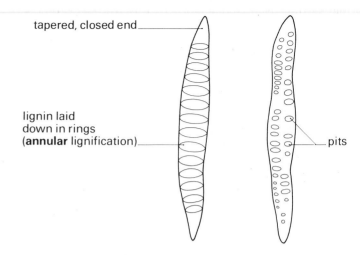

SAQ 139 How does water pass from one tracheid cell to another?

In most gymnosperms (the conifers and their allies) and also ferns, xylem tissue consists entirely of tracheids. It is most probable that xylem vessels have evolved from tracheids.

Fibres

Fibres found in xylem tissue, form an integral part of the xylem.

These are very long, slender, pointed dead cells with greatly thickened walls and comparatively small pits. They serve as strengthening cells. See figure 171.

171   Fibres

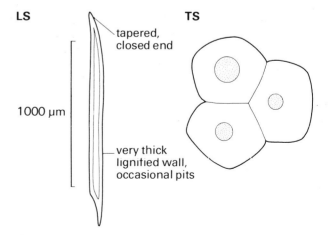

SAQ 140 Identify the cells **A, B, C** and **D** in the photomicrograph shown in figure 172.

6.3.3 The transition between roots, stems and leaves

The connection between the vascular tissue of a root and that of a stem is known as the **transition zone.** The structure of the transition zone varies in different groups of plants and is generally complex.

Figures 173, 174 and 175 illustrate the connections between the vascular tissue of the root, stem and leaves.

Look carefully at figures 173, 174 and 175 and answer the following questions.

SAQ 141 Describe the arrangement of vascular tissue in (*a*) the root and, (*b*) the stem.

SAQ 142 Explain the changes that occur in vascular tissue distribution when going from root to stem.

SAQ 143 Explain how a number of leaves that are directly above one another can be supplied with vascular tissue.

The main function of xylem is the transport of water and minerals. The structure of xylem vessels and fibres also aids in the support of the plant. This concept is considered in the unit *Support, movement and behaviour.*

172   Photomicrograph showing LS through a marrow stem

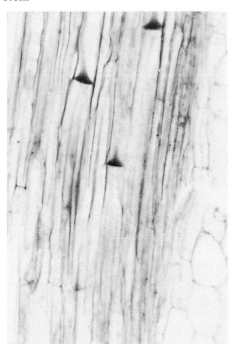

173   The distribution of vascular tissue in a plant

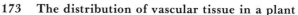

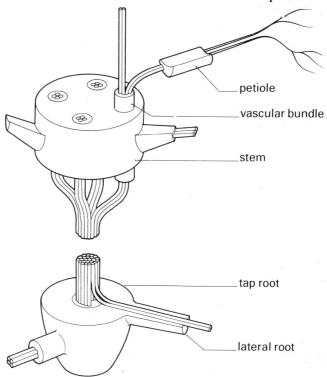

petiole

vascular bundle

stem

tap root

lateral root

174   Transition from root to stem

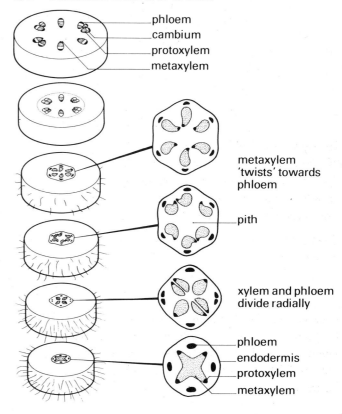

phloem
cambium
protoxylem
metaxylem

metaxylem 'twists' towards phloem

pith

xylem and phloem divide radially

phloem
endodermis
protoxylem
metaxylem

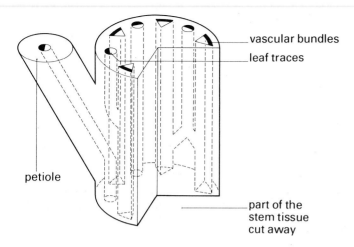

petiole

vascular bundles

leaf traces

part of the stem tissue cut away

6.3.4 Summary assignment 11

1 Draw annotated diagrams of transverse and longitudinal sections of each type of cell found in a dicotyledonous plant. Your annotations should, where possible, include notes on the structure and function of the cell. Figure 176 illustrates one way in which you could present your work.

176   Table for summary question 1

Cell type	Diagram TS	Diagram LS

2 Combining the results of practicals R and S, comment on the distribution of dyed water and lignin in the stem of a general dicotyledonous plant.

3 Your answer to SAQs 141, 142 and 143 will serve as a summary of the distribution of vascular tissue in a dicotyledon.

Show this work to your tutor.

Self test 9, page 127, covers sections 6.1, 6.2 and 6.3 of this unit.

6.4 The mechanism of water and mineral transport

The fact that xylem is the tissue responsible for the upward transport of water and mineral salts has been known for many years. As early as 1726, the English clergyman, Stephen Hales, who was one of the first to investigate plant physiology experimentally, observed the movement of water in xylem vessels. He also pointed out that xylem cells were not restricted to stems but continued via small branches into the leaves. Hales went on to carry out a large number of investigations into transpiration, and from the measurements he made, he calculated that *'the sunflower, bulk for bulk, imbibes and perspires seventeen times more fresh liquor than a man every twenty-four hours'*.

Evidence that xylem is the tissue tranporting water from the roots to leaves came from 'ringing' or 'girdling' experiments.

The effect of removing a piece of bark from a woody stem is shown in figure 177.

177   A ringing experiment

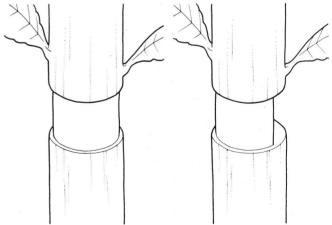

(a) bark and phloem removed   *(b)* xylem then removed from RIGHT HALF ONLY

SAQ 144 How does this simple experiment show that xylem transports water to the leaves?

For many years, biologists were puzzled as to how water could move to the top of tall trees through dead cells. A few suggested that metabolic energy must be used by living cells to push the column of water upwards.

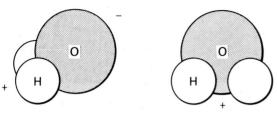

Positive and negative charges are distributed unequally due to the asymmetrical shape of the water molecule

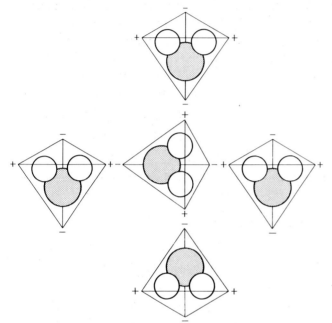

Because of its polarity, each water molecule can form hydrogen bonds with four other water molecules

In 1891, Strasburger showed that water movement in the xylem is a passive process. He immersed the cut base of a young oak tree in a barrel containing picric acid. This acid is highly toxic and kills living tissue. After three days, when the acid had reached the leaves, he replaced the picric acid in the barrel with a dye solution. The dye quickly rose to the top of the dead stem.

The water in xylem vessels consists of continuous threads or columns of water, possibly as much as 100 m in height in a tall tree. The long columns do not break under the weight of water held in them. The reason for this lies in the properties of liquids and the relatively narrow diameter of the xylem vessels.

6.4.1 Adhesion and cohesion of water

The polarity of water

A water molecule is asymmetrical — one 'end' of the molecule is positively charged and the other is negatively charged. In other words, the molecule shows **electrical polarity.** See figure 178.

As a result of this polarity, water molecules are strongly attracted to each other — they are strongly **cohesive.** In addition, the water molecules are attracted by other polar molecules in the wall of the vessel — they tend to **adhere** to the wall. These forces can be illustrated by the formation of drops from a tap — see figure 179.

179　Adhesion and cohesion of water

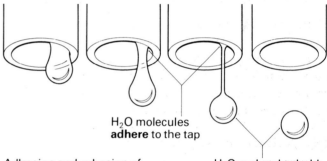

H$_2$O molecules **adhere** to the tap

Adhesion and cohesion of water molecules can be seen in the formation of a drip from a tap

H$_2$O molecules held together by **cohesion** to form drop

It is thought that a combination of these adhesive and cohesive forces prevents the column of water breaking when it is subjected to a pull.

A water-filled sealed tube with an open end dipped into water will support a column of water 10.3 m high at atmospheric pressure. The adhesion of the water molecules to the walls of the tube and the cohesive forces between them is sufficient to support this column. See figure 180.

SAQ 145 What forces will prevent the column of water rising higher than 10.3 m?

SAQ 146 Assuming that 1 atmosphere (atm) pressure will support a water column 10.3 m high, what pressure difference between the two ends of xylem would be required to support water columns in a giant redwood, 100 m high?

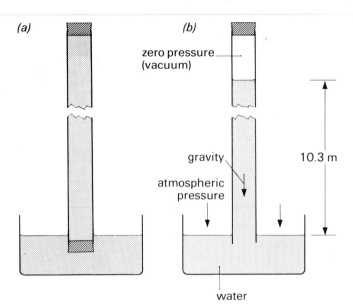

(a)   *(b)*

zero pressure (vacuum)

gravity

atmospheric pressure

10.3 m

water

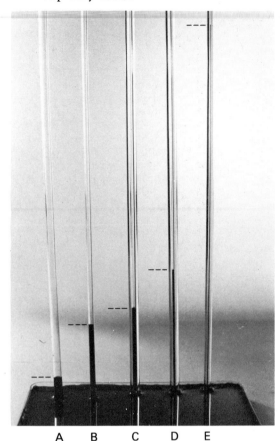

A   B   C   D   E

Capillarity

As a result of these cohesive and adhesive forces, water tends to rise up tubes against the force of gravity. This phenomenon is called **capillarity**.

Figure 181 shows a series of open-ended tubes immersed in water. The tubes have **bores** (holes) of different diameters ranging from the widest **A** to the narrowest **E**.

SAQ 147 Explain why the level of water in tube **E** is the highest.

SAQ 148 Water in xylem vessels of dead plants can rise to greater heights than in glass tubes with the same bore. Suggest a reason for this.

6.4.2 The cohesion–tension theory of water transport

To move water molecules to the top of xylem columns at the rates known to occur would need a pressure difference of about 30 atm. The cohesive forces between water molecules in xylem vessels are sufficiently large to sustain pressure differences of more than 30 atm and yet columns of liquids under tension are unstable. High winds bending the stems can 'snap' these columns which can be heard by using a sensitive microphone.

SAQ 149 How do you think that the plant overcomes this problem of broken water columns?

The cohesion of water molecules was first demonstrated experimentally by the Austrian botanist, Josef Böhm, in 1893. His apparatus and method are described in figure 182.

The Irish botanist, H.H. Dixon, and his collaborator, J. Joly, repeated this experiment but substituted a leafy shoot for the porous clay pot and achieved the same result, (that of) mercury being drawn up the tube. See figure 183. In 1894, Dixon and Joly formulated what has come to be known as the **cohesion–tension theory.**

According to this theory, water molecules are pulled up the xylem vessels as a result of transpiration. The water columns in the vessels do not break because of

182 Böhm's experiment

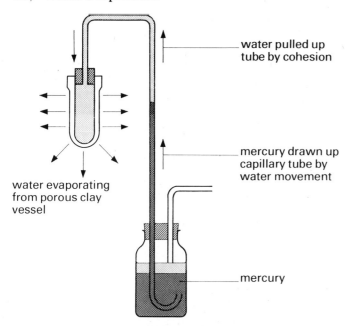

water pulled up tube by cohesion

mercury drawn up capillary tube by water movement

water evaporating from porous clay vessel

mercury

183 Dixon and Joly's experiment

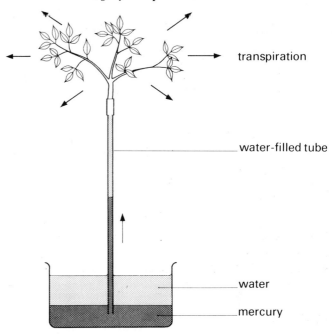

transpiration

water-filled tube

water

mercury

the cohesion of the molecules, but they are in a state of tension due to **transpiration pull** (the tension exerted by the evaporation of water from leaves).

Hales, and most of the early plant physiologists of the nineteenth century concluded that this rapid flow or **transpiration stream** in the xylem, provided a ready explanation for both the pathway and the mechanism of water and mineral movement from the roots to the aerial parts of the plant.

The mechanism of mineral ion uptake by the root and its movement into the xylem was considered in section 4.4. Once inside the xylem, the mass flow of water carries with it mineral ions to all parts of the plant.

6.4.3 Root pressure

Other observations, however, have shown that water can be pushed up the plant from below. Xylem sap frequently exudes from the freshly-cut stumps of plants. This can be demonstrated quite simply — see figure 184.

When the transpiration rate is very low, for example, at night and under conditions of high humidity, droplets of water often appear at the end of blades of

184 Experiment to demonstrate root pressure

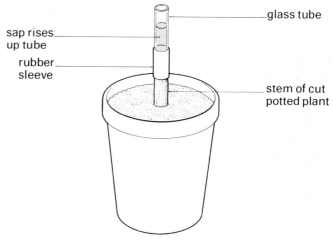

glass tube

sap rises up tube

rubber sleeve

stem of cut potted plant

185 Guttation

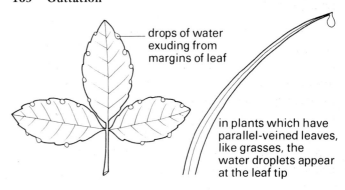

drops of water exuding from margins of leaf

in plants which have parallel-veined leaves, like grasses, the water droplets appear at the leaf tip grass or edges of leaves. These water droplets emerge from the stomata or special water pores called **hydathodes**. This phenomenon, called **guttation** contributes to the 'dew' that forms on plants at night. See figure 185.

In plants which have parallel-veined leaves, like grasses, the water droplets appear at the leaf tip.

In tropical rain forests, many plants guttate so profusely that a fine drizzle is created.

These observations suggest that, under certain conditions, a positive pressure is generated in the xylem by the root, hence its name, **root pressure.**

6.4.4 The roles of transpiration pull and root pressure in xylem transport

It seems possible that the two processes, transpiration pull and root pressure, lead to the flow of water in the xylem. Observations have been made which enable us to assess the importance of these two processes. In order to interpret this evidence, it is necessary to consider the implications of the two mechanisms — see figure 186.

186   Diagrammatic representation of root pressure and transpiration pull

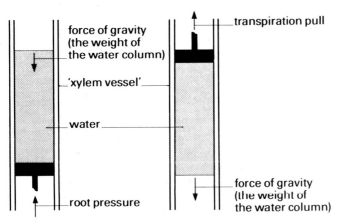

(a) Water being pushed up from below – root pressure

(b) Water being pulled up from above – transpiration pull

Both mechanisms tend to move water up the vessel but each has different effects on the vessel walls. In (a) the forces tend to compress the water column. As a result, the water pushes out against the walls of the vessel.

In (b), the forces tend to stretch the water column and, as a result, the water molecules tend to pull the wall of the vessel inwards.

If the xylem of a tree-trunk is cut into with a sharp knife, there is no exudation of sap but a hissing sound can sometimes be heard.

SAQ 150 Can this best be explained in terms of root pressure or transpiration pull? Explain your answer.

Evidence to support the theory that transpiration is the main cause of water movement came from investigations using a **dendrograph**. A dendrograph is a very sensitive instrument for measuring changes in the diameter of tree-trunks. It consists of a band of metal fitted tightly around the trunk in such a way that changes in its diameter may be recorded on a chart moving at constant speed. See figure 187.

187   A dendrograph

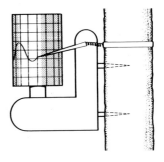

188   MacDougal's results with Monterey pine

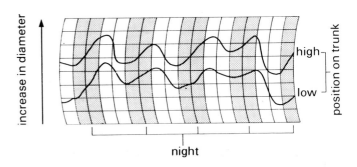

In 1936, MacDougal, using a dendrograph, measured changes in the diameter of a Monterey pine at two different positions up the trunk over a period of several days. Figure 188 shows an example of the results he obtained.

SAQ 151 (*a*) There appears to be a regular cycle of increase and decrease in trunk diameter. During which part of the day (i) does an increase occur; (ii) does a decrease occur?
(*b*) Suggest an explanation for these observations.
(*c*) When do the changes in diameter higher up the tree slightly precede those lower down?

When transpiration rate is high, the transpiration pull is much greater than the pressure that can be developed by roots. Hence, in an actively-transpiring plant, root pressure is effectively absent although the process of exudation continues. It is only when transpiration rate is low that the pressure of root exudation causes a significant effect.

For these reasons, root pressure is not considered to contribute significantly to the transport of xylem sap. However, it is thought that root pressure may provide a means of moving needed mineral ions from roots to shoots during periods of low transpiration.

6.4.5 Summary assignment 12

Outline the contributions made by each of the following people to the understanding of water transport:
Dixon, Hales, MacDougal, Joly, Böhm, Strasburger.

Show this work to your tutor.

6.5 The transport of organic materials

Even less is known about the transport of organic molecules and there are many different hypotheses. Even something as basic as the pathway of transport has been the subject of debate until relatively recently. Hales had shown, in 1726, that water and inorganic nutrients were transported in the xylem, and for a long time it was thought that organic molecules were transported in the xylem also. It was not until the 1930s that the transport of organic molecules was finally identified as the function of the phloem.

6.5.1 The structure of phloem

Like xylem, phloem tissue contains a variety of different cells. The cells which are unique to phloem are the **sieve tube elements** and the **companion cells** but, in addition, parenchyma cells are found in the phloem and possibly also fibres. Unlike xylem, phloem is not lignified and is composed of living cells. See figure 189 and 190.

Figure 191 summarises the main differences between phloem sieve tube elements and xylem vessel elements.

6.5.2 Ringing experiments

In the eighteenth century, Stephen Hales performed a number of investigations that gave information

189   Diagrams to show the structure of phloem sieve tube elements and companion cells

(a) Sieve tube

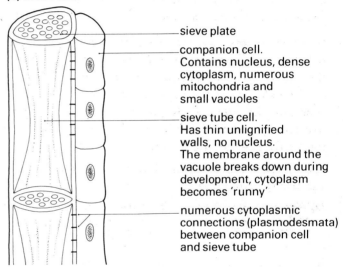

sieve plate

companion cell.
Contains nucleus, dense cytoplasm, numerous mitochondria and small vacuoles

sieve tube cell.
Has thin unlignified walls, no nucleus.
The membrane around the vacuole breaks down during development, cytoplasm becomes 'runny'

numerous cytoplasmic connections (plasmodesmata) between companion cell and sieve tube

(b) LS sieve plate region

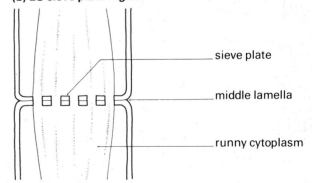

sieve plate

middle lamella

runny cytoplasm

perforations form in sieve plate when middle lamella closing adjacent pits in end walls breaks down

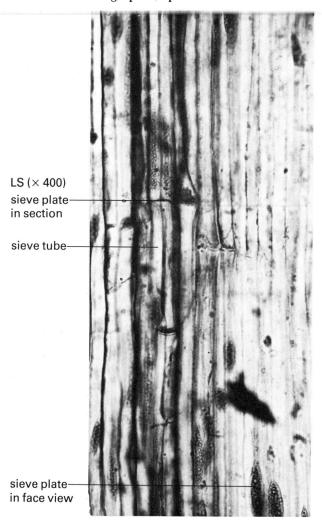

LS (× 400)

sieve plate in section

sieve tube

sieve plate in face view

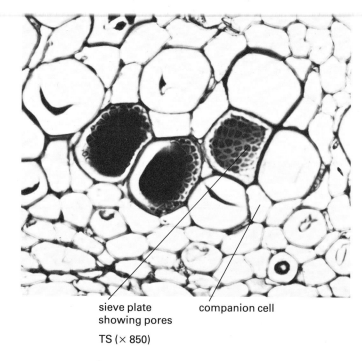

sieve plate showing pores

companion cell

TS (× 850)

191 Differences between phloem and xylem elements

Phloem sieve tube elements	*Xylem vessel elements*
1. Living cells.	1. Dead cells.
2. Smaller diameter, 10–50 μm on average.	2. Larger diameter, 20–200 μm on average.
3. Walls thin, flexible, composed of cellulose and pectic substances.	3. Wall thick, hard, impregnated with lignin.
4. Mature cells have lumen which is filled with disorganised protoplasm (no membranes or organelles) which is continuous with adjacent cells via numerous plasmodesmata.	4. Mature cells have lumen which is empty (contains no protoplasm).
5. End walls of adjacent sieve tube elements form sieve plates.	5. End walls of adjacent vessel cells break down.

concerning the transport of organic materials in plants. He removed a ring of bark and phloem from the branch of a tree. The results are shown in figure 192.

192 Hales' ringing experiment

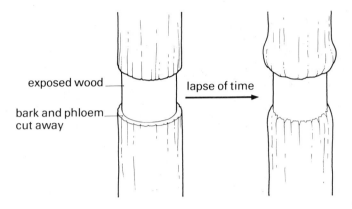

exposed wood

bark and phloem cut away

lapse of time

SAQ 152 What can you conclude from the changes just below and above the ring?

If this ringing is performed on the main trunk of a tree, the whole tree will die due to the death of the root system.

SAQ 153 How does this information support your conclusion from SAQ 152?

The changes shown in figure 192 do not take place if the experiment is performed in winter.

SAQ 154 In what way is this information relevant to your answer to SAQ 152?

These indirect methods of investigation only provide general information. Nowadays, much more refined and direct techniques can be employed; the use of radioactive isotopes. Organic compounds can be **'marked'** using the radioactive isotopes ^{14}C and ^{13}C (as opposed to the more common non-radioactive ^{12}C) and **'traced'** using photographic film. Radioactive isotopes cause a darkening of unexposed photographic film, thus showing the location of any radioactive compound. This process is called **autoradiography.**

Figure 193 shows the start of a ringing experiment using radioactive tracers.

Two young privet shoots were cut and placed in water. One was ringed about 8 cm from the apex,

the other control shoot was not ringed. See figure 193.

The waxy cuticle of the upper surface of a leaf was removed by rubbing a small area with fine emery paper. Radioactive sucrose was then introduced into the cells of the leaf. The same treatment was given to both privet shoots which were then left for twenty-four hours.

Excess sucrose was removed from the 'fed' leaf and each shoot was placed in contact with X-ray film in a light-proof folder for five days. The results, after the film had been developed, are shown in figure 194.

With reference to figure 194, answer the following questions.

SAQ 155 (*a*) What evidence is there that radioactive sucrose has been transported away from the leaf into which it was 'fed'?

(*b*) What evidence is there that the sucrose can be transported both up and down the stem?

193 Applying radioactive sucrose

control shoot

ringed-shoot

ring

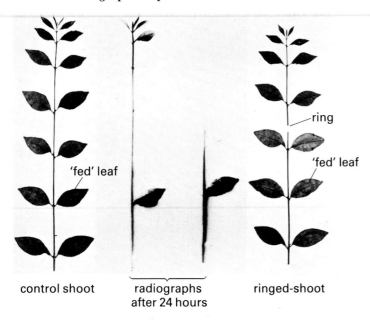

control shoot   radiographs   ringed-shoot
after 24 hours

(*c*) Is there any evidence that the xylem is responsible for transporting the sucrose?

(*d*) How far do the results support the hypothesis that phloem is responsible for transporting the sucrose?

(*e*) What hypothesis can you suggest to account for the appearance of radioactive sucrose in the young leaves but not in older ones?

(*f*) What other comments can you make on the distribution of radioactive sucrose in control shoot **A?**

SAQ 156 Suggest three possible causes for the movement of sucrose out of a leaf into which it has been introduced.

SAQ 157 Why should ringing a tree trunk kill the tree?

In 1945, Rabideau and Burr carried out a series of investigations using bean plants. They enclosed single leaves in glass chambers filled with an atmosphere containing carbon dioxide incorporating the radioactive isotope of carbon, **^{13}C**. The phloem of some of the plants was killed right around the stem, using either hot wax or a fine jet of steam. This ringing operation serves to leave the phloem structurally intact and in position but as non-living tissue.

SAQ 158 (*a*) Can the phloem be killed without affecting the xylem?
(*b*) How could this be checked?

The level of radioactive carbon in different parts of the plant was measured and calculated as the percentage of the total carbon content of the plant tissue.

The results of the experiments are presented in figure 195.

195   Results of Rabideau and Burr's ringing investigation

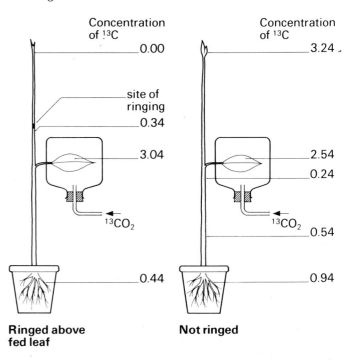

Ringed above
fed leaf   Not ringed

SAQ 159 What extra piece of information does this investigation provide about phloem transport?

6.5.3 Obtaining samples of phloem sap

Experiments using radioactive isotopes have provided a lot of information about the pathway, direction and rate of phloem transport. However, scientists needed to know more about what was going on inside the phloem sieve tubes, and about the composition of the sap they contained. Various mechanical methods of extracting sap from the phloem were devised, but it was difficult to be sure that only sieve tube contents were being sampled. In addition, these methods tended to damage the delicate phloem tissue.

An ingenious technique to overcome these difficulties was first developed by Mitler in the USA and is now used widely to study the phloem contents. An aphid ('greenfly') is placed on the stem of a plant and allowed to feed, which it does by inserting its **stylets** (tube-like piercing mouthparts). The feeding aphid is anaesthetised in a gentle stream of carbon dioxide. Using a fine splinter of glass, the anaesthetised aphid is severed from its stylets. Droplets of sap are formed on the end of the severed stylets, and may be collected in a fine capillary tube for analysis. This exudation may continue for several days. Subsequent examination of sections through the stem always reveal that the stylets have penetrated a phloem sieve tube.

SAQ 160 (a) How do these observations compare with what is observed when xylem is pierced with a sharp knife?
(b) What do they reveal about the sap in the phloem when compared to that in xylem?

Thus, aphid stylets provide a simple method of sampling the phloem sap which causes a minimum of damage to the plant.

This technique also illustrates one of the reasons for the great success of aphids, they need to expend very little effort in obtaining their food. An energy-rich nutrient solution is pumped into them by their host plant. So rich and abundant is their food supply that aphids actually excrete sugars in the form of droplets of honeydew — see figure 196.

6.5.4 The composition of plant sap

The compostion of both phloem sap and xylem sap varies with a number of different factors including:
1 The stage of growth of the plant.
2 The times of year (and the time of day).
3 Environmental factors, such as the availability of nutrients, factors affecting transpiration, and so on.

It is often stated that xylem sap is composed of water and inorganic mineral ions and phloem sap is composed of water and organic solutes.

196 Aphid 'honeydew'

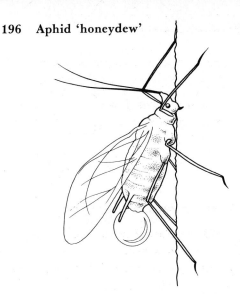

This is an over-simplification. Soluble carbohydrates have been detected in the xylem and inorganic ions are found in phloem sap. However, in both cases, the concentrations are small. It is true to say that inorganic ions are predominantly carried in the xylem, and organic solutes are predominantly carried in the phloem.

Analysis of phloem sap obtained by aphid stylet method (see section 6.5.3) has shown that it contains usually between 10 and 25% sugar, principally **sucrose.** In some plants, compound sugars, **tri- and tetra-saccharides** containing three or four simple sugar units are transported. In some plants, sugar alcohols such as **mannitol** and **sorbitol,** are also transported. Amino acids and other **organic nitrogenous compounds** are also present as are small quantities of mineral salts. **Plant growth hormones** also seem to be transported in the phloem, but they can also move across parenchyma tissue.

6.5.5 Theories of phloem transport

The mechanism of **translocation,** the transport of soluble products of photosynthesis is not well understood. To quote Zimmerman (1969):
'It sometimes appears as though there are as many concepts as there are workers ...'

In 1930, Munch proposed a theory of movement based upon turgor pressure gradients in plants.

Differences in turgor pressure cause a mass flow of water through phloem that transports organic substances. This is called the **mass-flow hypothesis.**

Figure 197 shows the demonstration model used by Munch.

Bulb **A** contains a high concentration of sugar. Water will diffuse into the bulb by osmosis and be forced out of **B** by hydrostatic pressure. **A** Represents a turgor pressure **source** and **B** a turgor pressure **sink.** Mass flow occurs between sources and sinks. After a period of time, in this model, mass flow will stop.

SAQ 161 Explain why mass flow will stop in the model.

Figure 198 relates Munch's model to tissues found within plants.

SAQ 162 Why would mass flow not stop after a period of time in this living system?

Munch originally considered this to be a purely passive process. Recent work has shown that translocation is active and requires energy expenditure. It is thought that there is active transport of sugars into and out of the sieve tube elements. It is the sieve tube elements themselves, therefore, that act as turgor pressure sources and sinks.

SAQ 163 Applying Munch's model (figure 197) to a living plant, what parts of the plant will correspond to
(*a*) the source (**A**);
(*b*) the sink (**B**);
(*c*) the tube through which mass flow of water and sugars occurs;
(*d*) the tube through which back flow of water occurs;
(*e*) the water surrounding **A** and **B**?

On the basis of events occurring in sieve tubes, other theories have been proposed. The main alternative to mass flow is the **streaming hypothesis.**

Cyclosis or streaming of the protoplasm has been observed in many plant cells including sieve tubes. It has been suggested that organic solutes may be carried along in the streaming protoplasm which aids

197 Munch's demonstration of mass flow

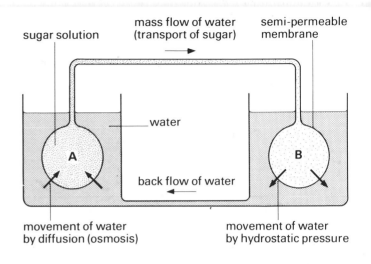

198 Mass flow in plant tissues

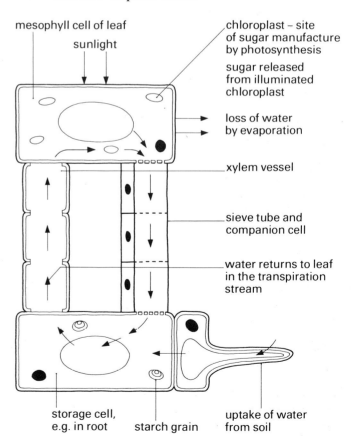

their diffusion through the sieve pores to adjacent sieve tube elements — see figure 199.

199   The streaming hypothesis

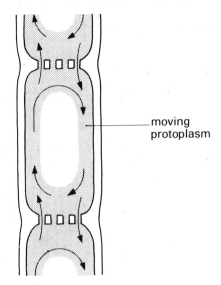

moving
protoplasm

The protoplasmic streaming hypothesis has been extended by Thaine to include a **transcellular strand** concept. Thaine has observed (and filmed) what he claims are strands of protoplasm which extend through the sieve tubes and which display directional streaming. See figure 200

200   The transcellular strand hypothesis

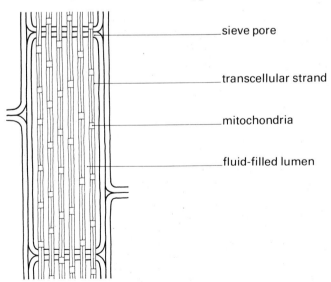

sieve pore

transcellular strand

mitochondria

fluid-filled lumen

However, other workers have argued that what was really being observed was streaming in parenchyma cells either above or below the phloem sieve tube.

SAQ 164 Below are given a number of pieces of evidence. For each say which, if any, of the hypotheses outlined above it supports or conflicts with, giving your reasons.
(*a*) Exudation of sap from severed aphid stylets.
(*b*) Sugars can be transported both up and down the plant.
(*c*) The dye fluorescein has been shown to move at a faster rate than the streaming cytoplasm.

6.5.6 Summary assignment 13

1 Draw a representative sample of phloem tissue and add annotations to show how its structure is related to its function.
2 Make notes to summarise the observations made on the transport of organic materials and the theories proposed to explain the mechanism of transport.

Show this work to your tutor.

Self test 10, page 129, covers sections 6.4 and 6.5 of this unit.

6.6 Extension: Evidence for the movement of assimilates in phloem

Read the following passage; then write short answers to all of the questions which follow it.

(Nuffield, Paper 2, June 1977)

(1) Hartig's discovery that the sap which exuded from cuts made into the phloem was rich in carbohydrates was confirmed in 1917 by Mangham who carrried out microchemical investigations on sieve tubes and showed that the carbohydrate content of these cells varied in relation to the environmental conditions.

(2) A more careful analysis of the normal pathway for transport of soluble carbohydrates was made by Mason and Maskell in 1928 using cotton (*Gossypium barbadense*) plants growing under field conditions. They removed a complete ring of phloem from plants in the morning and then analysed samples of both phloem and xylem from above and below the ring at intervals during the following twenty-hour period.

They found that ringing caused a marked accumulation of sugars in both the phloem and the xylem above the ring, and a marked decline in the phloem and the xylem below the ring.

(3) These early results were subject to a number of valid criticisms, the chief of which arose from the rather extended duration of the experiment. It is feasible that, during the twenty-hour period of the experiment, removal of the phloem might have led to harmful effects on the movement of water and dissolved substances in the xylem.

(4) In subsequent work, Mason and Maskell showed that there was a diurnal variation in the sugar content of the sap in the various parts of the cotton plant. Moreover, there was a much greater correlation between the varying contents observed in the leaves and in the phloem than there was between the values for the leaves and the xylem.

(5) In further experiments with cotton plants, Mason and Maskell levered up strips of bark and cut the phloem tissues away from the underlying xylem. Some of the strips of phloem were bound back into place immediately without further treatment (normal plants), while others were first coated with a layer of petroleum jelly on their inner surfaces and then bound back into position (treated plants). After varying periods of time, the tissues of the bark and the wood of plants treated in these different ways were analysed for their content of carbohydrates. In the normal plants, both the xylem and the phloem contained large quantities of carbohydrate, whereas in the treated plants, a much greater amount of carbohydrate was found in the phloem than in the xylem.

(6) The use of radioactive isotopes as tracers gradually facilitated convincing demonstrations by a number of physiologists that translocation downwards of organic assimilates occurs predominantly in the phloem. The advent of the electron microscope was also a further stimulus to the study of the structure of phloem.

(7) Biddulph and Markle (1944) studied the translocation of the radioactive isotope ^{32}P after it had been introduced into the leaves of cotton plants by immersing a small cut or flap on the surface of the leaf in the radioactive solution. A slit was made into the bark of the stem below the leaf to which the ^{32}P was administered, and a piece of waxed paper was inserted in such a way that it completely separated the phloem tissues of the bark from the xylem. After a short period of time, the tissues which had been separated by the waxed paper were harvested and analysed for radioactivity. Only minute traces of radioactivity were found in the xylem, while much greater amounts were observed in the phloem. If, however, the phloem and xylem below the treated leaf were separated but then placed together again without inserting the waxed paper, then subsequent analysis revealed appreciable amounts of radioactivity in the xylem as well as the phloem.

(8) An improved method of introducing a radioactive trace into a leaf, which did not involve the questionable technique of cutting into the leaf, was employed by Rabideau and Burr (1945). Single leaves of bean plants were allowed to photosynthesise in small glass chambers filled with an atmosphere containing $^{13}CO_2$. Prior to the feeding with $^{13}CO_2$, the cells of the stem of some of the plants were killed both above and below the leaf, by ringing with hot (100 °C) wax or a fine jet of steam. In these plants the ^{13}C assimilates did not penetrate the stem beyond either of the rings. Rabideau and Burr demonstrated at the same time that ringing the stem with hot wax or steam did not stop the transport of ^{32}P, supplied to the roots, to all parts of the plant.

(9) While it was conclusively demonstrated by these methods that the phloem was the tissue in which the organic assimilates produced in the leaves were translocated both upwards and downwards, there was still, however, some doubt as to which actual element of the phloem was involved. Early workers such as Hartig had hinted that it was the sieve tubes which were the actual channels of movement, and this was confirmed by Biddulph in 1956.

Using the information in this passage and your own knowledge of biology, answer the following questions. Short, concise answers are required.

1 Give the meaning of each of the following terms:
(a) microchemical investigations (para 1),
(b) greater correlation (para 4).

2 State two environmental conditions which may lead to variations in the carbohydrate contents of the sieve tubes (para 1).

3 What did the results of the work of Mason and Maskell in 1928 indicate (para 2)?

4 Why would you expect a diurnal variation in the contents of the phloem (para 4)?

5 In Mason and Maskell's subsequent experiments with cotton plants, the phloem was cut away from the underlying xylem (para 5).
(a) In the normal plants the strips of phloem were bound back without the insertion of a layer of petroleum jelly. What was the purpose of this procedure?
(b) In the treated plants a layer of petroleum jelly was placed between the xylem and the phloem. State a hypothesis which was being tested by this procedure.
(c) Was the hypothesis confirmed? Explain your answer.

6 (a) In 1944, Biddulph and Markle introduced ^{32}P into the plant through a cut on the leaf surface. Why was this a questionable technique (para 7)?
(b) What did the results of their experiment indicate?

7 (a) What conclusions can be made from Rabideau and Burr's experiments about pathways of transport in the plant of (i) ^{13}C? (ii) ^{32}P (para 8)?
(b) Briefly explain how you arrived at these conclusions.
(c) What is the meaning of the term ^{13}C assimilates (para 8)?

8 Briefly outline an experimental technique which would demonstrate that it is the sieve tubes in the phloem which are involved in the translocation of assimilates.

Show this work to your tutor.

Section 7 Exchange and transport of wastes

7.1 Introduction and objectives

Chemical processes occurring in the cytoplasm of unicellular and multicellular organisms consume and produce a variety of substances. See figure 201.

201   The exchange of materials by the cytoplasm

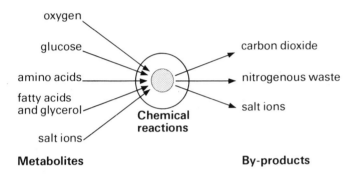

SAQ 165 What is the term used to describe the chemical processes of the cytoplasm?

SAQ 166 How would figure 201 need to be altered to take account of photosynthesis in plant cells?

From your answer to SAQ 166 you can see that a single substance, in this case carbon dioxide, may sometimes be a waste product and at other times an important raw material. Urea, a major waste in the urine of mammals is found in the saliva of ruminants. The urea passes back into the stomach and acts as a source of nitrogen for the microorganisms of the rumen. Urea is also retained in the blood of some rays and sharks to increase the osmotic pressure of their blood.

Conversely, some substances not usually thought of as wastes must be removed in certain situations to avoid serious disruption to body cells.

SAQ 167 What problem might arise if the water content of an animal became too high and why is this not such a critical problem for plants?

The problem of what constitutes a waste substance depends on the organism under study and indeed the state at that moment of its internal and external environments.

This section will look at a variety of wastes and the ways organisms remove them from their bodies.

After completing this section, you should be able to do the following.
(a) Describe what constitutes a waste.
(b) Distinguish between secretion, egestion and excretion.
(c) Explain why excretion is not such a problem for plants.
(d) Explain the relationship between the water availability and nitrogenous excretion in animals.
(e) Draw and label diagrams of the mammalian kidney.
(f) State the functions of the nephron.
(g) Describe the role of the kidney in homeostasis.
(h) State the function of aldosterone and ADH.
(j) Extension: Describe the evolution of the mammalian kidney.

7.2 Waste materials of plants and animals

A waste can be thought of as any substance that is poisonous or present in excess (cannot be stored or put to immediate use). Such wastes obviously need to be eliminated from the organism.

Carbon dioxide

This is the principal waste of carbohydrate breakdown. In animals, oxygen is thought of as the more important substance for life, yet it is carbon dioxide concentration that is monitored and precisely controlled. This reflects the toxicity of this waste to the animal.

Remember, in plants, carbon dioxide is also an important raw material for carbohydrate synthesis. The way animals and plants remove carbon dioxide has already been dealt with in this unit and will not be considered further in this section.

SAQ 168 What are the main organs of carbon dioxide removal in plants and animals?

SAQ 169 What do 'anabolic' and 'catabolic' mean, and how are they related to metabolism?

Ammonia

Unlike carbohydrates, excess protein cannot be stored by organisms. In the catabolism of proteins, the amino group of the amino acids is removed in a series of reactions. The rest of the molecule is then fed into the carbohydrate breakdown reactions.

This removal of the amino group takes place in the liver and is called **deamination** — see figure 202.

202   **Deamination of an amino acid**

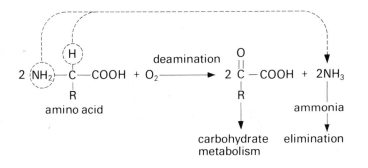

Ammonia is extremely toxic and organisms show a variety of strategies for safely removing this **nitrogenous** (nitrogen containing) waste.

In plants, carbon dioxide is the principal waste product yet, in animals, the main wastes are nitrogenous compounds.

SAQ 170 Why should there be this difference in the main waste product of animals and plants?

Water

The problem most organisms face is one of too little water and hence most systems are concerned with

water retention. However, water can be present in excess and the necessary removal occurs by relaxation of these conservation mechanisms. The problem of water and salt balance will be mentioned in this section but a fuller account of osmoregulation is in the unit *Survival — biological themes.*

Heat

Although generally not thought of as a waste, organisms can accumulate too much heat which can severely disrupt cell function. Animals and plants, therefore, need mechanisms to control the heat content of their bodies. Temperature regulation is covered in the unit *Response to the environment.*

7.2.1 Excretion, secretion and egestion

Some substances that are in excess are specifically formed to carry out special functions within the body. These substances are not considered as wastes but as **secretions** of the cells involved.

SAQ 171 List some such useful metabolic secretions formed in humans.

One obvious type of waste in animals is **faeces** — undigested and unassimilated matter that has never been a part of the body substance. Removal of such matter is termed **egestion.** The rest of this section will be concerned mainly with **excretion** of wastes. Excretion is defined as the removal of poisonous waste products formed as a result of the cell's metabolism.

Useful substances that are in excess and need to be removed from the body, e.g. water, do not really fall into the previous three categories. The term **elimination** will be used here to describe the removal of such substances.

SAQ 172 Define the terms: excretion, egestion, secretion and elimination.

7.3 Excretion in plants

Excretion in plants does not pose any serious problems. There are several reasons for this. First, the rate of catabolism in plants is generally much lower than in animals of the same weight. Consequently, metabolic wastes accumulate more slowly. Second, green plants use many of the waste products of catabolism in their anabolic processes. Water and carbon dioxide, produced by respiration, are used in photosynthesis. Waste nitrogen compounds, whose excretion makes such demands upon animals, can be used by green plants in the synthesis of new protein. Finally, the metabolism of plants is based mainly on carbohydrates rather than proteins. This reduces their excretory needs, as the end products of carbohydrate metabolism are far less poisonous than the nitrogenous wastes produced by protein metabolism; also, being gaseous, carbon dioxide can simply diffuse out of the organism. Of course, plants do produce protein from which a variety of important cell structures and all their enzymes are made. Nevertheless, protein metabolism plays a much smaller role in plants than in animals, whose general body structure is based to such a great extent upon protein.

Among aquatic plants, metabolic wastes are free to diffuse from the cytoplasm into the surrounding water. No cell is far removed from the water and the concentration of wastes within the cell exceeds the concentration of these substances in the water.

Among the terrestrial plants, the waste products of metabolism, such as salts and organic acids that cannot diffuse out of the plant, are simply stored in the plant. These wastes may be stored in solid form in crystals or they may be dissolved in the fluid of the central vacuoles. In herbaceous species, the wastes simply remain in the cells until the tops of the plants die in the autumn. In perennial plants, wastes are deposited in the non-living heartwood and are also eliminated when the leaves are shed.

7.3.1 Summary assignment 14

1 Explain what a waste substance is.

2 Copy and complete figure 203.

3 Give three reasons why excretion is not a major problem for plants.

Show this work to your tutor.

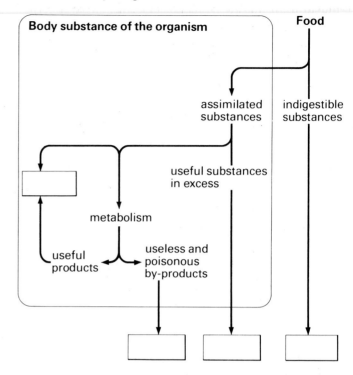

203 Summary diagram for section 7.2

7.4 Excretion in animals

Some of the more common nitrogenous compounds excreted by animals are shown in figure 204.

204   Chemical formulae of some nitrogenous wastes

urea

ammonia

trimethylamine oxide

uric acid

Ammonia, the product of deamination, is extremely toxic and if allowed to accumulate it will poison the animal. To reduce the toxicity, the ammonia is diluted with relatively large amounts of water before removal from the body. If, however, the organism is short of water, the toxicity can be reduced by converting ammonia into some other less toxic substance. See figure 205.

205 Nitrogenous wastes and toxicity

Waste	Relative toxicity
Ammonia	
Trimethylamine oxide	↑ (increase)
Urea	
Uric acid	

There is a relationship between the method of nitrogenous excretion and water availability in the animal's external environment.

SAQ 173 (*a*) What types of environment will pose problems of (i) water gain, and (ii) water loss? (*b*) Explain your answer to part (*a*).

Use figure 206 to answer the following question.

206 Water relations and nitrogenous excretion for a variety of animals

Organism	Habitat	Main excretory product
Paramecium	freshwater	ammonia
Flatworm	freshwater	ammonia
Carp	freshwater	ammonia
Frog	damp terrestrial	urea
Cod	marine	trimethylamine oxide
Dog	dry terrestrial	urea
Lizard	very dry terrestrial	uric acid
Insect	very dry terrestrial	uric acid

SAQ 174 (*a*) Outline the relationship that exists between water availability and nitrogenous excretion. (*b*) Explain fully the data shown in figure 207.

Figure 208 refers to one order of the reptile family, the tortoises and turtles.

SAQ 175 Comment, with reasons, on the likely habitats of each species.

7.5 Excretion in humans: the kidney

The main organs of excretion and water control in humans are the kidneys. These organs and their

207 Excretion in toads *Bufo* and *Xenopus*, during development

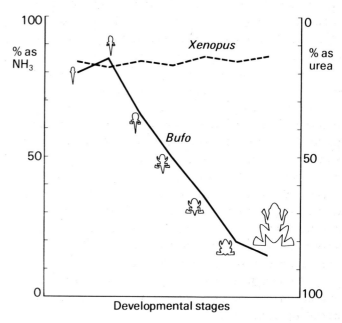

Xenopus laevis is fully aquatic.

208 Nitrogenous excretion in *Chelonia* species

Species	Habitat	% of urinary nitrogen		
		Ammonia	Urea	Uric acid
A		79	17	4
B		6	61	4
C		4	22	52
D		4	3	93

209 The urinary system

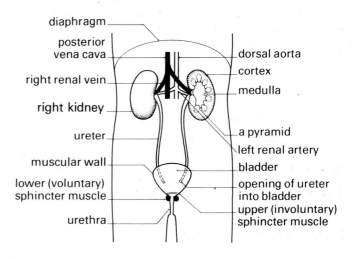

location in the body are shown in figure 209. The composition of the fluid urine produced by the kidneys is shown in figure 210.

To understand fully how this fluid is formed, we shall first look at the structure of the kidney. The overall structure of bisected kidney is shown in figure 211.

It is in the cortex and medulla that urine formation takes place. Urine collects in the pelvic space and is drained off to the bladder by the ureter.

210 The compostion of urine

Substance	Amount (g/24 hours)
urea	35.0
uric acid	0.8
hippuric acid	0.7
ammonia	0.6
creatinine	0.9
sodium chloride	15.0
phosphoric acid	3.5
sodium	2.5
sulphur	1.2
potassium	2.0
total solids	≈ 60
water	1440
total quantity of urine	1500

211 The gross structure of the kidney

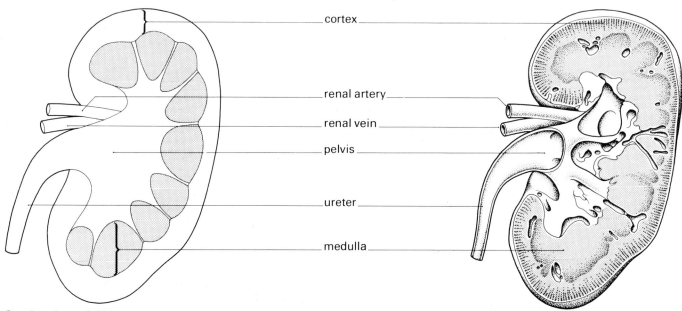

Section through kidney to show regions

cortex

renal artery

renal vein

pelvis

ureter

medulla

Kidney cut open to show internal structure

The kidney is mainly composed of small tubes: blood capillaries and kidney tubules or **nephrons.** Figure 212 shows a section through a kidney where the capillaries have been injected with a black dye. Note the change in appearance between the cortex and medulla.

212   Arrangement of capillaries in the kidney

The diagram in figure 213 shows more clearly the arrangement of capillaries and also the position of the nephrons.

The nephrons join into **collecting ducts** which empty

213   Diagram showing the arrangement of tubules in a kidney

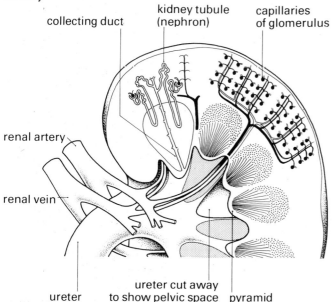

their fluid into the pelvic space. The structure of a single nephron is shown in figure 214.

214   Diagram of a single nephron

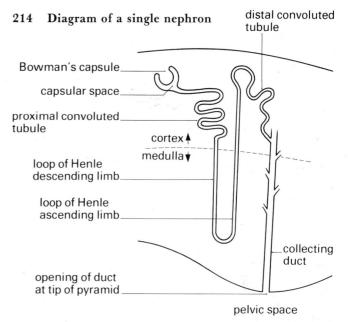

Nephrons and capillaries come into very close contact at the **Bowman's capsule** end of the nephron. The knot of capillaries in the capsule is called the **glomerulus.** See figures 213 and 215.

215   Bowman's capsule and glomerulus

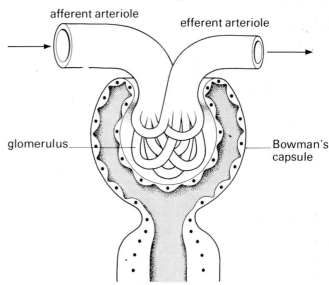

The capillary leaving the glomerulus branches to form a network of capillaries that is intimately linked around the convoluted tubules and loop of Henle. See figure 216.

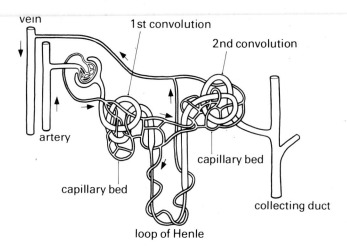

vein

1st convolution

2nd convolution

artery

capillary bed

capillary bed

collecting duct

loop of Henle

7.5.1 Kidney function

The nephron and its associated capillaries form the functional unit of the kidney. The kidney is an organ associated wih **homeostasis,** the maintenance of constant internal conditions. To keep the body fluid composition constant, it must remove waste products, conserve useful substances and regulate the balance of water and salts. These kidney functions are performed by the nephron. The blood pressure in the glomerulus is very high.

SAQ 176 Look again at figure 215. Explain why a rise in blood pressure should occur in the glomerulus.

This high hydrostatic pressure forces small molecules through the walls of the capillaries and the Bowman's capsule into the capsule space. This process is called **ultra-filtration.** As this fluid passes

down the nephron and collecting duct, its composition is modified before urine is released into the ureter.

Look carefully at the table in figure 217 and answer the following questions.

SAQ 177 (a) What percentage of the blood flowing through the glomerulus is filtered into the nephron? (b) Compare and explain the compositions of plasma and nephric filtrate.
(c) Compare and explain the compositions of nephric filtrate and urine.

From figure 217, you can see that small volumes of concentrated urine are produced by the action of the nephron. It is the **loop of Henle** that is responsible for this increase in fluid concentration. Sodium is actively transported out of the ascending limb into the surrounding kidney tissue, the tissue concentration being greatest at the tip of the loop. Some of the sodium enters the descending limb by passive diffusion and returns to be actively transported out into the tissue again to maintain the tissue concentration. See figure 218.

The walls of the ascending limb are impermeable to water (water cannot diffuse out from here to dilute the kidney tissues). The fluid in the ascending limb is **isotonic** (at the same concentration) with blood.

It is not until the fluid flows back through the kidney tissue in the collecting ducts that water leaves the filtrate by osmosis so forming the concentrated urine. See figure 219.

As water is *reabsorbed* from the filtrate back into the kidney tissue and then the bloodstream, the filtrate

217   Composition of fluids in the kidney

Component	Plasma (afferent capillary)	Nephric filtrate (Bowman's capsule)	Urine (collecting duct)
urea	0.03	0.03	2.0
glucose	0.10	0.10	—
amino acids	0.05	0.05	—
salts	0.72	0.72	1.5
proteins	8.00	—	—
Flow rate (lh^{-1})	14	2.8	0.05

All figures are g/100 cm^3 of fluid.

218   Sodium movement in the loop of Henle

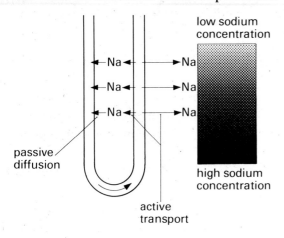

low sodium concentration

high sodium concentration

passive diffusion

active transport

219   Reabsorption of water from the collecting duct

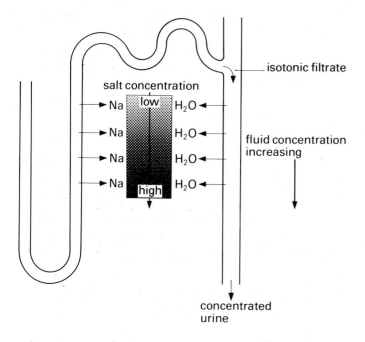

isotonic filtrate

salt concentration

low

high

H_2O

H_2O

H_2O

H_2O

fluid concentration increasing

concentrated urine

becomes more concentrated. An interesting feature is that the sodium concentration of the tissue around the duct also increases so ensuring that water does not move back into the collecting duct as the filtrate gets more concentrated. A capillary network associated with the loop of Henle prevents a build-up of water in the kidney tissue by taking water back into the general circulation.

SAQ 178 Briefly summarise how the kidney produces concentrated urine.

220   Simplified diagram of the nephron

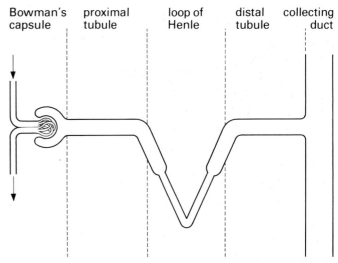

Bowman's capsule | proximal tubule | loop of Henle | distal tubule | collecting duct

Figure 220 should be referred to as you read through the following information.

Fluid in the Bowman's capsule is isotonic with blood plasma. At the first or proximal convoluted tubule there is *reabsorption* by active transport of useful substances by the tubular cells from the nephric filtrate into the surrounding capillaries. Substances reabsorbed include salts, glucose and amino acids. Water also tends to leave the tubule by passive diffusion into the blood.

As already mentioned, there is passive diffusion of sodium and water into the descending limb of the loop of Henle. The fluid tends to become **hypertonic** (more concentrated) to blood. In the ascending limb, active transport of sodium out of the tubule causes the fluid to become **hypotonic** (less concentrated) to blood. As the walls are permeable to sodium and impermeable to water, removal of sodium makes the filtrate less concentrated and the tissue more concentrated.

The second or distal convoluted tubule has a mainly **regulatory function,** there is a variable reabsorption by active transport of ions (e.g. H^+, Na^+, Cl^- and Ca^{2+}). The amount of ions being reabsorbed depends on the needs of the body at that time and the composition of blood.

The collecting ducts, being permeable to water, allow **conservation of water** by passive diffusion back into kidney tissue. However, here again, this process is regulated as the permeability of the collecting duct can be varied according to the body's need for water.

SAQ 179 Summarise the preceding information by copying figure 220 and adding brief comments.

7.5.2 Control of the kidney

Variable reabsorption by the nephron is controlled by hormones circulating in the blood. **Aldosterone** from the adrenal cortex controls Na^+ and Cl^- reabsorption. An increase in the hormone level stimulates reabsorption, that is retention of these ions in the body.

The permeability of the collecting ducts to water depends upon the blood level of the **anti-diuretic hormone** (ADH), released by the posterior pituitary. The more ADH present, the more permeable are the collecting ducts.

SAQ 180 Do high ADH levels cause more or less water reabsorption from the collecting ducts? Explain your answer.

This regulation of water and ion concentration is of great importance in maintenance of the osmotic pressure, volume and hydrostatic pressure of blood.

Figure 221 shows these control mechanisms.

SAQ 181 Using figure 221 to help you, draw a flow diagram to show the sequence of events that would occur after the intake of a relatively large amount of salt.

7.5.3 Summmary assignment 15

Your answers to SAQ 174 to 181 form a summary for the work on excretion in animals.

Show this work to your tutor.

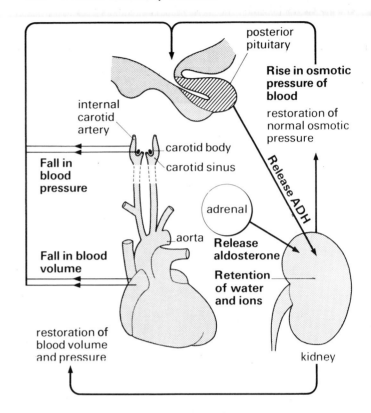

Self test 11, page 129, covers section 7 of this unit.

7.6 Extension: Evolution of the mammalian kidney

Outline the stages of evolution with reference to kidney function from the earliest chordates to mammals.

One suitable reference is *The Kidney* By Homer W. Smith (Scientific American, January 1953, pp. 40–48).

Show this work to your tutor.

Section 8 Self tests

Self test 1

1 (*a*) Complete the table (figure 222) by drawing a box against each substance which may be taken up or given out by an animal or a plant.
(*b*) Write the appropriate letter within each box to indicate which of the following major processes each substance is associated with: Nutrition (N), Respiration (R), Excretion (Ex), Egestion (Eg).

The first line has been completed for you.

2 Copy the diagrams (figure 223) and, for each organism, indicate as precisely as possible the surface for gas exchange, the surface for food and water uptake and the surface for elimination of waste.

3 How does size and shape affect the use of the external body surface as a respiratory surface?

4 Outline the similarities and differences between diffusion and mass flow.

5 List the characteristics of a respiratory surface.

6 What are the two main advantages of an internal respiratory surface for terrestrial organisms?

7 Why do some organisms need an internal transport system?

222 Uptake and output of substances by organisms

	Animals		Plants	
	uptake	output	uptake	output
oxygen	R		R	N
carbon dioxide				
organic food				
minerals				
water				
nitrogenous waste				
faeces				

223 Sites of uptake and output

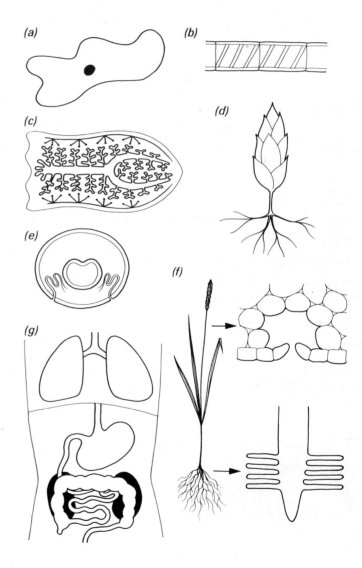

8 Why do higher plants not require a specialised transport system for carrying gases around the body?

9 Name the mechanism by which fresh air (or water) is carried from the environment to the respiratory surface.

Self test 2

1 Name the respiratory surface in an insect, a fish, a mammal and a flowering plant.

2 Which of the following characteristics apply to the respiratory surface of an insect, a fish, a mammal and a flowering plant?
(a) large surface area;
(b) thin;
(c) moist;
(d) associated transport system

3 The tracheae of an insect are lined with cuticle.
(a) What is the function of this cuticle?
(b) What structure has the equivalent function to this cuticle in the trachea of a mammal?

4 Describe, with the aid of a diagram, the gills of a fish.

Self test 3

1 How does ventilation occur in a locust?

2 State two ways associated with the gas exchange mechanism in which a locust is adapted to conserve water.

3 The apparatus shown in figure 224 was used to measure oxygen uptake of root tips.
(a) Name the apparatus.
(b) Name the structure labelled **X**.
(c) Name the solution in tube **B**.
(d) What would you expect to happen to the fluid in structure **X** during the experiment?
(e) Explain this change.
(f) What is the function of tube **A**?

4 In the ventilation mechanism of a fish, water is drawn into the buccal and opercular cavities by means of a pressure pump in front of the gills and a suction pump behind the gills. Explain how these work.

5 What causes water to leave the opercular cavity?

6 Make a drawing of the blood vessels in the gill region of a dogfish. Name the main blood vessels.

Indicate which vessels carry oxygenated blood and which carry deoxygenated blood.

224 **Apparatus for measuring oxygen uptake in root tips**

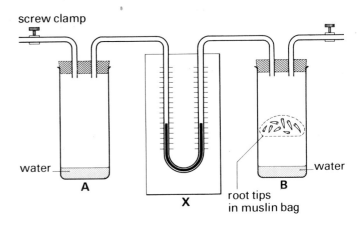

7 (a) Explain what is meant by the counter-current mechanism.
(b) Why is this important in gas exchange in a fish?

8 Draw a diagram to show the structures associated with ventilation in a mammal.

9 Complete the following account of ventilation in mammals by copying it out and filling in the blanks.

The mechanism of ventilation or (1)____ in a mammal depends on changes in (2)____ which occur in the (3)____. This is an (4)____ chamber bounded by the (5)____ and intercostal muscles and the diaphragm.

During inspiration, the (6)____ intercostal muscles contract causing the ribs to move (7)____ and (8)____. The diaphragm muscles (9)____, pulling the diaphragm (10)____. These movements cause the (11)____ in the cavity to increase and hence the (12)____ decreases, becoming (13)____ than atmospheric pressure. As a result, (14)____ is drawn into the lungs which expand.

During expiration, the (15)____ intercostal muscles contract causing the ribs to move (16)____ and (17)____. The diaphragm muscles (18)____ causing the diaphragm to (19)____ upwards. These movements cause the volume in the thoracic cavity to (20)____ and hence the pressure (21)____ becoming greater than (22)____. As a result, air is forced out of the lungs.

The lungs are lined by membranes known as the (23)____. The small space between the membranes contains a (24)____ which acts as lubricant to reduce (25)____ as the different structures move during breathing.

10 The apparatus in figure 225 can be used to measure oxygen consumption in humans.

225 Apparatus for measuring oxygen consumption in humans

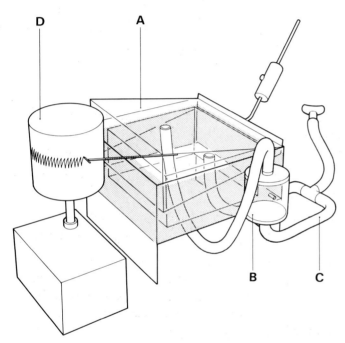

(a) Name the apparatus.
(b) Name and state the function of the structures labelled **A–D.**
(c) Draw the sort of trace you would expect if the apparatus was set up to measure oxyygen consumption. Indicate on your diagram what represents oxygen uptake.
(d) Name six other things, besides oxygen uptake that can be measured with this apparatus.

11 During breathing in humans, what is
(a) the percentage of CO_2 in inspired air?
(b) the percentage of O_2 in inspired air?
(c) the percentage of CO_2 in expired air?
(d) the percentage of O_2 in expired air?

12 Draw a diagram to show the relationship between the alveoli and the blood supply in the lungs.

Indicate on your diagram the direction of movement of inspired air, expired air and the net movement of oxygen and carbon dioxide.

Show on your diagram the mechanism of movement for each of these substances.

13 How is the concentration gradient of oxygen maintained in the lungs?

14 (a) Define the term respiratory cycle.
(b) Define the term tidal volume.
(c) What is the tidal volume for the average person?

15 (a) What is the major factor controlling breathing rate in a human?
(b) How is it detected?
(c) By what means is information carried from the detectors to bring about changes in breathing rate?

16 State the route and mechanism of movement of gases:
(a) from a cell in the spongy mesophyll of a leaf to the outside;
(b) from a cell in the phloem of a tree trunk to the outside;
(c) from a cell in the inner cortex of a root to the outside;
(d) from a root-hair cell to the outside.

17 In which direction does oxygen move in a plant (a) during the day, (b) at night?

How is the concentration gradient necessary for diffusion to occur maintained (c) during the day, (d) at night?

18 State five reasons why diffusion alone is sufficient to carry oxygen to all parts of a plant.

Self test 4

1 Figure 226 shows the changes in mass in two plants, one with roots intact and the other with its roots removed. Both plants were kept in beakers of water covered with oil and under identical conditions. The mass of the apparatus was measured each hour.
(a) Describe the changes in mass for the two plants.
(b) What is the main cause of this loss of mass?

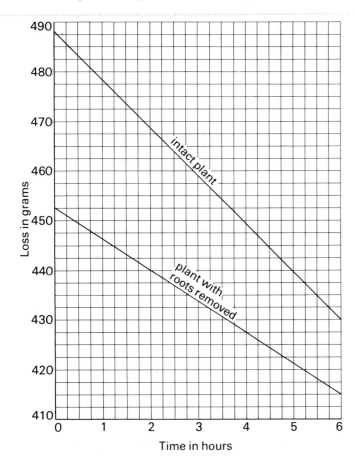

Time in hours

(Graph axes: Loss in grams (410–490) vs Time in hours (0–6); curves labelled "intact plant" and "plant with roots removed")

(c) Suggest a reason why the apparatus with the intact plant lost more mass?

(d) State one other possible cause for loss in mass of the plants.

(e) What hypothesis could you propose on the basis of these results?

2 (a) Draw a diagram of a TS through a root in the region of the piliferous layer. Label the main features of your diagram.
(b) What is the main source of water for plants?
(c) In what part of the plant is water taken up?
(d) State one way in which this part is well adapted for its absorptive function.
(e) How does the plant tap progressively new areas for water absorption?

3 Explain the terms apoplast and symplast.

4 Name the tissues through which water and ions move in passing from the soil to the xylem.

5 Name three ways in which water can move along this route and state the mechanism of movement involved.

6 (a) Which of the above three ways has a barrier at one point in the route from soil to xylem?
(b) What causes this barrier?

7 Ions may move into and through the plant by diffusion and/or active transport. For each of the following state which process(es) could be involved.
(a) Movement from the apoplast to the symplast.
(b) Movement through the symplast.
(c) Movement from the symplast to the cell vacuoles.
(d) Movement from the symplast of the pericycle to the xylem.
(e) Movement through the apoplast.

8 State four findings which indicate that active transport is involved in ion movement.

9 The apparatus in figure 227 is used to measure transpiration.
(a) Name the apparatus.
(b) The apparatus does not directly measure transpiration. What does it actually measure?
(c) Why is it valid to use measurements recorded from this apparatus as an indication of transpiration?
(d) Two of the above sets of apparatus were assembled. The leaves on the shoot in one were 'Vaselined' on the upper surface. In the other apparatus, the leaves were 'Vaselined' on the lower surface. Bubbles were introduced into each apparatus.

After two minutes, which bubble would you expect to have moved the greater distance?

10 State three pathways of water movement from the xylem in the leaf veins through the mesophyll to the stomatal pores. For each, state whether diffusion or osmosis is involved.

11 Complete the following account of the mechanism of stomatal movement by copying it out and filling in the blanks.

The stomata control transpiration by opening and closing. Changes in size of the (1)____ depend on changes in the shape of the surrounding (2)____ cells. When these cells are (3)____ the opening is large.

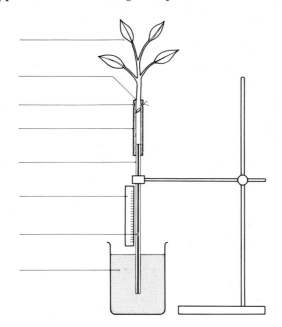

When these cells are (4)_____ the opening is small or closed. These changes depend on the uptake and loss of (5)_____ by the guard cells.

As the cells take up water and become turgid, their (6)_____ stretch. Because of the uneven (7)_____ of the walls, they cannot stretch uniformly. Consequently, they assume a curved (8)_____ shape which results in a (9)_____ pore between them.

Investigations have show that, in general, darkness, (10)_____ concentrations of carbon dioxide and (11)_____ shortage cause stomatal closure.

The classical hypothesis proposed to explain why these conditions caused closure was that they are associated with a cessation of photosynthesis and a conversion of (12)_____ to (13)_____. This reduces the (14)_____ concentration in the guard cells which consequently lose water by (15)_____.

The alternative hypothesis proposed to explain why stomata close is that (16)_____ ions are pumped from the guard cells hence lowering their (17)_____ concentration and causing water loss by (18)_____. A potassium (19)_____, possibly using (20)_____ from photosynthesis, is thought to move potassium into the guard cells during the day causing (21)_____ of water by osmosis, increased turgor and stomatal (22)_____.

There is also some evidence of a (23)_____ rhythm of stomatal (24)_____, possibly involving the pigment (25)_____.

12 Which of the following conditions will cause high rates of evaporation and hence increased transpiration?
(*a*) high humidity, (*b*) dry air, (*c*) wind, (*d*) still air, (*e*) high temperature, (*f*) low temperature.

13 For each of the following plants, state one adaptation which suits it for living in a dry environment.
(*a*) Marram grass.
(*b*) Cactus.
(*c*) Stonecrop.
(*d*) Date palm
(*e*) Pine.

Self test 5

1 Define (*a*) mass flow, and (*b*) diffusion.

2 Which of the following does not involve mass flow?
(*a*) Movement of water over gills in a fish!
(*b*) Movement of gases in and out of a leaf.
(*c*) Movement of fluid around a *Daphnia*.
(*d*) Movement of oxygen around an earthworm.

3 What does the term cyclosis mean?

4 Explain how a transport system can increase the concentration gradient between the internal and external environment at an exchange surface.

5 Using the letters on figure 228 indicate points where (*a*) mass flow, and (*b*) diffusion, take place.

6 (*a*) Which of the following is the cavity through which body fluid is circulated?
A Coelom.
B Peritoneum.
C Haemolymph.
D Blastocoel.
(*b*) What is the cavity called in adult insects?

7 What are the main differences between an open and a closed circulation?

8 What is the main advantage of a closed circulation?

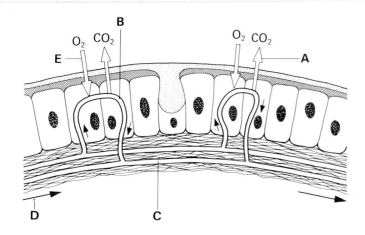

9 Which of the following functions of blood is shown by earthworms but not by insects?
(a) Transport of carbon dioxide.
(b) Transport of hormones.
(c) Transport of inorganic salts.
(d) Transport of assimilates.

10 Draw a simplified diagram of the circulatory system of a fish.

11 What *two* terms can be used to describe this type of circulation?

12 Which of the following is the best explanation of the term double circulation?
(a) There are two hearts side by side.
(b) There are two sets of vessels in the body.
(c) Fluid passes through the heart twice in one circulation.
(d) Blood is pumped through two capillary networks in one circulation.

13 What is the advantage of a double circulation?

14 What effect do capillary networks have on blood flowing through them?

15 Which of the following have a double circulatory system?
(a) Zebra finch.
(b) Whale.
(c) Octopus.
(d) Frog.
(e) Shark.

Self test 6

1 Figure 229 shows a section through a mammalian heart. Write labels for each of the numbered lines.

2 What is the function of the coronary artery?

3 What is the function of the heart?

4 Explain the relationship between wall thickness of chambers of the heart and blood pressure.

5 What role do the chordae tendinae play in the opening and closing of the cuspid valves?

6 Figure 230 shows a simplified diagram of the circulatory system of humans. Arrange the letters shown in order of decreasing blood pressure (highest pressure first).

7 What do the terms (a) systole, and (b) diastole, mean?

8 What is the cardiac cycle?

9 Outline the events that occur during the cardiac cycle with reference to figure 231.

10 What is the function of the semi-lunar and cuspid valves?

11 Distinguish between myogenic and neurogenic muscle.

229   Section through a mammalian heart

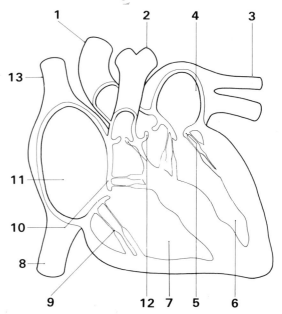

12 How is the structure of cardiac muscle suited to the rapid spread of contractions across the whole heart?

13 What is the function of (*a*) the sino-atrial node, (*b*) Purkinje fibres, and (*c*) the atrio-ventricular node?

14 What effect do the parasympathetic and sympathetic nervous systems have on heart-beat?

15 Explain how the heart-beat can respond to changing demands of the body.

230   Simplified diagram of circulatory system of humans

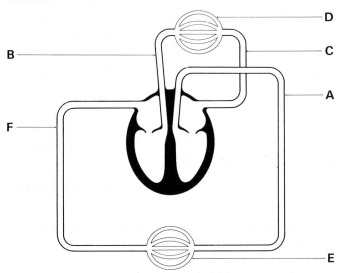

231   Diagram for question 9

Self test 7

1 (*a*) State the name, composition and function of the regions labelled **A, B, C, D, E, F** and **J** on figure 232.
(*b*) Explain the differences between **ABC** and **GHI** on figure 232.

2 (*a*) Explain the term elastic recoil.
(*b*) What effect does this have on the nature of blood flow?

3 Why do arteries not contain valves?

232   Diagram for question 1

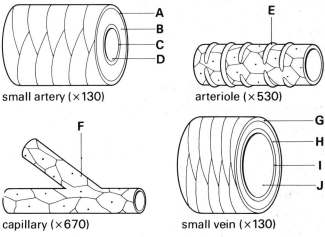

small artery (×130)   arteriole (×530)

capillary (×670)   small vein (×130)

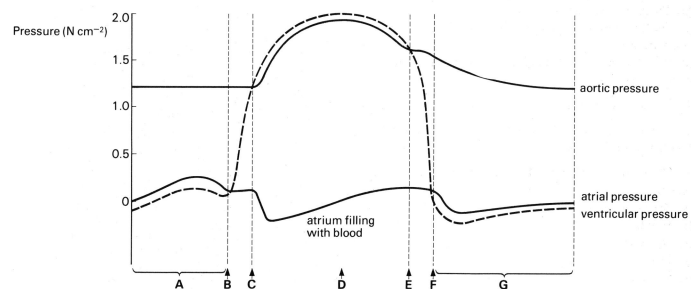

4 How does skeletal muscle help ensure a flow of blood back to the heart in the veins?

5 (*a*) How does hydrostatic pressure change as blood flows through a capillary?
(*b*) Explain the relationship between hydrostatic pressure and the movement of substances across a capillary wall.

6 State two distinct functions of the lymphatic system.

7 Name each of the structures labelled in figure 233.

233 Diagram for question 7

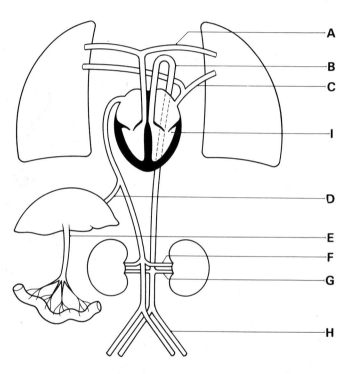

8 What is the significance of muscular sphincters at the entrance to capillary beds?

9 What effects does the sympathetic nervous system have on arteries and veins during exercise?

10 What hormone produces similar effects to the sympathetic nervous system?

11 What is the function of (*a*) the carotid body, and (*b*) the carotid sinus?

12 How do temperature and carbon dioxide affect vasodilation and vasoconstriction in capillaries?

13 During exercise, what causes an increased flow of blood through muscle tissue?

14 What is the main difference between nervous and hormonal control of blood circulation?

Self test 8

1 State two properties of respiratory pigments.

2 Name three respiratory pigments and the animals which possess them.

3 Briefly describe the structure of haemoglobin.

4 What do the terms association and dissociation refer to with respect to respiratory pigments?

5 What is an oxygen–haemoglobin equilibrium curve?

6 What does the term sigmoidal mean?

7 What information does a dissociation curve give?

8 Define the Bohr effect.

9 Where in a living animal would you expect the Bohr effect to occur?

10 How does the Bohr effect contribute to the efficiency of haemoglobin as a respiratory pigment?

11 Write equations to summarise the carriage of (*a*) oxygen, and (*b*) carbon dioxide by human blood.

12 Which of the following enzymes is associated with the transport of respiratory gases?
A Carbonic oxidase.
B Carbonic dehydrogenase.
C Carbonic anhydrase.
D Carbonic synthetase.

13 What is the chloride shift and where does it occur?

14 Explain the function of the chloride shift.

15 Distinguish between whole blood, serum, plasma, tissue fluid and lymph.

16 Where are granulocytes and agranulocytes formed in the body?

17 Give the meaning of the term immune response.

18 Which of the following cells are phagocytic?
A Basophils.
B Neutrophils.
C Eosinophils.
D Lymphocytes.
E Monocytes.
F Macrophages.

19 What is the difference between active and passive immunity?

20 Which of the following blood groups could be donated to a B-group recipient.
A A
B AB
C B
D O

21 Explain the role of the platelets in the defence of the body.

Self test 9

1 Give the meaning of the term cotyledon.

2 Figure 234 shows part of a LP tissue plan.

List the labels for each of the regions lettered.

3 Figure 235 shows regions of stems from a monocotyledon and a dicotyledon.
(*a*) Which stem is typical of a monocotyledon?
(*b*) Comment on the differences shown in figure 235 that enabled you to answer part (*a*).

4 (*a*) What is lignin?
(*b*) What reagent could be used to stain lignin and what colour would the lignin become after staining?

5 In which of the following cells would you expect to find lignin?
A Phloem.
B Xylem
C Cambium.
D Parenchyma.
E Sclerenchyma.

6 What is a pit?

234 Diagram for question 2

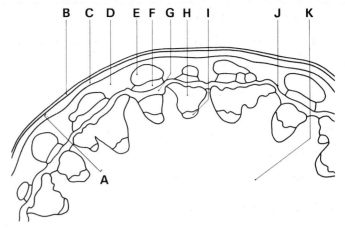

235 Figures for question 3

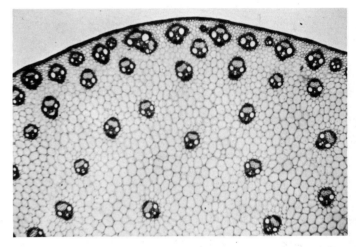

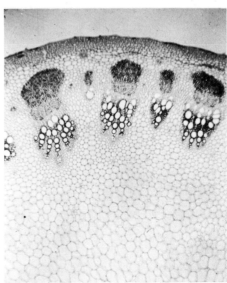

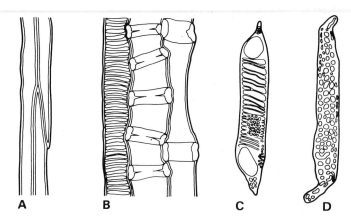

A   B   C   D

7 Name the cells shown in figure 236.

8 State one *difference* between xylem vessel elements and tracheids.

9 What two types of cell can be found in sclerenchyma tissue?

10 Give the names of the two types of cell shown in figure 237.

237   Diagram for question 10

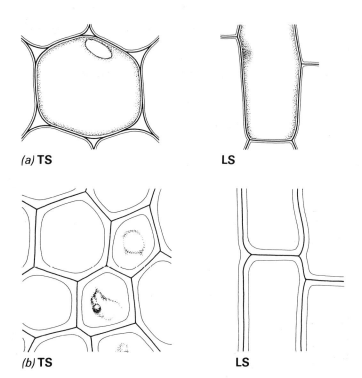

(a) TS   LS

(b) TS   LS

11 The following definitions are taken from a botanical dictionary. List the word or words that should appear for each entry (they are not alphabetically arranged).
(1) Tissue derived from the ground meristem and occupying the central portion of the stem.
(2) A strand of tissue composed of primary phloem and primary xylem (and cambium if present) and usually surrounded by a bundle sheath, which functions in transport of materials.
(3) An elongated, tapering, thick-walled cell that imparts rigidity to a plant.
(4) Collective term referring to the three primary tissues: cortex, pith ray, and pith.
(5) Waxy layer on outer walls of epidermal cells.
(6) Tissue derived from the procambium and vascular cambium and serving as both a water and mineral conductor and a mechanical support for plants; wood.
(7) The tissue surrounding vascular bundles in a stem or leaf.
(8) An elongated, thick-walled, tapering, conducting cell of the xylem.
(9) A plant whose embryo has two cotyedons.
(10) Primary tissue of a stem or root that develops from the ground meristem and is bounded externally by the epidermis and internally by the phloem.
(11) Cells with extensively lignified walls, serving as a supporting tissue.
(12) Tissue composed of thin-walled, loosely compacted cells; often retains meristematic potentialities.
(13) A series of vessel members joined end-to-end and forming a continuous tube; its function is to conduct water and minerals.
(14) A pit in secondary xylem having a distinct rim of the cell wall overarching the depression of the pit.
(15) Causing to become woody.
(16) An organic material imparting strength to certain cell walls, notably xylem.
(17) A segment of a vessel derived from a single xylem cell.
(18) Secondary xylem.
(19) The surface layer of roots, stems and leaves.
(20) A cortex tissue in young stems, composed of cells that fit rather closely together and have walls thickened at the angles of the cells.

(21) An area of a cell wall that lacks secondary thickening.

(22) Cells capable of division and differentiation; located between xylem and phloem tissues.

Self test 10

1 With reference to water
(*a*) What do the terms cohesion and adhesion mean?
(*b*) What is it about water molecules that gives rise to these effects?

2 Explain the cohesion–tension theory of water transport.

3 Give two observations that led to the idea of root pressure.

4 (*a*) What effects will transpiration and root pressure have on the diameter of xylem vessels?
(*b*) Explain your answer to (*a*).

5 What is a dendrograph and how can it give information concerning the relative importance of transpiration and root pressure in water transport?

238   Diagram for question 6

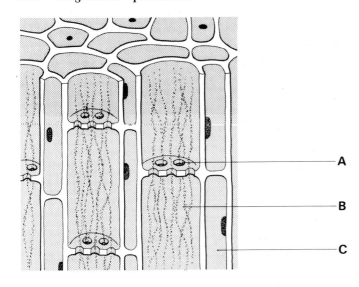

6 (*a*) Add labels to the diagram shown in figure 238.
(*b*) What name is given to this tissue?
(*c*) State five differences between this tissue and xylem tissue.

7 What is a ringing experiment?

8 What is autoradiography?

9 Give two advantages, to botanists, of using severed aphid stylets as a method for collecting phloem sap.

10 Briefly describe the contents of phloem sap.

11 Give the meaning of the term translocation.

12 (*a*) State two theories that have been proposed to account for translocation.
(*b*) Briefly distinguish between these two theories.

13 Give observations that could support or conflict with the two theories mentioned in question 12.

Self test 11

1 (*a*) How could you deliberately decrease the concentration of your blood?
(*b*) What effect would this have on your nephrons?

2 What would be the effects of drinking 1 l of salt solution that was isotonic to blood plasma?

3 Distinguish between ureter and urethra.

4 In which organ does the synthesis of urea occur?

5 Why is the problem of excretion less complex in an oak-tree than in an owl?

6 Distinguish between excretion and egestion.

239   Diagram for question 8

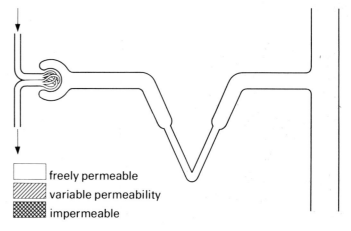

☐ freely permeable
▨ variable permeability
▩ impermeable

7 Carnivorous mammals excrete a higher concentration of urea than herbivorous ones. Explain.

8 Copy figure 239 and, using the key, shade areas of the nephron with the appropriate water permeabilities.

9 Figure 240 shows the change in amount of a substance in urine when a hormone concerned with kidney functioning is injected into a subject.

What does the line represent and what hormone was injected?

240 Diagram for question 9

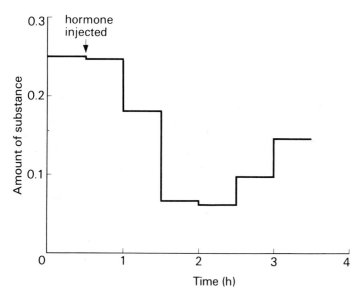

10 Using the letters from figure 241, state where you would expect to find each of the following structures: Bowman's capsule, glomerulus, collecting ducts, convoluted tubules, loop of Henle and capillaries.

11 Draw a diagram of a nephron and add brief notes to summarise the functions of the various parts.

241 Diagram for question 10

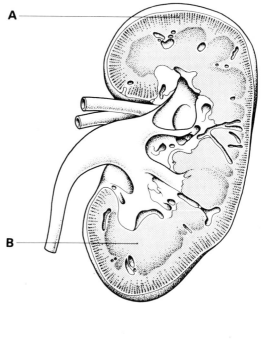

Section 9 Answers to self tests

Self test 1

1 (*a*) and (*b*) See figure 242.

2 See figure 243.

3 As organisms increase in size (assuming shape remains constant) the external surface area to volume ratio decreases. Gas exchange depends on the area of the respiratory surface whereas oxygen requirements and carbon dioxide production depend on the volume of the organism. Therefore, eventually a size is reached at which the surface area is insufficient to supply the oxygen requirements for the body.

The surface area of an organism can be increased by altering its shape from a compact form to a flattened form. Thus, larger organisms may be able to use their surface area as the respiratory surface if they have a flattened shape.

4 Both are ways in which substances move. In diffusion, the energy for movement comes from the motion of the molecules themselves. In mass flow, the movement is due to externally applied pressure.

In diffusion, random movement of molecules occurs which eventually results in their even distribution. In mass flow, the direction of movement is not random but is determined by the direction of the applied pressure.

242   Uptake and output of substances by organisms (completed)

	Animals		Plants	
	uptake	output	uptake	output
oxygen	R		R	N
carbon dioxide		R	N	R
organic food	N			
minerals	N	Ex	N	
water	N	Ex	N	Ex
nitrogenous waste		Ex		
faeces		Eg		

243   Sites of uptake and output (completed)

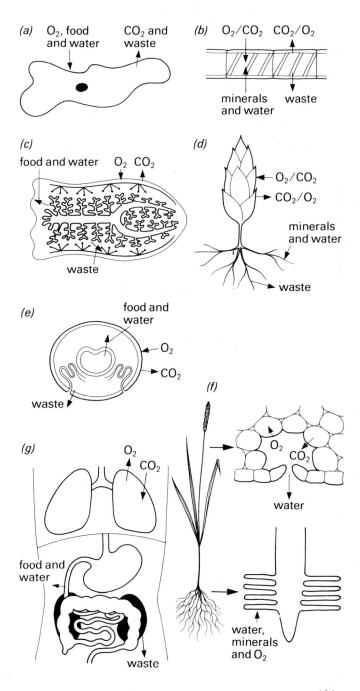

Mass flow does not usually result in even distribution of molecules, rather it results in a buildup in the direction of the pressure.

5 (*a*) Large surface area in relation to the volume of the organism. (*b*) Thin and permeable to gases. (*c*) Moist.

In larger and more complex animals it must also be associated with a transport system.

6 (*a*) An internal respiratory surface may have a much larger surface area which allows greater gas exchange. (*b*) Its moist surface is protected from the desiccating effects of the atmosphere.

7 As organisms increase in size and specialisation there are considerable distances between the respiratory surface and some parts of the body. Diffusion alone would be too slow to carry gases to and from these regions. Being unable to obtain its requirements fast enough, the organism would not survive.

Therefore, a transport system becomes necessary enabling substances to be carried around the body at greater speeds than diffusion. The transport system is also important to carry other substances, e.g. food, from areas of uptake to areas of requirement and wastes from areas of formation to areas of elimination.

8 The plant body has a diffuse and branching shape and no part is far from the external environment and a source of oxygen. Therefore, the distance which gas must move between the environment and the respiratory surface and between the respiratory surface and sites of requirement/formation are short. In fact, they are short enough for diffusion alone to be an efficient mechanism of movement. Thus, a specialised transport system for carrying gases is not required.

9 Ventilation mechanism.

Self test 2

1 Insect — walls of tracheoles. Fish — gill surface. Mammal — walls of alveoli. Flowering plant — cell walls bordering intercellular spaces.

2 Insect — *a, b, c.*
Fish — *a, b, c, d.*
Mammal — *a, b, c, d.*
Flowering plant — *a, b, c.*

3 (*a*) The cuticle supports and holds the tubes open. (*b*) The incomplete rings of cartilage have an equivalent function in a mammal.

4 The gills are soft, thin, reddish structures associated with the gill bars in the pharyngeal region. They comprise a series of layered sheets called filaments. The upper and lower surfaces of these filaments are covered with a series of perpendicular plates. See figure 244.

244 A gill

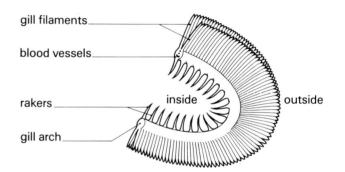

Self test 3

1 Ventilation occurs by diffusion and muscular movements of the abdomen. Carbon dioxide is passed into the inner tubes of the tracheal system by respiring cells and oxygen is removed from the tubes into the cells. This sets up a concentration difference with respect to oxygen and carbon dioxide between the inside and the external environment. Oxygen moves down a concentration gradient into the body and carbon dioxide moves down its concentration gradient to the outside.

In larger insects and most insects when active, ventilation is aided by pumping movements of the abdominal muscles.

2 The moist respiratory surface is internal. The spiracles leading to the respiratory surface can be closed by valves periodically. Both these features reduce evaporation from the respiratory surface.

3 (*a*) Respirometer.
(*b*) Manometer.
(*c*) Potassium or sodium hydroxide.
(*d*) The fluid in the left arm would go down while that in the right arm would go up.
(*e*) Oxygen is taken up from the air in tube **B** during respiration of the root tips. The carbon dioxide that is evolved is absorbed in the potassium hydroxide. Therefore, there is an overall decrease in volume and pressure in **B**. This causes the fluid levels to change.
(*f*) Tube **A** acts to compensate for any changes in environmental pressure and temperature during the experiment.

4 Pressure pump. Water enters the pharynx via the mouth. The pharynx floor is lowered. The mouth then closes. The floor of the pharynx is raised and water is forced under pressure over the gills.

Suction pump. The operculum valve is closed. The operculum wall bulges out. Waste is then sucked into the operculum cavity.

5 The operculum wall moves in and the opercular valve opens.

6 See figure 245.

7 (*a*) If a substance has to be exchanged from one medium to a second medium, the exchange will be greater if the two media flow in opposition to each other rather than in parallel. With this so-called counter-flow, the concentration difference between the two media is always such that diffusion is greater from the first medium to the second.
(*b*) The counter-current mechanism is used in gas exchange in a fish. Water carrying oxygen flows over the gills, while blood into which oxygen must diffuse flows in capillaries in an opposite direction. This ensures maximum uptake of oxygen and, in a similar way, maximum output of carbon dioxide.

8 See figure 246

9 (1) breathing, (2) pressure (volume), (3) thoracic cavity, (4) airtight, (5) ribs (6) external, (7) up, (8) out, (9) contract, (10) downwards, (11) volume, (12) pressure, (13) lower, (14) air, (15) internal, (16) down, (17) in, (18) relax, (19) arch, (20) decrease, (21) increases, (22) atmospheric pressure, (23) pleural membranes, (24) fluid, (25) friction.

10 (*a*) Spirometer.
(*b*) **A** — chamber containing air for breathing.
B — cannister of soda-lime to remove carbon dioxide.
C — tube through which subject breathes.

245 Gill region of a dogfish

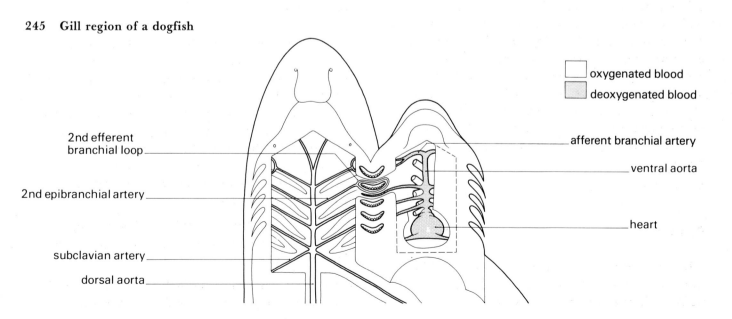

oxygenated blood
deoxygenated blood

2nd efferent branchial loop

2nd epibranchial artery

subclavian artery

dorsal aorta

afferent branchial artery

ventral aorta

heart

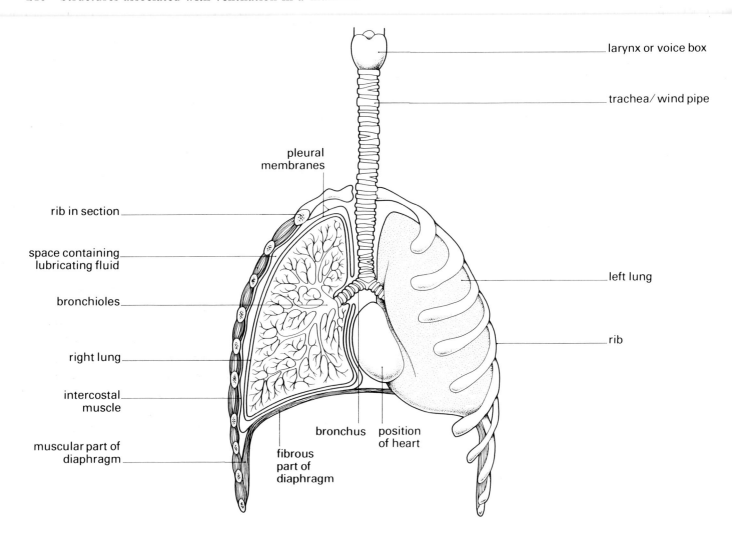

larynx or voice box

trachea/ wind pipe

pleural membranes

rib in section

space containing lubricating fluid

bronchioles

left lung

right lung

rib

intercostal muscle

muscular part of diaphragm

bronchus

position of heart

fibrous part of diaphragm

D — kymograph for recording traces of breaths.

(c) See figure 247

(d) Tidal volume, inspiratory reserve volume, expiratory reserve volume, vital capacity, respiratory rate at rest, effects of exercise on respiratory rate.

11 (a) 0.03%

(b) 21.00%

(c) 4.10%

(d) 16.40%

12 See figure 248.

13 Oxygen is continually brought into the alveoli of the lungs by the breathing mechanism. Oxygen is continually removed from the lungs via the blood capillaries. This means the oxygen concentration will always be high in the alveoli and low in the capillaries. This ensures continued diffusion from the lungs into the blood capillaries.

14 (a) The respiratory cycle is one inspiration followed by one expiration.

(b) The tidal volume is the amount of air normally inspired or expired by an adult.

(c) 0.5 dm³.

15 (a) Carbon dioxide levels in the blood.

(b) Chemoreceptors in the respiratory centre of the medulla of the brain respond to changes in pH caused by altered levels of carbon dioxide.

247 Kymograph trace for measuring oxygen consumption

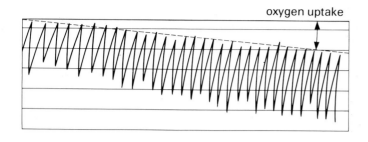

oxygen uptake

248 Relationship between alveoli and blood supply

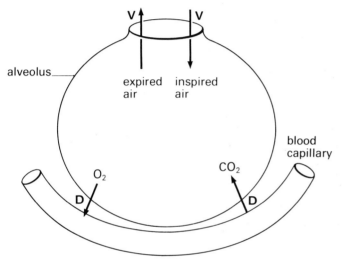

alveolus

V ⬆ V ⬇

expired air   inspired air

O_2 CO_2

D   D

blood capillary

V – ventilation due to movements of intercostal muscles and diaphragm   **D** – diffusion

To a lesser extent, chemoreceptors in the walls of the carotid and aortic arteries are involved. These are called carotid and aortic bodies respectively. They detect changes in the carbon dioxide levels in the blood.
(c) The information is carried by nerve impulses to the medulla of the brain and further impulses pass to the breathing muscles in the thorax.

16 (a) spongy mesophyll cell→network of intercellular spaces→stomata→external atomosphere.
(b) phloem cell→network of intercellular spaces→lenticel in bark→external atmosphere.
(c) inner cortex cell→network of intercellular spaces→stoma/lenticel in leaf or stem→external atmosphere.

(d) root hair→soil water.

All movement is by diffusion.

17 (a) Out of the plant.
(b) Into the plant.
(c) During the day, oxygen is produced in plant cells by photosynthesis at a greater rate than it is used up by respiration. Therefore, the oxygen concentration is higher in the plant than in the atmosphere. Therefore, oxygen diffuses outwards.
(d) At night, oxygen is no longer produced but it continues to be used up during respiration. Therefore, the oxygen concentration is lower in the plant than in the atmosphere. Therefore, oxygen diffuses inwards.

18 (a) The branching shape means that no part of the body is far away from the external environment.
(b) Metabolic rate is low compared with animals.
(c) Oxygen diffuses much faster through the air-filled intercellular spaces than it would through a liquid.
(d) During the day, oxygen is produced within the cells by photosynthesis. This oxygen has only a short distance to travel to reach the mitochondria for respiration.
(e) Much of the tissue of trees is dead and therefore does not require oxygen.

Self test 4

1 (a) Both plants lost mass at a constant rate. The rate was greater for the plant with roots than for the plant without roots.
(b) Loss of water by transpiration.
(c) The apparatus with the intact plant probably lost more mass since the plant was able to absorb more water through the larger surface area of its roots. The water absorbed was then lost by transpiration.
(d) If the respiration rate exceeded the photosynthetic rate, this would lead to a net decrease in mass.
(e) Plant roots are involved in water uptake in plants.

2 (a) See figure 249.
(b) Soil water.
(c) The root-hair region (piliferous layer).

249 TS through root in region of piliferous layer

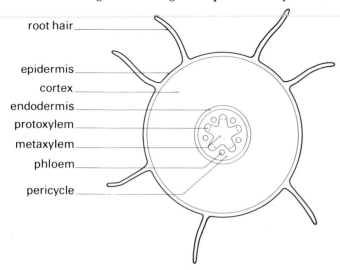

root hair
epidermis
cortex
endodermis
protoxylem
metaxylem
phloem
pericycle

(*d*) The root hairs are numerous and are long, fine structures. Collectively, they have a large surface area in relation to volume. This increases the amount of water that can be absorbed.

(*e*) The roots are continuously growing and develop new root-hair zones. These develop in contact with new areas of soil and this enables new sources of water to be tapped.

3 The apoplast is the sum total of all the cell walls and intercellular spaces in the plant. This forms a continuous network throughout the plant.

The symplast is the sum total of all the cytoplasm in the plant. This forms a continuous network throughout the plant including the cell cytoplasm together with the plasmodesmata connections.

4 Soil — root hair — cortex — endodermis — pericycle — (phloem) — cambium — xylem.

5 (*a*) Through the apoplast — diffusion.
(*b*) Through the symplast — diffusion.
(*c*) From cell vacuole to cell vacuole — osmosis.

6 (*a*) Apoplast.
(*b*) The endodermis cells have a band of waterproof corky material in their walls which prevents water passing to the inside of the plant through their walls.

7 (*a*) Active transport.
(*b*) Diffusion or active transport.
(*c*) Active transport.

(*d*) Active transport.
(*e*) Diffusion.

8 (*a*) Ions are selectively absorbed.
(*b*) Ions are absorbed against a concentration gradient.
(*c*) Ion absorption is temperature dependent.
(*d*) Ion absorption is related to respiration.

9 (*a*) Potometer.
(*b*) Water uptake.
(*c*) Water uptake is directly related to water loss.
(*d*) The bubble would have moved a greater distance in the apparatus in which the leaves were 'Vaselined' on the upper surface.

10 (*a*) Through the apoplast — diffusion.
(*b*) Through the symplast — diffusion.
(*c*) From cell vacuole to cell vacuole — osmosis.

11 (1) pore, (2) guard, (3) turgid, (4) flaccid, (5) water, (6) walls, (7) thickening, (8) sausage, (9) wider, (10) high, (11) water, (12) sugar, (13) starch, (14) solute, (15) osmosis, (16) potassium, (17) solute, (18) osmosis, (19) pump, (20) ATP, (21) uptake, (22) opening, (23) diurnal, (24) movement, (25) phytochrome.

12 (*b*), (*c*), (*e*).

13 Any one for each of (*a*)–(*e*).
(*a*) Inrolled leaves, hairy leaves, sunken stomata, extensive fibrous root system.
(*b*) Low surface area to volume ratio of leaves, water storage.
(*c*) Water storage.
(*d*) Long taproot.
(*e*) Low surface area to volume ratio of leaves, sunken stomata, thick cuticle.

Self test 5

1 (*a*) The bulk movement of materials from one area to another due to differences in pressure.
(*b*) Movement of substances over short distances by random motion from an area of high concentration to an area of low concentration.

2 (*b*).

3 The circulation of cytoplasm within cells.

4 At an exchange surface, useful substances tend to accumulate at the internal side of the surface as movement away by diffusion occurs relatively slowly. Mass flow of fluid away from the surface decreases this concentration so ensuring a greater concentration gradient.

5 (*a*) **B, C** and **D.** (*b*) **A** and **E.**

6 (*a*) **D.**
(*b*) Haemocoel.

7 An open circulation does not confine blood to a continuous series of vessels. Cells are bathed by blood rather than tissue fluid. Blood pressure of an open circulation cannot be as high as a closed system.

8 A high blood pressure can be developed which enables the system to function more efficiently.

9 (*a*).

10 See figure 250

250 **Simplified diagram of the circulatory system of a fish**

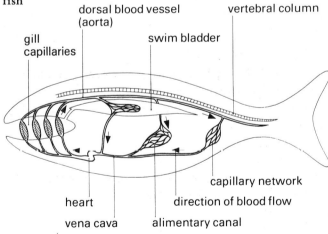

dorsal blood vessel (aorta)

vertebral column

gill capillaries

swim bladder

heart

capillary network

vena cava

direction of blood flow

alimentary canal

11 Closed and single.

12 (*c*).

13 High pressure blood can be supplied to capillaries of the lung or gill and the body capillaries.

14 They greatly reduce the velocity and pressure of blood flow.

15 (*a*), (*b*) and (*c*).

Self test 6

1 1. aorta, 2. pulmonary artery, 3. pulmonary vein, 4. left atrium, 5. mitral (bicuspid) valve, 6. left ventricle, 7. right ventricle, 8. posterior vena cava, 9. valve tendon (chordae tendinae), 10. tricuspid valve, 11. right atrium, 12. semi-lunar valves, 13. anterior vena cava.

2 It supplies the heart muscle with oxygen and other essential materials.

3 The heart raises the pressure of the blood to a point where it can circulate through the body. It is the driving force for mass flow.

4 The thicker the walls of a chamber, the greater the pressure that can be produced in the blood.

5 The tendons play no part in the opening or closing of the valves. Changes in blood pressure cause opening and closure. The tendons, however, prevent the valves, when closing, from being inverted or blown open by the increase in pressure in the ventricles.

6 A, E, B, D, F, C.

7 (*a*) Phase of heart-beat when heart muscle contracts.
(*b*) Phase of heart-beat when heart muscle relaxes.

8 The succession of muscular contractions and movement of heart valves that occur between one beat and the next.

9 A — Atrium contracting, ventricle filling.
B — Ventricle contraction starts, cuspid valve closes.
C — Aortic semi-lunar valve opens, blood flows into aorta.
D — Ventricles start to relax.
E — Aortic valve closes, elastic recoil pushes on blood in aorta.
F — Cuspid valves open, ventricles start to fill with blood.
G — Atrium filling with blood from veins.

10 The heart valves help maintain a one-way flow of blood through the heart.

11 In myogenic muscle, the stimulus for contraction arises within the muscle itself. Neurogenic muscle must receive an external stimulus for contraction.

12 Highly-branched cardiac muscle fibres form a network over which contraction stimuli can rapidly spread across the whole heart.

13 (*a*) Initiates the stimulus for contraction and the frequency of stimulation — the heart rhythm.
(*b*) Rapid conduction of stimulus to all parts of the ventricular muscle mass so ventricles contract simultaneously.
(*c*) Responsible for a slight delay in conduction of impulse between atria and ventricles. This ensures atrial and ventricular contractions never occur together.

14 Parasympathetic system — inhibits heart-beat, i.e. produces a slower rate of beating.
Sympathetic system — stimulates the heart-beat.

15 The 'inherent' rhythm of the heart, produced by the SAN can be modified by varying levels of activity in the sympathetic and parasympathetic nervous systems. The balance of the stimulatory and inhibitory effects can adjust the heart to any level of output required by the body.

Self test 7

1 (*a*)
A — Tunica adventita, collagen. Non-elastic fibres to oppose pressure of the blood.
B — Tunica media, elastic fibres and some muscle. Elastic fibres allow expansion of artery wall followed by elastic recoil to help flow of blood. Alternations in extent of muscle fibre contraction allow vasodilation and vasoconstriction.
C — Tunica intima — elastic fibres. Performs same function as **B** and is usually fused with it.
D — Endothelium, squamous cells. Forms a smooth lining to reduce resistance to blood flow.
E — Arteriole, smooth muscle fibres. Alter diameter of arteriole allowing control of local blood flow.
F — Capillary, squamous epithelia. Allows movement of substances in and out of blood.
J — Lumen, space in centre of the vessel for the flow of blood.
(*b*) The three outer walls of arteries and veins have the same names and functions. In veins, however, (**GHI**) the walls are much thinner and contain smaller amounts of muscle, elastic and collagen fibres. This can be related to the low pressure of the blood they carry.

2 (*a*) Elastic recoil refers to the return of elastic fibres to their normal length after being stretched by an increased volume of blood in arteries. This pulse of blood is caused by heart contraction.
(*b*) Near the heart, blood flows in pulses due to successive contractions of the ventricles. Elastic recoil tends to force the blood along when the heart is relaxing. As distance from the heart increases, the energy of the pulse is dissipated and a smooth steady flow of blood results.

3 The pressure developed by the heart and elastic recoil maintains a one-way flow of blood. Valves are unnecessary.

4 Contractions of skeletal muscles often press against veins so increasing the blood pressure. This increased pressure and action of valves help move blood back into the heart.

5 (*a*) Hydrostatic pressure falls by approximately half when blood flows from arterioles to venules.
(*b*) When hydrostatic pressure is high, substances are forced across the capillary wall from blood. When hydrostatic pressure drops, substances can move back across the wall by diffusion.

6 (*a*) Prevention of fluid accumulation in tissues by draining away excess tissue fluid.
(*b*) Defence of the body against infection, mainly by the lymph nodes.

7 A pulmonary artery, **B** aorta, **C** pulmonary vein, **D** hepatic vein, **E** hepatic portal vein, **F** renal vein, **G** renal artery, **H** iliac artery, **I** left ventricle.

8 Sphincters that can open and close give a great control over local flow of blood and usage of oxygen and glucose by different parts of the body.

9 Dilation of arteries supplying limbs.
Constriction of arteries supplying other organs.
Constriction of veins.

10 Adrenalin.

11 (*a*) Carotid body detects blood carbon dioxide concentration.
(*b*) Carotid sinus detects blood pressure.

12 Increased carbon dioxide and temperature causes vasodilation, decreased carbon dioxide and temperature causes vasoconstriction in capillaries.

13 Vasoconstriction of peripheral arterioles raising general blood pressure along with dilation of muscle arterioles and capillaries cause increased flow of blood to muscle tissue.

14 Nervous systems adjust the circulatory system to changes in demand of the body while the *hormonal* system prepares the body for *anticipated* demand.

Self test 8

1 Should load and unload gases with relative ease and be able to carry large quantities of gases.

2 Three examples from figure 143, page 79.

3 Haemoglobin consists of a folded globin–protein chain associated with an iron-containing prosthetic group. Blood haemoglobin contains four such 'units'.

4 Association refers to the uptake of oxygen by haemoglobin while dissociation is the release of oxygen.

5 This equilibrium curve is a graph showing the relationship between the percentage saturation of haemoglobin with oxygen when blood is in equilibrium with samples of air differing in oxygen content.

6 S-shaped.

7 Information concerning the amount of oxygen released by a blood sample when exposed to *decreasing* partial pressures of oxygen.

8 A shift in the oxygen–haemoglobin equilibrium curve in response to changes in carbon dioxide concentration.

9 The Bohr effect will occur wherever there is a change in blood carbon dioxide concentration, principally in capillary beds. It results in a shift in equilibrium to the right in body capillaries and a shift in equlibrium to the left in lung capillaries.

10 The shift in equilibrium in areas rich in carbon dioxide make more oxygen available to tissues actively using up oxygen. The reverse occurs in areas rich in oxygen and with little carbon dioxide.

11 (*a*) Oxygen
$$Hb + 4O_2 \rightleftharpoons Hb(O_2)_4$$
haemoglobin   oxyhaemoglobin
(*b*) Carbon dioxide
(i) Red cells
$$Hb + CO_2 \rightleftharpoons HbCO_2$$
                    carbamino compounds

$$H_2O + CO_2 \xrightarrow{\text{carbonic anhydrase}} H_2CO_3 \rightleftharpoons H^+ + HCO_3^-$$
                        carbonic
                        acid

(ii) Plasma
$$H_2O + CO_2 \rightleftharpoons H_2CO_3 \rightleftharpoons H^+ + HCO_3^-$$

12 C

13 The exchange of chloride ions and hydrogen carbonate ions between red blood cells and blood plasma. The shift occurs in body and lung capillaries, chloride ions entering red cells in body capillaries and leaving the cells in lung capillaries.

14 To maintain ionic and electrical neutrality within the red blood cells.

15 See figure 251.

16 Granulocytes are formed in bone-marrow. Agranulocytes are formed in the lymph nodes.

17 The production of antibodies in response to antigens.

18 B, E and F.

19 In active immunity, the body produces its own antibodies as a result of antigens. In passive immunity the body receives antibodies from another individual, e.g. a baby acquires some antibodies from its mother.

20 C and D.

21 Platelets are involved in the first line of defence of the body. When skin is damaged, oxygen in the air

Whole blood		Plasma	Serum	Tissue fluid	Lymph
red cells					
white cells:	granulocytes			some	
	agranulocytes			some	✓
platelets					
water		✓	✓	✓	
ions and small molecules		✓	✓	✓	✓
proteins:	fibrinogen	✓			
	others	✓	✓	✓	✓

causes platelets to disintegrate and release an enzyme that causes the formation of a blood clot. The clot helps prevent the entry of microorganisms.

Self test 9

1 The term given to the leaf formed by a plant embryo during early development in the seed.

2 A Vascular bundle, B Epidermis, C Collenchyma (cortex), D Parenchyma (cortex), E Fibres, F Phloem, G Cambium, H Metaxylem (primary xylem), I Protoxylem (primary xylem), J Intervascular cambium, K Pith (medulla)
3 (a) Section A.
(b) Vascular tissue is dotted throughout the pith of the stem. In dicotyledons, vascular tissue is restricted to a ring around the outside edge of the stem.

4 (a) A complex organic material derived from phenylpropane and often associated with cellulose.
(b) Phloroglucinol and hydrochloric acid, red or purple.

5 B and E.

6 Pits are thinner areas of cell walls where lignin has not been deposited.

7 A Fibres.
B Annular and spiral xylem vessel.
C Xylem vessel element.
D Tracheid.

8 Tracheids have end walls containing pits, xylem vessel elements do not.

9 Fibres and sclereids (or stone cells).

10 A Parenchyma.
B Collenchyma.

11 (1) Pith, (2) Vascular bundle, (3) Fibre, (4) Ground tissue, (5) Cuticle, (6) Xylem, (7) Bundle sheath, (8) Tracheid, (9) Dicotyledon, (10) Cortex, (11) Sclerenchyma, (12) Parenchyma, (13) Xylem vessel, (14) Bordered pit, (15) Lignification, (16) Lignin, (17) Vessel member, (18) Wood, (19) Epidermis, (20) Collenchyma, (21) Pit, (22) Cambium.

Self test 10

1 (a) Cohesion — attraction between water molecules.
Adhesion — attraction between water molecules and molecules of the water container.
(b) The asymmetry of the water molecule resulting in electrical polarity.

2 Transpiration exerts a pull on water columns in xylem vessels. Due to the cohesive forces of water, this pull is transmitted along the whole length of the water column which is drawn up the plant.

3 (a) Exudation of xylem sap at freshly-cut stumps of plants.
(b) Exudation of water from leaves when transpiration rate is low (guttation).

4 (a) Transpiration will tend to decrease and root pressure will tend to increase vessel diameter.
(b) Transpiration pull will result in a tension (negative pressure) so pulling the vessel walls inwards. Root pressure pushing water upwards will tend to make the walls bulge outwards.

5 A dendrograph is a device for measuring changes in diameter of tree trunks. By measuring rate of water transport and diameter of trunk it can be found whether increase in diameter (root pressure) or decrease in diameter (transpiration) coincides with maximum water transport.

6 (*a*) **A** Sieve plate and pits, **B** sieve tube element, **C** companion cell.
(*b*) Phloem.
(*c*) (i) Cells are living.
(ii) Smaller diameter.
(iii) Walls do not contain lignin.
(iv) Mature cells contain protoplasm.
(v) Vessels contain pitted cross walls.

7 An experiment where a ring of surface tissue is killed or removed from a plant stem or branch.

8 The method of obtaining a photographic picture of the localisation of radioactive substances in plant or animal tissue.

9 (*a*) Minimal damage to plant tissues.
(*b*) Only sieve tubes being sampled.

10 Sap contains between 10 and 25% sugar, mainly sucrose although tri- and tetra-saccharides are also transported. Amino acids and other nitrogenous compounds, small quantities of mineral salts and plant growth hormones can also be found.

11 The transport of soluble products of photosynthesis in plants.

12 (*a*) Mass-flow hypothesis and the streaming hypothesis.
(*b*) Mass flow: active transport of sugars into and out of phloem sieve tubes establishes turgor pressure gradients down which there is a mass flow of water. Sugars are carried along with the water flow.

Streaming: sugars are carried along sieve tubes by streaming protoplasm and diffusion between sieve tube elements.

13 Mass flow supported by exudation of sap from severed stylets and the transport of certain substances at a faster rate than the streaming cytoplasm. These conflict with the streaming hypothesis. Transport of sugars up and down the plant tends to support the streaming hypothesis.

Self test 11

1 (*a*) Drink water or stop taking in salt.
(*b*) To increase blood concentration, the nephron would increase salt reabsorption and decrease water reabsorption.

2 General blood volume would increase. This increase would inhibit the release of ADH by the pituitary. This decrease in ADH would decrease the permeability of the collecting ducts and less water would be reabsorbed so reducing blood volume. Salt reabsorption would also be decreased.

3 The ureter connects the kidney to the bladder and the urethra the bladder to the outside.

4 The liver.

5 In plants: (*a*) metabolic rate is lower; (*b*) many waste products are also used as raw materials, e.g. carbon dioxide; (*c*) metabolism is based on carbohydrates whose waste products are more easily excreted than urea; (*d*) any waste product can be simply stored in older parts of the plant.

6 Excretion is the removal of waste products of the body's metabolism, while egestion is the removal of undigested food matter.

7 The protein-rich diet of carnivores supplies a greater amount of amino acids that need to be broken down and removed. Urea is the final product of excess protein catabolism.

8 See figure 252.

252 Answer to question 8

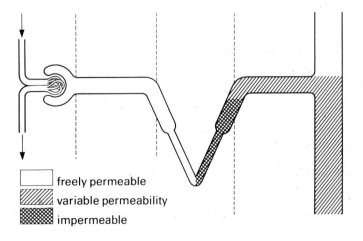

freely permeable

variable permeability

impermeable

9 Water in urine and ADH *or* salts in urine and aldosterone.

10 A — Bowman's capsule, glomerulus, convoluted tubules and capillaries.
B — Collecting ducts, loop of Henle and capillaries.

11 See figure 265 (answer to SAQ 179).

Section 10 Answers to self-assessment questions

1 (a) Respiration and photosynthesis, (b) respiration.

2 (a) In the day carbon dioxide is taken up and oxygen evolved. At night oxygen is taken up and carbon dioxide evolved.
(b) Oxygen is taken up and carbon dioxide evolved.

3 All over the surface of the organism, i.e. the plasma membrane in *Amoeba* and the cell wall in *Spirogyra*.

4 See figure 253.

5 With increasing size of cube, the surface area increases but at a gradually decreasing rate. At the same time, the volume increases, but at an increasing rate.

6 See figure 254.

7 With increasing size, the rate of increase of volume is greater than the rate of increase of surface area. Therefore, beyond a certain size, the body surface alone becomes an inadequate area for gas exchange to cope with the metabolic needs of the body.

8
	Shape **A**	Shape **B**
	SA = 6 mm²	SA = 10 mm²
	V = 1 mm³	V = 1 mm³
	SA : V = 6 : 1	SA : V = 10 : 1

9 Organisms of the same size may have different surface area/volume ratios depending on their shape. Compact shapes have a lower surface area/volume ratio than flattened shapes.

Thus, organisms with flattened shapes will have a greater surface for the gas exchange necessary for their metabolism compared with organisms of a similar size with a compact shape.

10 Diffusion is the net movement of a gas or liquid, due to the random motion of its molecules, down a concentration gradient from regions of high concentration to regions of low concentration until the concentration is even.

253 **Graph comparing surface area and volume for seven cubes**

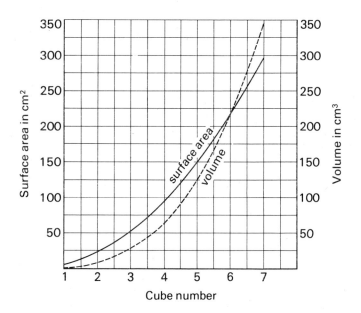

254 **Comparison of number of cm² of surface per cm³ of substance in different cubes**

Cube number	Number of cm² of surface/cm³ of substance
1	6.00
2	3.00
3	2.00
4	1.50
5	1.20
6	1.00
7	0.86

11 Their body surfaces are permeable to oxygen. Oxygen is continuously used up by the metabolic processes of the body. Therefore oxygen concentration is higher outside the body than inside. This sets up a concentration gradient so that oxygen moves inwards.

12 A blood system.

13 There are small branches of the blood transport system which carries oxygen away from the respiratory surface and brings carbon dioxide to it.

14 See figure 255.

255 Comparison of respiratory surfaces and oxygen transport in humans and grass plants

Human	Grass plant
Special respiratory surface	No special surface. Respiratory surface is the walls of the plant cells boardering the intercellular spaces
Oxygen moves by mass flow in a specialised blood transport system and then diffuses into cells	Diffusion alone is involved in conveying oxygen from the respiratory surface to sites in cells where it is required

15 Large surface area in relation to volume of body.

16 *Spirogyra* — cell walls and membranes.

Moss — surfaces of leaf, stem and rhizoids.

Grass — walls of leaf cells (spongy mesophyll — CO_2)
— root hairs (water and minerals).

17 *Amoeba* — contractile vacuole (water)
— body (cell wall) (other wastes).
Human — kidney tubules (water and other wastes).
Planaria — flame-cells (water and other wastes).
Grass — walls of spongy mesophyll cells of a leaf (water).

18 Blood vessels and veins — i.e. transport system.

19 External body surface.

20 Nephridia.

21 The former are internal surfaces. The latter are on the external surface of the body.

22 A crude estimate of surface area of the body can be obtained by measuring the girth of the body at the widest part and multiplying this by the height. Alternatively, the surface area of the individual parts, head, trunk, arms, fingers, etc. can be calculated separately and then the total estimated.

23 5.6 m^2

24 Approximately 400–500 times greater.

25 The greater surface area allows more oxygen to enter the body. Oxygen is required for aerobic respiration. This means a much higher respiration rate and the organism can be more active. This can be important for feeding, avoiding predators, finding a mate, etc.

26 A respiratory surface must be kept moist. Water loss from an external respiratory surface is considerable. This is why organisms with external respiratory surfaces can only survive in aquatic or moist habitats. Water loss from an internal respiratory surface is very much less, enabling the organism to survive in dry habitats.

27 In humans, the respiratory surface is inside the body so a special mechanism is required to allow fresh supplies of air to pass to and from it. In *Amoeba,* the body surface is the respiratory surface. This is in contact with the external water containing supplies of oxygen. Movements of the animal may also play a role in ensuring it is always in contact with water containing sufficient oxygen.

28 The cuticle supports the tubes and keeps them open allowing free movement of gases.

29 (*a*) It has a very large surface area — comprising parts of the walls of virtually *all* the living cells in the plant body.
(*b*) The surface comprises the walls of individual cells. This is a relatively short distance for diffusion.
(*c*) The outer surfaces of the cell walls are surrounded by a film of moisture necessary to dissolve the diffusing gases.

30 Water is an important component of all living organisms but on land, terrestrial organisms are continuously subject to water loss by evaporation from any moist surface. The spiracles lead to the respiratory surface, therefore some evaporation will occur from the respiratory surface through them. The fact that there are relatively few spiracles, that they are small holes and that they may be closed, all tend to reduce the rate of evaporation. This is an advantage for water conservation.

31 Oxygen moves by diffusion from the external

environment to the respiring cells.
Carbon dioxide moves by diffusion from the respiring cells to the external environment.

32 Air pressure in the front section is reduced, suggesting a reduction in volume. Air pressure in the back section is increased, suggesting an increase in volume.

33 It suggests that air passes into the insect's body in front of the diaphragm and leaves it via the abdomen. It also suggests that air can move within the body of the insect from the anterior to the posterior region.

34 (*a*) Pressure would increase.
(*b*) The fluid level in arm **A** would fall.
(*c*) The fluid level in arm **B** would rise.

35 (*a*) This would indicate a decrease of pressure in **A** due to a decrease in volume of gas. This means oxygen uptake is greater than carbon dioxide production.
(*b*) This would indicate an increase of pressure in **A** due to an increase in volume of gas. This means carbon dioxide output is greater than oxygen uptake.

36 Potassium hydroxide or sodium hydroxide both absorb carbon dioxide and could be used.

37 It is assumed that the atmospheric pressure remains constant. Atmospheric pressure does, in fact, vary. Therefore, this assumption is not justified.

38 Temperature could affect (*a*) volume of the fluid, (*b*) dimensions of the glassware and (*c*) volume and pressure of gas in the flask.
(*c*) would affect the pressure on fluid levels in arm **A** only and could, therefore, significantly affect the accuracy of the readings. (*a*) and (*b*) would affect arms **A** and **B** equally.

39 (1) inspiration, (2) floor, (3) pharynx, (4) reducing/lowering/decreasing, (5) water, (6) increasing/raising, (7) forces, (8) over/across, (9) gills, (10) opercular cavity, (11) operculum wall, (12) out, (13) access, (14) remains, (15) passing water out, (16) in, (17) increases, (18) opercular cavity, (19) opens, (20) continuous, (21) water, (22) gills, (23) continuous, (24) oxygen, (25) removed.

40 Blood reaches a much higher percentage saturation after flowing over the gills with a counter-current flow system than with a parallel flow system. This, in turn, provides more oxygen for the respiring cells of the fish.

41 (1) water, (2) pharynx, (3) gill slits, (4) gill filaments, (5) gill plates, (6) deoxygenated, (7) afferent branchial artery, (8) blood capillaries, (9) connect, (10) oxygenated, (11) gill arch, (12) outer, (13) opposite, (14) exchange, (15) counter-current, (16) concentration, (17) concentration, (18) greater, (19) water, (20) blood, (21) blood, (22) water.

42 1. larynx or voice box
2. trachea or wind-pipe
3. left lung
4. rib
5. position of heart
6. bronchus
7. fibrous part of diaphragm
8. muscular part of diaphragm
9. intercostal muscle
10. right lung
11. bronchioles
12. space containing lubricating fluid
13. rib in section
14. pleural membranes

43 They would collapse.

44 In.

45 Potassium hydroxide or sodium hydroxide.

46 Potassium pyrogallate.

47 See figure 256.

48 See figure 257.

49 Diffusion.

50 Investigate the breathing rate using a spirometer with different partial pressures of gases in the chamber. The partial pressure of oxygen should always be the same, but varying levels of carbon dioxide should be used.

51 The thickness of the walls varies.

52 A lenticel is larger since it is made up of many cells. A stoma is composed of just two cells surrounding a pore.

	Inspired air	Expired air
Volume 1 Total volume of air (cm³)	200	150
Volume 2 Air less carbon dioxide (cm³)	199.04	143.8
Volume 3 Volume of carbon dioxide in air sample (cm³)	0.06	6.2
Volume 4 Air less carbon dioxide and oxygen (cm³)	157.04	119.2
Volume 5 Volume of oxygen present in the sample (cm³)	42.00	24.6
% carbon dioxide present in original air sample $= \dfrac{\text{vol. of } CO_2}{\text{total vol. air}} \times 100$	$\dfrac{0.06}{200} \times 100$ $= 0.03\%$	$\dfrac{6.2}{150} \times 100$ $= 4.1\%$
% oxygen present in original air sample $= \dfrac{\text{vol. of } O_2}{\text{total vol. air}} \times 100$	$\dfrac{42}{200} \times 100$ $= 21\%$	$\dfrac{24.6}{150} \times 100$ $= 16.4\%$

257 Gas exchange in an alveolus

53 In stomata it is a simple opening. In lenticels it comprises many tiny spaces between loosely packed cells.

54 Water vapour.

55 Decrease in size of opening would reduce loss of water vapour. This is important for water conservation.

56 The direction of diffusion of oxygen and carbon dioxide is reversed.

57 See figure 258.

58 For the intact plant, the rate of mass loss over the whole investigation

$$= \frac{488.1 - 430.0}{6} \text{ g h}^{-1}$$

$$= 9.7 \text{ g h}^{-1} \text{ (approx.)}$$

For the plant with the root system removed, the rate of mass loss over the whole investigation

$$= \frac{452.3 - 415.1}{6} \text{ g h}^{-1}$$

$$= 6.2 \text{ g h}^{-1}$$

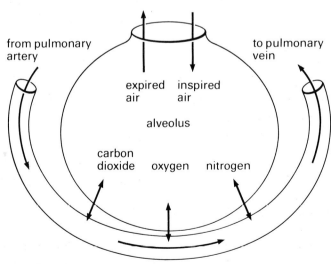

CO_2. There is a net diffusion of CO_2 from a region of high concentration (the blood) to a region of lower concentration (the alveolus). Blood in the pulmonary vein has less CO_2 than blood in the pulmonary artery.

O_2. There is a net diffusion from a region of high concentration (the lungs) to one of lower concentration (the blood). Blood in the pulmonary vein has more O_2 than blood in the pulmonary artery

N_2. This diffuses in both directions, to and from the alveolar air and the blood. Nitrogen is not used at the tissues, so blood in all vessels will have the same N_2 content

258 **Graph showing mass loss in plants with and without roots**

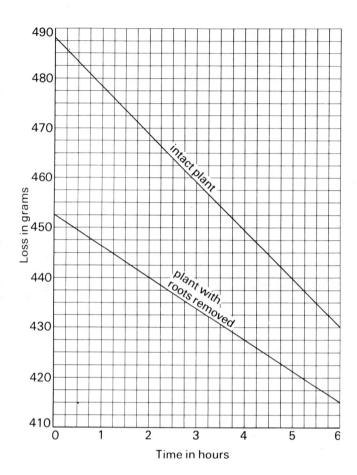

59 The rate of mass loss is not absolutely constant, ranging between 9.0 g h^{-1} and 10.1 g h^{-1} for the intact plant and between 6.0 g h^{-1} and 6.5 g h^{-1} for the plant without roots. This degree of fluctuation is quite normal for biological investigations, but the fact that the graphs are straight lines rather than curves, shows that the rate of mass loss is more or less constant under standard conditions.

60 The two assumptions being made are:
(a) that the loss in mass is due only to water loss;
(b) that the mass of water lost is equal to the mass of water taken up.
(a) There are other processes going on in the plant which could lead to mass changes, such as photosynthesis and respiration. However, over such a short period of time, mass changes due to these processes would be very small indeed compared to

those due to water loss and it seems reasonable to discount them in an investigation in which extreme precision is not essential.
(b) If the amount of water taken up was not the same as that lost from the plant, visible changes in the plant would result. It seems unlikely that the water taken up would exceed that lost but, if so, a general increase in turgor and possible guttation (see section 6.4.3) would be observed. If the amount of water taken up was less than that lost (due to blockage in the conduction system, for example) the plant would lose turgor and wilt. As long as these possibilities are borne in mind, it seems reasonable to use this method as a means of measuring (approximately) both water uptake and water loss.

61 The results show that a root system increases water uptake by (9.7 − 6.2) = 3.5 g h^{-1}. Expressed in percentage terms, this means that a root system increases water uptake by (3.5/6.2) × 100 = 56% approx.
Note: The significance to roots under natural conditions is much greater than in this artificial situation. A cut shoot immersed in water is able to take up water, but a plant without roots would be quite incapable of taking up water from the soil.

62 The oil film prevents water loss by evaporation from the beaker.

63 To prevent air entering the vascular system and blocking it with bubbles.

64 The large number of thread-like hairs greatly increase the surface area to volume ratio of the root. Therefore, more water can be absorbed than across a smooth root surface.

65 Cortex, endodermis, pericycle, (phloem), cambium.

66 It will enable new areas of the soil to be progressively tapped for water supplies.

67 (b)

68 (b)
Water could not pass from **XX** to **YY** through the cell walls since it would have to cross the part of the wall containing the Casparian strip which is impermeable to water. Therefore, water could only pass through the cytoplasm.

69 Any two of the following:
(*a*) Movement of ions from apoplast to symplast in root hairs or cortical cells;
(*b*) Movement of ions through symplast.
(*c*) Movement of ions from symplast into cell vacuoles;
(*d*) Movement of ions from cell vacuoles into symplast;
(*e*) Movement of ions from symplast of pericycle into xylem cells.

70 (*a*) 3, (*b*) 4, (*c*) 1, 4, (*d*) 2.

71 Carbon dioxide. The high concentration of carbon dioxide released from organic acids during the day appears to have a greater effect, causing closure. This happens despite the presence of light which causes opening in most plants.

72 Stomata closed $\underset{\text{dark, high CO}_2\text{ conc.}}{\overset{\text{light, low CO}_2\text{ conc.}}{\rightleftarrows}}$ stomata open

Note: The carbon dioxide concentration is low in the day as it is used up by photosynthesis. It is high at night because it is not used in photosynthesis.

73 No.

74 Closure could be related to a fall in water content of the plant as a result of transpiration during the morning.

75 (*b*), (*c*), (*d*).

76 No.

77 See figure 259.

259 Environmental conditions affecting transpiration

Environmental factor	Transpiration rate	
	High	Low
1 Temperature	high	low
2 Air movement	windy	still
3 Humidity	low	high
4 Light	high	low/absent
5 CO_2 level	low	high
6 Soil water	high	low

78 1, 2 and **3** affect evaporation. **4, 5** and **6** affect stomatal movement.

79 Stomata are found in depressions on the leaf surface. Water vapour passing out of the stomata during transpiration will get trapped in these hollows creating a humid micro-environment. Humid conditions reduce transpiration.

80 The stomata are found in depressions on the upper surface of the leaf. The leaf itself rolls inwards. It also bears hairs on the upper surface. All these factors will trap a layer of humid air over the stomata, thus reducing transpiration.

81 The mucilage-filled parenchyma cells in the cactus act as a water store.

82 Marram grass and the cactus both have extensive root sytems to tap a greater area of soil for water.

83 Thick cuticle (pine), reduced surface area to volume ratio (pine and cactus).

84 The arthropod contains a much larger blastocoel, the cavity that will later carry blood.

85 Through the tracheal system.

86 (*a*) Carry food from digestive organs to cells.
(*b*) Carry waste products from cells to exoretory organs.
(*c*) Carry hormones, aids in defence, etc.

87 (*a*) The gill capillaries.
(*b*) Diffusion at other capillary networks will be less efficient because of the lower blood pressure they receive.

88 (*a*) Increased blood flow by faster heart-beat.
(*b*) Increased blood pressure by more forceful contractions.

89 Blood mixing in the heart means tissues will receive blood with a lower oxygen concentration.

90 Atrium has moved dorsally. Ventricle has moved ventrally. All chambers enlarged. Atrium and ventricle have thicker walls. Valves between chambers to ensure one-way flow.

91 A body, **B** lungs, **C** vein, **D** ventricles, **E** oxygenated, **F** high pressure.

92 See figure 260

93 The cuspid valves close under the increasing pressure of blood during ventricular contraction and prevent back flow into the atria so allowing the atria to fill with blood from the attached veins. The semi-lunar valves, closing under pressure of blood in the

260 Answer to SAQ 92

Ventricular diastole

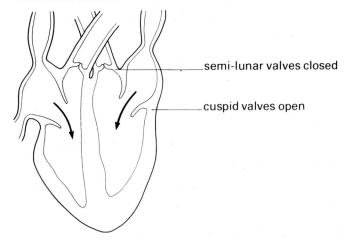

semi-lunar valves closed

cuspid valves open

Ventricular systole

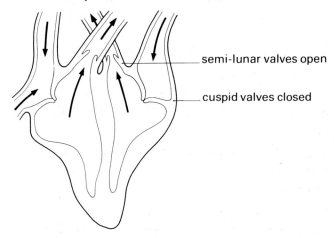

semi-lunar valves open

cuspid valves closed

arteries, prevent back flow into the ventricles. Both sets of valves help maintan a unidirectional flow of blood through the heart.

94 *Normal* means the average value of a representative sample of the population.

95 The QRS complex is a record of the electrical activity of the ventricular muscle mass which is much larger than the atrial muscle mass.

96 90 beats per minute.

97 (*a*) (i) 0.1 second; (ii) 0.06 second; (iii) 0.23 second; (iv) 0.2 second.
(*b*) (i) duration of P wave; (ii) duration of the QRS complex (the Q–S distance); (iii) time from T wave to point R; (iv) time from T wave to next P wave.

98 The time delay means atrial contraction is not disrupted by ventricular contraction which is delayed for a short time.

99 Muscles of the septum contract first, followed by the apex and outer walls of the ventricle. Blood is squeezed out smoothly.

100 The SAN is the origin of the heart-beat. Impulses from the two nerves can modify the rhythm by affecting the functioning of the SAN. During exercise, for instance, the sympathetic nerve passes impulses. During rest, the parasympathetic would operate. A balance of nerve action can 'fine tune' the heart rhythm to the needs of the body.

101 Elastic tissue allows the vessels to expand and accommodate greater volumes of blood while the non-elastic collagen will oppose too great an expansion so stopping the vessels from bursting.

102 Veins contain less elastic tissue and collagen fibres, the *tunica adventitia* and *media* being thinner than arteries. This may be due to veins carrying fluid at lower pressures, hence less collagen fibres. The fluid also probably undergoes less dramatic changes in volume, hence less elastic tissue.

103 Alternate contraction and relaxation of the ventricles.

104 Venules and veins have large diameters and offer less resistance to the flow of blood.

105 Although moving slower, there is a larger *volume* of blood in the vein due to its larger lumen.

106 (*a*) Arteriole end:
Effective pressure = (4.3 − 1.1) − (3.3 − 1.3)
                   = + 1.2

Venule end:
Effective pressure = (1.6 − 1.1) − (3.3 − 1.3)
                   = − 1.5

(*b*) Diffusion of substances across the capillary wall would decrease or stop if the pressures fell significantly.

107 1. pulmonary vein, 2. aorta, 3. carotid artery, 4. dorsal aorta, 5. hepatic artery, 6. mesenteric artery, 7. hepatic portal vein, 8. hepatic vein, 9. renal artery, 10. renal vein, 11. iliac artery, 12. iliac vein, 13. vena cava, 14. anterior vena cava, 15. pulmonary artery.

108 6 and 7 — 7 will contain less oxygen and much more assimilates.
1 and 15 — 1 will contain more oxygen and less carbon dioxide.
9 and 10 — 10 will contain less urea and, depending on body conditions, may have less salt and water.

109 However slight the exertion, there is bound to be an increase in metabolic rate. This will result in an increase in the amount of oxygen used and carbon dioxide produced. The oxygen content of the blood will, therefore, fall and carbon dioxide will rise.

110 (*a*) The body responds by increasing the rate and depth of breathing (ventilation rate) and the rate at which the heart beats (cardiac frequency). These responses tend to reduce and increase carbon dioxide and oxygen levels respectively.
(*b*) The arterioles supplying those structures that are running short of oxygen and accumulating carbon dioxide will increase their diameter. This local vasodilation encourages the flow of blood through those structures that need it. Vasoconstriction of other vessels will reduce blood supply to inessential regions.

111 When blood carbon dioxide concentration *increases,* impulses pass from chemoreceptors in the carotid and aortic arteries via sensory nerve fibres to the cardiovascular centre in the medulla. Impulses reaching the cardiovascular centre initiate impulses which travel down the spinal cord via the spinal nerve and ganglia to the sino-atrial node. These excitatory impulses cause the SAN to increase heart-beat.

112 An increase in general blood pressure and dilation of muscle arterioles will greatly increase the flow of blood through the muscles where carbon dioxide is building up.

113 Oxygen is loaded and carbon dioxide is unloaded in the capillaries of the lungs or gills. The reverse process occurs at the tissue capillaries.

114 The volume of gas that can be taken up by the respiratory pigment.

115 (*a*) Haemoglobin, in corpuscles.
(*b*) Annelids.

116 If the reaction were not reversible, once haemoglobin picked up oxygen at the lungs, it could not release it at the tissues.

117 Water — maximum 0.6% saturation.
Haemoglobin — maximum 30% saturation.
Haemoglobin is fifty times more efficient than water at carrying oxygen.

118 The collision of gas molecules on the wall of the balloon causes the gas pressure. Fifty per cent of the gas molecules are from gas B. They must therefore cause 50% of the total pressure: 25 kN m^{-2}.

119 (*a*) Gas A contributes 20% of the total pressure: 20% of 50 kN m^{-2} = 10 kN m^{-2}.
(*b*) Gas A produces 10 kN m^{-2}, gas B produces 25 kN m^{-2} (SAQ 118). The remaining pressure would be $50 - (10 + 25)$ kN m^{-2} = 15 kN m^{-2}. This is, of course, the partial pressure of gas C.

120 (*a*) See figure 261.
(*b*) See figure 262.

261   Answer to SAQ 120(*a*)

Partial pressure O$_2$ of air (kNm^{-2})	% saturation Hb with O$_2$
0	0
1	10
2	22
3	42
4	67
5	81
6	88
7	93
8	94
9	95
10	96

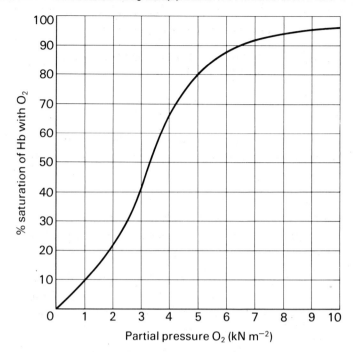

121 Between 2 and 4 kN m^{-2} of oxygen the percentage saturation of Hb changes most quickly.

122 (*a*) Increasing the partial pressure will çause haemoglobin to take up oxygen.
(*b*) Decreasing the partial pressure will cause the haemoglobin to liberate oxygen.

123 (*a*) (i) High p.p., e.g. 5. (ii) Low p.p., e.g. 1.
(*b*) Between 1 and 5 kN m^{-2} percentage saturation changes from 10% to 80%. A change of 70%
(*c*) It is advantageous to have the steepest part of the curve over normal body partial pressures because this represents the largest change in oxygen/haemoglobin saturation. Hence, a large amount of oxygen can be taken up quickly as blood reaches the lungs. A large amount of oxygen can be liberated quickly as blood reaches the tissues.

124 Increasing carbon dioxide partial pressures shift the equilibrium curve, over most of its length, to the right. For a given partial pressure of oxygen, an increase in carbon dioxide concentration causes percentage saturation of haemoglobin to decrease. OR decreasing carbon dioxide partial pressures shifts the curve to the left, increasing haemoglobin percentage saturation.

125 (*a*) Decrease in saturation for **X** = 70% (90 − 20).
(*b*) Decrease in saturation for **Y** = 70% (80 − 10).
(*c*) Decrease in saturation for **Z** = 80% (90 − 10).

126 Although the curve shifts to the right, the *shape* of the curve between partial pressures oxygen 9 and 3 kN m^{-2} remains the same.

127 If blood carbon dioxide partial pressures increase in capillaries, the change in percentage saturation is larger due to the curve shifting to the right. In other words, more oxygen is given off if the partial pressure of carbon dioxide increases.

128 See figure 263.

263   Answer to SAQ 128

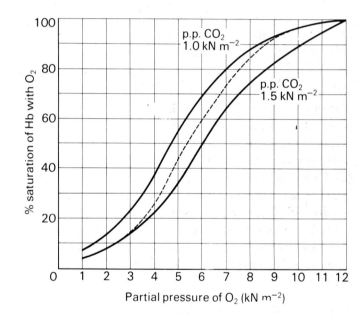

129 Actively respiring tissues; e.g. liver, muscle.

130 The partial pressure of carbon dioxide in blood entering the lungs *decreases* and so the equilibrium curve shifts to the left. Haemoglobin can then become fully saturated at lower oxygen partial pressures than if the shift did not occur.

131 Increased carbon dioxide causes (*a*) increased acidity, (*b*) decreased pH.

132 Temperature and pH may affect the tertiary structure of the globin protein and so alter its functioning slightly.

133 Respiring tissues would have a relatively low pH due to the production of acids and carbon dioxide. This would have the effect of shifting the equilibrium curve to the right, i.e. oxyhaemoglobin would tend to dissociate in the tissues, providing them with more oxygen.

During exercise, body temperature rises. This would also move the curve to the right, again making oxygen more readily available in the tissues.

134 (a) Hb2.
(b) The animal containing Hb2 may be aquatic. Water contains less oxygen than air. The organism's haemoglobin is therefore likely to be adapted to associate at lower partial pressures of oxygen.

135 If the equilibrium curves shifted to the right with an increase in carbon dioxide, the curve could be shifted outside the range of oxygen partial pressures that the organism encounters.

136 An accumulation of H^+ ions decreases the pH which causes the curve to shift to the right.

137 See figure 264.

264   Answer to SAQ 137

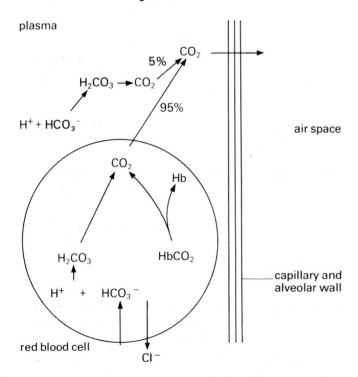

138 The pits allow lateral transfer of water.

139 Vertically, through the pits in the tapering end walls and sideways (laterally) through the pits in the side walls.

140 A Tracheid.
B Fibre.
C Fibre.
D Xylem vessel.

141 (a) Xylem and phloem occur separately. Protoxylem occupies the outer regions of the xylem tissue. The vascular tissue occurs in the centre of the root as a compact mass.
(b) Xylem and phloem occur together in the same radii in discrete bundles. Protoxylem occupies the inner regions of the vascular bundles. The vascular tissue is distributed around the margin of the stem in bundles.

142 The regions of phloem and xylem split into equal numbers of groups with pith developing between each group. The xylem tissue twists so that the metaxylem lies next to, and on the same radius as, the phloem tissue. The vascular bundles so formed move to the outside of the stem, just below the epidermis separated by larger amounts of pith.

143 Vascular tissue is supplied to the leaf by small leaf trace bundles. Once a leaf trace has diverted out of the stem into a petiole, another leaf trace is immediately formed above by the branching of adjacent vascular bundles. See figure 175.

144 Interruption of the xylem on one side prevents water moving into the leaves situated vertically above the cut — these leaves, therefore, wilt. Leaves elsewhere remain turgid.

145 The mass of the water in the column and gravity.

146 A column of water 100 m high would need a pressure difference of approximately 10 atm.

147 The narrower the bore in a tube, the higher the liquid will rise because the adhesive forces of the water molecules to the side of the tube and their cohesion to each other, are greater relative to the force of gravity.

148 Water molecules are more strongly attracted to lignified cell walls of xylem than to the walls of glass tubes.

149 The plant produces new xylem vessels arising from the vascular cambium, thus new intact columns of water are formed.

150 This phenomenon is best explained in terms of transpiration pull. As the columns of water in the vessels are broken by the knife, because they are under tension, the water below the cut falls back down the tree while the water above the cut is pulled up. As a result, air rushes into the vessels, causing the hissing sound. If the water was being pushed up the tree by root pressure, you would expect it to spurt out under pressure when the vessels are punctured.

151 (a) (i) During the night and early morning, reaching a peak about mid-morning.
(ii) A decrease begins about 10.00 a.m. and continues through the day until dusk.
(b) When the columns of water in the xylem are pulled up as a result of transpiration, they are stretched and the water molecules tend to pull in the walls (rather as an elastic band gets thinner when stretched. The net result is that the tree actually gets thinner when transpiration is at a maximum (i.e. during the heat of the day). During the cool, humid night, transpiration is considerably reduced and the diameter of the trunk increases.
(c) As the changes in diameter are due to transpiration pull which begins in the leaves, you would expect them to occur first higher up the tree.

152 The swelling of the branch above the ring could be due to the accumulation of materials whose downward movement has been interrupted. The shrivelling of the bark below the cut could be due to the lack of supply of nutrients from above (it).

153 The death of the root system due to ringing shows that phloem is probably involved in the downward movement of nutrients.

154 In winter when the leaves have fallen, rate of production of nutrients and their transport around the plant will have greatly decreased. This tends to support the view that the swelling is caused by accumulating nutrients.

155 (a) The film has been affected by other parts of the plant than the 'fed' leaf.

(b) The film has been affected by the stem both above and below the 'fed' leaf.
(c) There is the merest trace of radioactivity in the tissue above the ring. This could be the result of slight wounding of the xylem during ringing.
(d) Very strongly. Interruption of the phloem to all intents and purposes stops the flow of ^{14}C sucrose.
(e) It is being used in some way by the younger leaves.
(f) It is not evenly distributed in the young leaves. This suggests that most of it travels up the same side of the stem as the 'fed' leaf with little transverse movement.

156 (a) Diffusion down a concentration gradient out of the leaf.
(b) Some mass-flow system which removes it.
(c) Active transport through cells.

157 By cutting off the flow of food supplies to the roots from the aerial parts.

158 (a) As the phloem is situated on the outside of the vascular bundle, it should be possible to cut or block the phloem without affecting the xylem, which is a dead tissue and, therefore, not likely to be damaged by the ringing techniques used by Rabideau and Burr.
(b) This could be checked by repeating the experiment, but studying, in addition, the movement of a substance known to be transported in the xylem, such as an inorganic salt.

159 This investigation indicates that *living* phloem is required for transport of organic substances.

160 (a) When xylem is pierced with a sharp knife, air rushes in, showing that the xylem sap is under tension (see SAQ 150).
(b) These observations show that conditions in the phloem are opposite to those in xylem — the phloem sap exerts an outward pressure on the sieve tube walls.

161 As sugar molecules are transported from region **A** to **B,** after a time sugar concentrations will become equal. Regions **A** and **B** will take up water by osmosis which will stop when the hydrostatic pressure reaches a high enough level.

162 In the living system, the sugar concentrations do not become equal because of the continued supply of sugars to the source from photosynthesis and the continued removal at the sink by respiration.

163 (a) The 'leaf end' of phloem tubes where active transport from mesophyll cells occurs.
(b) The 'root end' of phloem tubes.
(c) Phloem sieve tubes.
(d) Xylem vessels.
(e) Mesophyll cells at the end of phloem sieve tubes.

164 (a) Supports the mass-flow hypothesis which predicts that the contents of the phloem will be under pressure. Does not conflict seriously with either of the other hypotheses.
(b) Could support both the transcellular strand and cyclosis hypotheses. Conflicts with mass flow which only accounts for unidirectional movement at any one time.
(c) Conflicts with cyclosis hypothesis and tends to support mass flow.

165 The chemical processes taking place in the cytoplasm are collectively termed *metabolism*.

166 In a plant, carbon dioxide should be shown entering the cell and oxygen being produced under the influence of light.

167 Too much water in animals can cause rupture of cells due to influx of water by osmosis. Plant cells are not prone to rupture because of their cell wall.

168 The organs of carbon dioxide removal in animals are the lungs of gills, and in plants, the leaves.

169 Metabolism is the sum total of all chemical reactions taking place in a cell and can be divided into synthesis (anabolism) and degradation (catabolism).

170 The difference in waste depends upon the main body consitituent. Plants are mainly carbohydrate (producing waste carbon dioxide); animals are mainly protein (producing waste ammonia).

171 Useful products in man include: hormones, enzymes, mucus, tears, etc.

172 Definitions of:
excretion — the removal of waste products of the body's metabolism.
egestion — removal of undigested matter that has not been part of the body's metabolism.
secretion — the production and release of substances by cells to perform some useful function.
elimination — the removal of useful substances that are in excess.

173 (a) (i) Water gain from a freshwater environment. (ii) Water loss from marine and terrestrial environments.
(b) Freshwater will cause an influx of water into an organism due to osmosis, the body tissues being more concentrated than the surrounding medium. A marine environment being more concentrated than body fluids, will cause a loss of water by osmosis. A terrestrial environment will produce a loss of water by evaporation.

174 (a) When an animal has a plentiful supply of water, ammonia is excreted as it can be sufficiently diluted to prevent a risk of the animal poisoning itself. As water becomes in short supply, animals tend to excrete urea as this is less toxic and requires less water for removal. In very dry habitats uric acid, the least toxic waste product, is excreted with very little water being lost.
(b) Toads excrete a mixture of ammonia and urea. In *Bufo,* during metamorphosis, the percentage of urea excreted increases. This can be correlated with its increasing time spent on land. Excretion of urea requires less water loss. *Xenopus,* however, maintains its chief excretory product as ammonia. Being aquatic for its whole life, water is in plentiful supply.

175 A — Freshwater aquatic, high percentage of ammonia.
B — Moist terrestrial, urea is the main excretory product which requires a certain amount of water loss.
C — Dry terrestrial, a larger amount of uric acid which requires less water loss.
D — Desert — uric acid is the main waste. Little water loss occurs on its elimination.

176 The diameter of the arteriole leading to the glomerulus is greater than that leaving. As blood tries to force its way out of the smaller tube an increase in pressure will occur.

177 (*a*) 2.8 l h^{-1} are filtered off from 14 l h^{-1} passing through the glomerulus, i.e 1/5 or 20%.
(*b*) The concentration of substances in plasma and nephric filtrate are exactly the same except for the absence of protein in the nephron fluid. This is as would be expected from straightforward filtration, the larger particles being unable to pass through the capillary walls.
(*c*) As fluid flows along the nephron the useful amino acids and glucose are removed from the fluid while the concentration of wastes such as salts and urea increases by their excretion into the nephron. A large part of the water is also removed, as shown by the decrease in flow rate.

178 In summary, the function of the loop of Henle is to create and maintain a high sodium concentration in the medulla by active transport. This sodium tissue concentration then causes the reabsorption of water, by osmosis, from the collecting ducts so forming concentrated urine.

179 See figure 265.

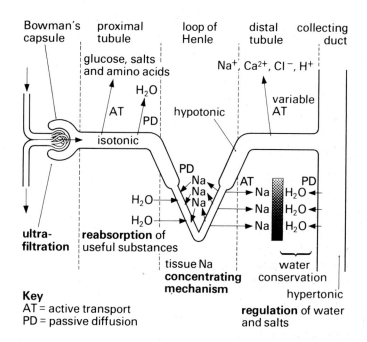

Key
AT = active transport
PD = passive diffusion

180 High ADH levels cause *more* water reabsorption. As the ducts are more permeable, more water can diffuse from the filtrate back into the kidney tissue.

181 See figure 266.

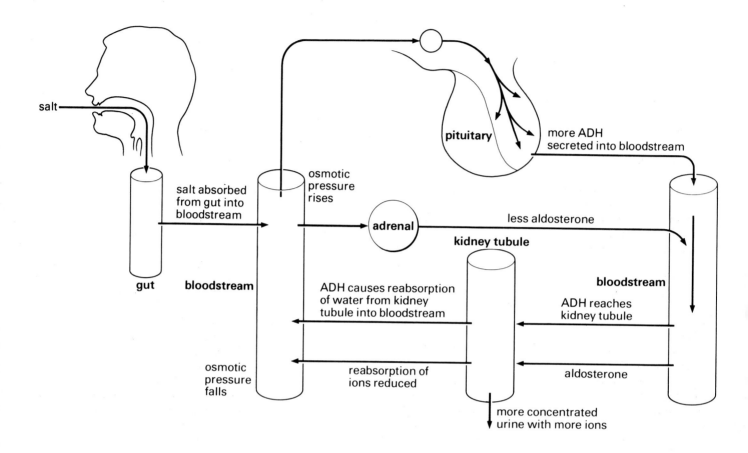

salt

salt absorbed
from gut into
bloodstream

osmotic
pressure
rises

pituitary

more ADH
secreted into bloodstream

adrenal

less aldosterone

kidney tubule

bloodstream

gut   bloodstream

ADH causes reabsorption
of water from kidney
tubule into bloodstream

ADH reaches
kidney tubule

osmotic
pressure
falls

reabsorption of
ions reduced

aldosterone

more concentrated
urine with more ions

Index